THE ABANDONED

Victims of Jack the Ripper

DAVID STEPHENS

WOODBRIDGE
PUBLISHERS

Forest House, 3rd Floor 16-20
Clements Road Unit #2048
Ilford, IG1 1BA

Copyright © 2025 David Stephens

ISBN (Paperback) : 978-1-917760-26-3

ISBN (Hardback) : 978-1-917760-27-0

ISBN (eBook) : 978-1-917760-28-7

All rights reserved

No part of this publication may be reproduced, stored in a retrieval system, copied in any form or by any means, electronic, mechanical, photocopying, recording or otherwise transmitted without written permission from the publisher. You must not circulate this book in any format.

Under no circumstances will any blame or legal responsibility be held against the publisher, or author, for any damages, reparation, or monetary loss due to the information contained within this book, either directly or indirectly.

Cover Design by Ruthie Stephens.

CONTENTS

PART ONE: THE NIGHTMARE BEGINS   iii

PART TWO: PANIC IN NEW YORK   207

PART THREE: A *RIPPER* LEGACY   249

PART FOUR: LOOSE ENDS   261

KEY

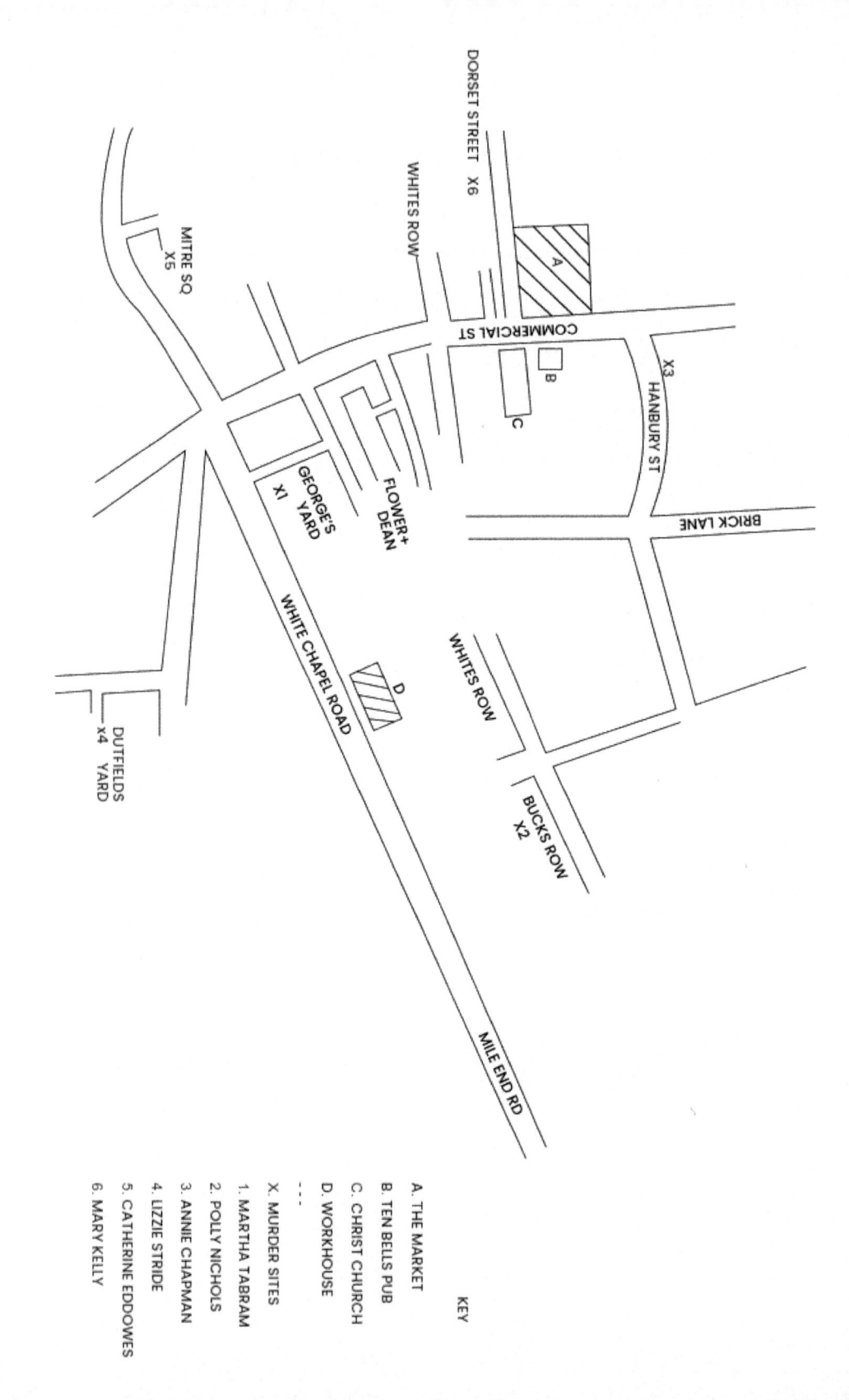

A. THE MARKET
B. TEN BELLS PUB
C. CHRIST CHURCH
D. WORKHOUSE
X. MURDER SITES
---
1. MARTHA TABRAM
2. POLLY NICHOLS
3. ANNIE CHAPMAN
4. LIZZIE STRIDE
5. CATHERINE EDDOWES
6. MARY KELLY

PART ONE

THE NIGHTMARE BEGINS

The Abandoned: *Victims of Jack the Ripper*

Part One: The Nightmare Begins

CHAPTER ONE

THE KILLING GROUNDS

1888 – Spitalfields, East London

Jack McCarthy and Billy Crossingham, not yet middle-aged, owned all the common lodging houses, the miserable rented properties in Dorset Street, a short, dank lane near Spitalfields market. Over a thousand people were crammed into them. McCarthy and Crossingham were close friends, more like brothers. During their early years as landlords, at least three brutal murders of prostitutes took place in the rooms they had rented, one at least being the most dreadful of all the *Jack the Ripper* killings; McArthy gave evidence at the inquest. According to a 1901 report in the *Daily Mail*, there was an attempted murder on Dorset Street nearly once a month, at least one murder in every house, and in one house, a murder in every room.

McCarthy and Crossingham became wealthy men by renting those rooms to people desperate enough to need them, and owned the stores from where the tenants would buy meagre provisions. It was hardly surprising that the two men also set up illegal prize fights as violence in all its forms happened to be the background to their lives.

If there was a leader, it was McCarthy. He was not quite a crime boss; he didn't set out to be one, but he flourished in the putrid atmosphere of prize fights, gambling, and the exploitation of the poor, knowing the rent he demanded was obtained by his tenants not only by the lowest paid casual work but also by begging, theft and prostitution. He kept thugs on hand to enforce his will and collect his rent.

Born in France, where his Irish parents briefly resided, and despite playing down his Irish heritage, he was most comfortable amongst the Irish immigrants of East London. It was mostly them he exploited, although it mattered little to him where his tenants came from.

In 1888, the year of the terrible *Jack the Ripper* killings, all the victims, at one time or another, lived in the properties owned by McCarthy, Crossingham, or their close friends. McCarthy was not *Jack the Ripper*, and neither was Billy Crossingham, but they and their like sustained the conditions that spawned his victims and facilitated his anonymity.

***

Spitalfields Market, squatting opposite the great Church on Commercial Street, dominated the lives of those who lived and worked in the decaying, struggling lanes, streets, roads, alleyways, yards, tenements, brothels, lodging houses and pubs in that grubby, malodorous, small part of East London. It was sad to think that the area had long ago been home to elegance, decency and propriety. Huguenot silk weavers once had set up homes and businesses there, as did the London branch of the Wedgwood pottery company, both drawing in royal and wealthy patrons. Driven out by changing economic circumstances, weavers and potters left the area to the swirl of immigrant humanity centred on the Market, its commercial hub.

By the beginning of Victoria's reign, Spitalfields Market was a major centre for fruit and vegetables, especially potatoes, for all of London. Men arrived to work as porters and clerks, often hired by the day for the lowest possible wage or to buy goods for costermongers, supplies for hotels and retail by greengrocers across the metropolis.

As the demand for meat grew, Spitalfields increased its scope with stalls selling mutton, pork and beef, as well as poultry of every kind. Busy though it was, it was not a serious rival to the other markets nearby, Billingsgate for fish and Smithfield for meat, and was a class beneath the modern and beautiful Leadenhall Market. It was

Part One: The Nightmare Begins

always a poor comparison. Nevertheless, drovers arrived there from towns and villages far away, as did buyers.

Catering for the needs of so many workers and traders, the public houses thrived, springing up on almost every corner and street near the Market. The pubs let rooms to those who needed to prolong their stay for a night or two, but the demand for rooms was so great that rooms in family houses were often rented out.

Empty properties were bought up and converted into cheap accommodation for a transient population. The building of ever more such places as cheaply as possible followed. Indeed, some were so poorly constructed that they simply collapsed. It seemed that no matter how many places were built, the demand continued to grow.

Word spread that casual work could be picked up in and around the Market, work that would at least pay for a bed for the night and something to eat. For the poorest, many second-generation Irish immigrants, and later the Jewish immigrants from Poland and Russia, what other choice did they have but to grasp at whatever accommodation was available, however squalid? Despite having the worst and most overcrowded slums in London, life in the streets around the Market was still preferable to the workhouse or the pogroms of Russia and Eastern Europe.

Local shopkeepers like McCarthy were quick to avail themselves of the opportunity to be landlords and bought or built all the property that could be crammed into the streets near the Market. Following their example, itinerants and drifters who raised money by criminal means, usually robbery and burglary, also got in on the business. They bought into nearly worthless, derelict properties and rented them out, keen to exploit those from whose ranks they themselves had emerged.

The design of the resultant common lodging houses was universal: a large kitchen for every tenant to use, but with few utensils, not much in the way of crockery, and forks available only if a deposit was left with the landlord. Rooms were furnished with narrow beds and straw mattresses. It was usual for two or more people to share a bed as they cost 3 pennies a night, not a trifling sum if pennies were all you had.

The places stank, ran with vermin and were disease-ridden. They were most overcrowded in winter when the poor would otherwise freeze to death on the streets. In summer, the lodging houses would empty out a little as about half the population drifted away to the countryside, mostly south to Kent, to work on the farms and in the hop fields.

The common lodging houses catered to those barely scratching a living. The owner landlords were described by local police as being greater criminals than any of the poor wretches who had to live in such squalor.

Like McCarthy, all landlords employed 'deputies' whose job it was to collect the rent, and a 'night watchman' who was no more than a brute who could throw out anyone who did not pay. McCarthy favoured employing burley former soldiers for the callous, rough work. Those most likely to be evicted would be the old, the sick, and pregnant women with children, as they had no earning capacity beyond begging and were likely to face nights huddled on the streets.

Alongside the lodging houses were the tenements. Here, houses were divided into small rooms that were let out by the week. Each room came with a bed and rudimentary furniture. The rooms would be filled with whole families, sometimes two, and even three in winter. They backed onto other tenements, old yards and every sort of ugliness. The rooms were populated by prostitutes, 'the unfortunates', women who had fallen into such poverty and hopelessness, often alongside wretched husbands or partners, that beneath them now was only the common lodging house and doorways on the street.

The reputation for filth and vermin in the lodging houses was so well known that local laundries refused to take in their laundry. Dorset Street, Whites Row, Thrawl Street, and Flower and Dean Street were the worst, though there were many contenders for that unwanted title.

Avarice and lust for power first bred amorality, then immorality, and ultimately, wickedness amongst the landlords. The owners of the common lodging houses and tenements soon tumbled to the idea that if prostitutes were going to trade in their area, which they did openly as an alternative to starvation, then landlords would ensure they had rooms for them to work from, with higher rents or charges levied against these clients, and sometimes, protection money to be paid too. The established landlords of the tenements and lodging houses took control of as many shops and pubs as they could and then happily rented to prostitutes to bring in trade from the Market and the streets.

Part One: The Nightmare Begins

As the number of prostitutes increased in the streets and pubs near the Market, sailors from the nearby docks knew where to find them in great number and availability, spending far more money in the pubs in the area than on the women. So rose another profession, the Bullies.

Usually former soldiers, these brutal men were employed to act as doormen in tenements and lodging houses which were occasional brothels. They enforced payment on behalf of the women, if required, and would occasionally help themselves to the contents of their client's pockets should they be too drunk to resist.

They ended up forming a relationship with the prostitutes who would, at times, rely on them for protection. There was always a fear amongst the women that when they were soliciting for trade on the streets, they might be confronted by gangs of youths from the boroughs north and east of Spitalfields, intent on robbing them. The mere sight of the Bully coming along the street was enough to chase them away. From this simple arrangement grew more regular agreements for protection, and some enterprising Bullies formed their own brothels of women, becoming pimps.

The Bullies were fearsome fellows who were afraid of only their employers and the police. Always amongst the most exploited were women driven by desperation into prostitution.

The alleyways and dank streets were not only home to the prostitutes. The area was known for its thieves' kitchens, whole tenements of villains of every kind who had contacts through the pubs, the shops, the Market, and their landlords to sell whatever they stole. Most of what they stole was through pickpocketing. They did not travel far for burglary or robbery, so they often did not manage to steal much of value unless they ventured into the city itself, where they too easily stood out from the crowd, betrayed by their ragged poverty. They kept watch for the police as the Metropolitan Police under its Commissioner, the professional soldier Sir Charles Warren, had become well organised, more numerous, more disciplined and determined. The police were not open to petty bribery, and this class of criminals could manage and work to a strict code of conduct.

However, the newly organised police were a little too regimented, and criminals learned the routes of the police beats, their timings, and found how to avoid them.

Pubs were largely unregulated, and drunkenness was the norm. The price of a prostitute was rarely more than six pence, more usually only four pence, the price of a glass of gin. It was often the case that the population of the area was alcoholic and daily faced the dilemma of choosing between a drink or a bed for the night.

The victims of *Jack the Ripper* lived there and died there.

Part One: The Nightmare Begins

CHAPTER TWO

INSPECTOR REID

The detective inspector with a new responsibility for Spitalfields, part of the Whitechapel district of East London, Edmund Reid, was an unlikely police officer. Born in Canterbury but moving when still young to a part of the Old Kent Road in South London known as the village, he had cast about for a profession. Always agile and quick, both physically and intellectually, he had tried many trades, including delivering immensely heavy bags of sugar for a grocery business, delivering newspapers that were rented out for reading, working as a pastry cook and also as a seaman.

Then, in 1872, upon seeing an advertisement for fit men to enrol in the Metropolitan Police, he left the sea and applied. There must have been something special about him, for, despite failing to reach the minimum height requirement for a police officer, he was taken on anyway, the shortest police officer in the country.

Policing proved to be another part of a fascinating life. Eighteen months after joining, he was a detective, taking pride in always dressing smartly, always noted for his courtesy and politeness to everyone. He spent three years in that rank, always receiving commendations for his work and his alertness. By 1885, he was a Detective Inspector.

Meanwhile, his athleticism and love of adventure saw him become famous across the country for exploits unrelated to his police work. He was the first man to parachute from a balloon, making the jump at about a thousand feet above the Bedfordshire countryside. He carried on in such ballooning exploits by making a record ascent from The Crystal Palace, for which he was awarded a gold medal. Such awards sat alongside the regular commendations he received from the courts for his police work.

An energetic man, Reid loved the theatre and readily took to amateur dramatics, where his ability was remarked on as being exceptional. He visited the Music Halls and the Opera House and got to know many of the professional acts. He could surprise his colleagues with his conjuring tricks, especially card tricks. He also sang so well he might have ventured off into another profession entirely. As his curiosity fitted him well for detective work, it also led him into a strange avenue of spiritual fulfilment. Always recognised as a decent, moral, kindly man, it bemused his senior officers, as well as his colleagues, that he drew his upstanding morality and spiritual strength not from mainstream religion but from paganism; he was a Druid.

He stood out from others not only for his eccentric religious practices and courageous exploits but also because of his clarity of method when conducting investigations. He referred to 'the facts' as being of greater value than opinions, the latter likely to draw too misleadingly on prejudice.

Specifically, he stood apart from his senior officers in two opinions, in his case based on facts, in theirs on prejudice: as far as he was concerned, the Whitechapel Borough as a whole was not endemically criminal as they opined, unlike the Spitalfields part of it which he did think to be thoroughly criminal. Secondly, he held the unfashionable opinion that the ongoing Jewish migration was fundamentally a civilising process, often remarking that he rarely saw a drunken Jew. He was enraged at the suggestion from many of the nominally Christian criminal residents of the slums, as well as from some fellow officers, that Jews had murdered the saviour, and so were by nature untrustworthy.

In his opinion, the Christ, if he had existed, had been killed by Romans, not Jews, but once the Romans embraced Christianity, it was a crime they conveniently shifted off onto someone else, an approach so familiar to him in working amongst the criminals of the grimy streets of H Division and elsewhere. His colleagues found it easy to tolerate his views even given they were so very different from

Part One: The Nightmare Begins

their own, and his popularity was unparalleled. His superiors found themselves drawn to his assertion that the Jewish immigrants were a civilising force, reluctantly accepting the facts he placed before them, troublingly different to their prejudices.

Reid loved police work. He lived at the police station and when he married, his wife lived there too. Indeed, his children were born there. Since at least the days of Warren, police stations were often like army barracks with family living quarters. When his much-loved daughter eventually married a policeman, she too lived at a police station and the birth of her child upheld the family tradition of being born in police stations.

Policing was his passion and his home. He was widely regarded as a very good detective too, but it saddened him that often the worst of crimes went unsolved whilst the unfortunate found themselves drawn into illegality by circumstance and were more readily apprehended and punished. He had a profound sense of pity.

So, it was with a solid foundation of reality and experience that Reid was called upon to investigate a series of murders of women in and around Spitalfields. Throughout what was to come, and in the years of reflection that followed, Reid remained calm and considered whilst many around him gave way to the hysteria of the time.

The Abandoned: *Victims of Jack the Ripper*

Part One: The Nightmare Begins

CHAPTER THREE

EMMA SMITH AND MARY RUSSEL

The start of dark deeds to come.

The gangs which roamed around H Division were a nuisance. They avoided the police but caused a great deal of anguish to almost everyone else in the area. Dealing with them was not made easier by the police borders with other Divisions, particularly J Division. However, when it came to detective work, that ceased to be a major issue as Reid, newly appointed to Whitechapel's H Division, had been the Detective Inspector in both areas and had many contacts. It was he who helped break down barriers and improve cooperation across these areas of policing. The roving gangs were mainly youths seeking to rob street vendors and prostitutes, but they could be very violent, and the women of the street were always in fear of them.

In early April 1888, a file arrived on the desk of Detective Inspector Reid concerning an attack by one of the High Rip gangs on one Emma Smith. He noted that the uniformed sergeant had stated on the case log that the attack looked to be the work of a street gang, probably motivated by robbery, but with an abhorrent aspect of sadism thrown in, which was unusual. There was something not right about it.

Reid did what he always did. He gathered all the facts he could. He called in two of his detectives and asked for the uniformed Police

Sergeant Thick to be present. He needed Thick as he was one of the most experienced and reliable officers in the Metropolitan Police and was a decent man. Reid liked to work with decent men.

Thick was a sturdy man of the West Country, a Wiltshire farm labourer's son and had come late to the city. When the detectives start making enquiries, it would be best to have Thick and his men on hand as parts of Spitalfields were too dangerous for policemen to go along unsupported. Reid knew that Thick would have men placed within police whistle distance of each other.

In the briefing session when Reid set out the list of enquiries he wanted made, he noted that Thick knew the victim. This was not particularly surprising because Sergeant Thick knew hundreds of criminals and prostitutes in the Spitalfields area and had probably arrested most of them at one time or another. His local knowledge was useful.

Emma Smith, he said, checking an old notebook, had lived in George Street with a man the locals called 'Fingers' or 'Fingers Freddy'. He had never been arrested under that name but was certainly part of a street distraction gang. Fingers would perform card tricks in the street, gaining the attention of a crowd whilst his pickpockets went to work. The Sergeant suggested talking to a Rose Mylett whom he knew for certain was lodging at 18 George Street, the same address as given for Emma Smith.

Rose was a well-known drunk who kept body and soul together by prostitution. She had already made a garbled statement to his beat officers suggesting how the assault had come about. They should also speak to the woman who ran the common lodging house where both women lived, one Mary Russell, and another lodger there he did not know so well, a woman called Annie Lee. It was these two women, Russell and Lee, who had managed to get Emma Smith to the hospital when they found her in a state of severe injury.

Reid let Thick speak, knowing the man brought authority to the enquiry. However, he already had the statements of Russell and Lee and would be interviewing them at length. What bothered him more was the whereabouts of Fingers Freddy. He ordered a search for him.

Reid started to piece together the movements of Emma Smith on the night she was assaulted. He found this to be easy to do, given that various women were giving information to his detectives. He had her police file on his desk, so he knew her for being a woman in

Part One: The Nightmare Begins

her mid-40s, a notorious drunk who was liable to be aggressive at times.

It seems that somehow, probably when plying her trade as a prostitute, she had met the man Fingers Freddy, who was taken with her. Women in her position were often trying to find a man to live with as it gave them at least rudimentary security. These relationships frequently failed under the pressure of poverty, degradation and drunkenness, yet Emma and Freddy still seemed to be partners at least a year after first setting up together in the Rookeries on George Street.

From the description given by Mary Russell, amongst others, he was a man capable of taking care of himself when things turned nasty and capable of taking care of Emma, too. At the very least, he tolerated Emma working as a prostitute – they needed her earnings as well as whatever he brought in, as often only in this way could they afford rent, food and gin. What disturbed Reid was the report from the hospital and, especially, the autopsy report.

Emma Smith was methodical. She worked set hours as, from experience, she knew where and when to find customers. She had left George Street a little after 6 p.m. but, unlike many of the other women in the area, tended to work a little further away, in Limehouse. She would drink a lot and, in the pubs, would either find her customers or take them there so they would buy her a drink before buying her services. Often, she would take the drink in lieu of additional payments, trapped by her alcoholism.

It was Easter Monday, a bank holiday when there was a lot of drunkenness about but no trade from the Market which was shut. There was, however, still trade from the docks. A little after midnight, she was seen by another prostitute, Margaret Hayes, on Fairance Street in Limehouse. It had been a slow night for business; it was cold and that was probably her last planned business of the night. A couple of hours later, she was walking home.

Reid then pieced together what Russell and Lee claimed she had told them. Emma got to Whitechapel church when she realised she was being watched. She moved a little quicker in the darkness but made out three figures closing in on her. She knew she had to get away as quickly as possible and ran. She made it as far as the corner of Brick Lane and Wentworth Street before they caught her.

She was drunk, but not so drunk she failed to recognise that these three meant to do her harm. Expecting robbery and being too far from home for the protection of Freddy or any of the Watchmen, she accepted the loss of her earnings, but this was more than that. One of the three, she guessed, was about 19 years of age. ('How could she be so specific', thought Reid). The other two were older. They attacked her viciously, beating and raping her, stealing her money and then, in an act that shocked Reid and was entirely new to him, rammed a blunt instrument into her vagina with such force that it tore the perineum, an injury causing a great loss of blood, eventual septicaemia and within days, her death.

Reid, a logical, careful man, found himself suddenly full of anger for what this woman had suffered. He knew he had to calm down and take a steady, careful approach to this. Emma had somehow struggled back to George Street, where Lee and Russell had seen her staggering in. They took her to the hospital on the Whitechapel Road, passing again the site of the assault. She was admitted and cared for, but there was little that could be done. There was another feature that caught his eye; her earlobe was torn, and her earring had been ripped out, a common cruelty perpetrated by street gangs.

A week later, Reid held another briefing meeting with his detectives and some of the uniformed men investigating the murder. The consensus was that many in the Spitalfields rookeries were angry about the brutality meted out to Emma Smith. Whether people knew her, whether they had liked her or not, did not matter. A new sense of fear was abroad. The detectives started questioning known gang members but got nowhere. The gangs themselves were not organised as such and had no hierarchy or structure. So, Reid put together a new way of thinking about the case and what his men needed to look for.

'We know some, but not all, of the facts of this case,' he said. 'We know that Smith was an 'unfortunate', a prostitute and that she was set upon by at least three men, though we have no witness to it except Smith herself. We are told one of the gang was about 19 years old. I want to know why she was able to pick out one so precisely in age. Did she know them? Find out which of the so-called High Rip Gangs are older but have a younger member with them. I have a bad feeling about this gang business. What do we know about this gang that does not fit the usual pattern?' It was a rhetorical question. 'We know that High Rip gangs are invariably gangs of youths, and they usually target lone individuals, especially in the docks areas, that they exist all over the city and in every city in the kingdom for that matter.

We know they use knives freely. Their motivation is intimidation and robbery, and they are not averse to rape. Why, then, am I unusually uncomfortable about this gang and this attack?' He let the silence hang for a few heavy seconds. 'It is the viciousness that marks it out, makes it different – she was not stabbed or slashed, but even more cruelly used. Is there something we are missing? There were older men involved, which is odd. This does not feel like the usual gang, the usual attack. What did the poor woman know about these attackers that she did not share with us? Or is it the case that she told the women Lee and Russell more than they have let on? Have they been intimidated, told to keep silent?'

He watched his detectives taking notes. He had renewed their enthusiasm to solve the case by steering them away from preconceived answers. This was not a street robbery; it was something more. Reid went on:

'I also want you to think about Fingers Freddy. Talk to the main fences in the area and find out when he last produced goods for sale. Ask why he has suddenly gone missing. Was he at the lodging house when the victim staggered back there? Apparently, he usually hangs around there when she returns in the early hours. If he was not there this time, where was he? Find him. I think he has something to tell us. A man like that would have looked for revenge and gone out to avenge the attack, but we have no indication that he did. We also need to eliminate him as a suspect, although it seems unlikely, given what we do know of the assault. Nevertheless, we cannot dismiss the proposition that Fingers Freddy was involved, and if he was, did she make up the story about the three men in a fit of loyalty? Not likely, I know, but keep it in mind. I will contact all the Criminal Investigation Departments across London. If Freddy is around, he will emerge somewhere to earn money as a card-sharp or street distraction thief and we will spot him. I want two of you back around the pubs finding out everything you can about Freddy and his paramour, the deceased Emma Smith. There is something not right about this case.'

He turned to Sergeant Thick, who had joined them.

'If we are going to ask around the pubs about two people who have been residents of George Street for an unusually long time, over a year, where might we start?'

The policeman did not hesitate.

'There is the Frying Pan pub, and that is your best bet. The Ten Bells, of course, is also there. I suggest you start there. There is the Horn of Plenty on the corner of Dorset and Crispin Streets, but I think it is safer to go there mob-handed, a show of force might be necessary, but be aware they will all clam up as soon as they spot us. The Blue Coat Boy in Dorset Street will have been used by Smith at some time or another, and upstairs is really no more than a brothel. The largest pub is The Britannia on Commercial Street, which is used a lot by market workers, but no, I think, stick to smaller places. I suppose we might also try The City of Norwich pub on Wentworth Street.'

'Right, that is a start,' said Reid. 'I also want you to talk to the landlords of the lodging houses and shops around George Street, Flower and Dean, Brick Lane, Thrawl Street and Wentworth Street. They run everything around there and know most of what is going on. Persuade them to talk to you. If you come across any Jews, let me know, of course, but be aware that a lot of them do not speak much English and none of them is in a High Rip Gang as far as I know, so don't waste too much time pressing them. It is possible they might have seen something, but not likely at that time of the morning. I want two of you to call on Jimmy Smith in Brick Lane. Make sure it is Jimmy Smith, the younger, not his father. His father is unlikely to tell us anything without first seeking advice from his friend McCarthy. The Smiths own most of the lodging houses around the south side. Then, speak with young Jimmy's sister, Elizabeth and her husband, Johnny Cooney, in Flower and Dean Street. They keep the lodging house where Emma Smith and Freddy lived.'

Sergeant Thick interrupted.

'Johnny Cooney keeps the Sugar Loaf Inn in Hanbury Street. It's a little out of the way for Emma Smith, but we might add that one to the list. Another thing is that young Jimmy Smith might be a bit of a rogue and up to all sorts of things, but he is well-liked around Brick Lane, and they call him The Governor. I very much doubt he will have had any part to play in this, but I can be sure he will let me know if anyone he deals with is involved.'

Then, in a softer voice, Thick added, 'he is a useful source of information at times, but we should keep that to ourselves.'

Reid nodded. Much as he respected Sergeant Thick, he was also aware that Thick had spoken up for Jimmy Smith in Court, ensuring the young man did not go to prison for some gambling offence or

Part One: The Nightmare Begins

other, something else involving McCarthy and Crossingham, he thought. He also heard the rumours that Smith was known to straighten up the police to ensure that street gambling went on without any harassment. Smith was a man who got his way by bribery whenever he could and not by violence unless he couldn't find another way out of a situation. Reid was suspicious that it was Thick who managed the pay-off to the police on the beat, making sure they turned a blind eye to illegal gambling. Smith and his sister would not want too much attention in the area as it was bad for business. They wanted the murder cleared up quickly.

'I'll take your judgment into account, Sergeant', said Reid. 'Meanwhile, find out if you can if anyone has suddenly left the lodgings Jimmy Smith controls, particularly women who might be so-called midwives. I know it's like looking for a needle in a haystack with these people moving every five minutes, but it's worth a try.'

Reid dismissed his team to discover what they could. He was already of the opinion that the trail was getting cold and that without Fingers Freddy, he would not have gotten to the bottom of this.

The Abandoned: *Victims of Jack the Ripper*

CHAPTER FOUR

ROSE MYLET, ANNIE MILWARD AND PEARLY POL

The general opinion, the only one accepted at the beginning of the investigation, was that Emma Smith had been violently assaulted by a High Rip Gang simply seeking to rob her. In robbing her, it was opined that their animal bloodlust led them to sexually assault her, humiliate her, and then, without remorse, they left her to die.

The gang had consisted of three men, although later re-examination of statements suggested there might have been four of them. No search among police informers turned up any gang matching the description.

Inspector Reid, however, was not so ready to accept that this had been a random assault, a victim in the wrong place at the wrong time. What if this had been a targeted attack, planned? He was sure that the gang had not meant to kill her, for if that had been their intention, they would have stabbed her. The perverted additional sexual assault might have been one of the men losing control of his sadistic impulses, but equally, it might have been an additional warning. If it was so, if Emma Smith had been selected for a reason other than robbery, perhaps as a warning, a warning of what, aimed at whom?

His detectives had lost sight of several of the prostitutes who had at first been keen to help. There may be nothing in that, and the women drifted between lodging houses and tenements. It all made life difficult for him. He could build theories but not cases. Another puzzling feature was the disappearance of Fingers Freddy. Reid knew that this man habitually drank in the Frying Pan pub every evening when his mistress, Emma Smith, was out soliciting for prostitution. The police could not get a fix on his movements on the final evening when Smith was out working the streets and pubs of neighbouring Limehouse. Some recalled him being in the pub for only a short time that evening, others thought it the day before. No one admitted to seeing him on the days following the murder. Usually, this would indicate to Reid that Fingers Freddy should be the main suspect, but that did not ring true if the assault was by a gang. The rambling, semi-coherent descriptions given by the sorry, dying woman to the policeman stationed by her bed in the hospital continued to refer to the gang. The only other motive for the attack that Reid thought plausible was revenge. He thought the woman Rose Mylett had hinted as much, but now she couldn't be found.

According to Mrs. Russell, Fingers and Emma Smith seemed to rub along as well as any couple in their circumstances do, but Fingers had returned early from the pub one night in a state of agitation; she did not remember whether it was the night of the attack or a previous night. On reflection, she thought it was the previous one and that he had possibly waited up for Emma, but she was not sure. She did think that there had been no argument between them but that Freddy had been 'up to something'. Was he seeing another woman? More likely, did he need an alibi for something, or money to pay off a debt, get more drinks?

The matter would go before the Coroner's Court, and yet another verdict of 'Murder against persons unknown' would be recorded. He tried one more ploy. He arranged for narks, police informants, to be in the pubs in the area, especially the Ten Bells and the Frying Pan and talk to customers about Freddy. He brought in some undercover detectives to sit in the pubs and listen in to the conversations. The Deputy Commissioner himself was willing to organise the undercover work, as he was experienced in secret police work.

A new line of enquiry arose from the information fed back to Reid. There was a particular story about Fingers and Emma, varying from place to place, depending on the teller and her state of sobriety. It concerned a scheme Freddy had hatched. Through his association with Emma, he knew that the younger prostitutes would sometimes need the services of a 'midwife'. This was the euphemism commonly used to refer to an abortionist. Such abortionists were often women practising in their own kitchens, women with little or no medical training. There were qualified medical practitioners who would carry out the illegal procedure, but no woman in Spitalfields could afford their services. The secret abortionists tried to keep a very low profile, not wanting to attract the attention of the law. The story in the Ten Bells, repeated in a similar fashion in the Frying Pan, the Blue Coat Boy and elsewhere, was that Freddy knew through Emma's many prostitute contacts who one of the local abortionists might be, a woman in Brick Lane. Unfortunately, no one was brave or foolhardy enough to mention her name to any of the narks and certainly did not do so in earshot of the waiting secret policemen. She was, by some accounts, a fearsome woman who had previously practised her trade in the Rookeries near south Camden. Her own man had several prostitutes working for him.

Reid set his detectives to find what they could about this abortionist, but they came up with very little. There was much confusion between abortionists and women who did offer perfectly legal services as genuine midwives. It was difficult to pin down where the abortionist midwives might be located or how to differentiate them from any woman performing more usual midwifery, especially as both tasks were sometimes on offer by the same woman. Indeed, as no sane abortionist would advertise her real occupation to the world, the term 'midwife' was always the euphemism used. Of the women called midwives whom he could trace, there was no evidence to suggest any of them did anything illegal, even though he suspected some of them of undertaking both services from time to time. Concentrating on Brick Lane did not bring anything new. More stories emerged of a 'midwife' in South Camden who was certainly an abortionist, but Reid decided not to follow that as it was too far from the usual area where Fingers Freddy and Emma Smith frequented. Given her age and state of alcoholism, Reid assumed that Emma would have little reason to have had personal need of a 'midwife' but would surely have known of some.

The scraps of information obtained from the now missing Rose Mylett supported the tales in the pubs that Freddy, Emma or both had used local knowledge to blackmail an abortionist based in Brick Lane. Could this have been the motivation for the attack on Emma – to warn off Freddy and herself? Had the abortionist paid a Bully to set up an attack using some of the High Rip boys? It might be the sort of thuggery her own 'husband' might get up to. Once commissioned, how far the thugs might go in carrying out their task would be down to them. Meanwhile, where and when had Freddy gone? Adding fuel to this theory was the rumour that Emma might have recently visited the abortionist with Rose Mylett, who was thought to have been pregnant, being one of the younger women in the business. Finding Freddy and finding Rose was what he needed to happen.

Meeting that evening with the uniformed officers mustering for the parade, Reid took a sound. He wanted a collective view of the Emma Smith murder. The views of the men fell into two camps. The first was that it had been a random attack by High Rip boys from Limehouse. They couldn't explain the sadistic cruelty, though, and none had come across it before. It also did not explain the disappearance of Fingers Freddy unless he had been the cause of the attack or even set it up, which seemed unlikely. The second theory was that the story in the pubs was correct. Freddy had tried to blackmail the unknown Brick Lane abortionist; she had used her influence to have him silenced, and Emma warned off. The attack on Emma was probably not meant to result in murder. Reid feared that if the latter were true, Fingers Freddy was at grave risk as he might point out to police who the abortionist was, should the police find him before the gang got him.

The chances were that Fingers would not be found unless his body was washed up in the Thames estuary one day. Whatever the truth of the matter, Reid would scale back the enquiry in the morning. It would remain an unsolved case unless he could find Rose Mylett, and she could shed some light on this. He shifted the focus of his investigation to finding Rose Mylett. She just might hold the key to the investigation.

Back in his office, he continued his research. He had a file sent over about another unsolved case, an attack on a woman in Mile End, Ada Wilson, just a few weeks earlier. This had not been in his area, but he had been curious about attacks on women in case there was a similarity with the Emma Smith killing.

Part One: The Nightmare Begins

There was no similarity in the cases as far as he could see apart from the profession of the women. Ada claimed to be a dressmaker and probably was for some of her time, as many of the women in the Whitechapel area had similar occupations. His own reports showed she was a prostitute working mostly in the dock area and had been receiving visitors at 19 Maidman Street. This was a lone assailant whom she says was asking for money, and when she refused, he attacked with a clasp knife, stabbing her in the throat. Her screams alerted neighbours, and the man only just got away. Ada Wilson had a good view of her attacker and, unlike Emma Smith, gave a description of the man who had stabbed and cut her about with a knife.

She was lucky to survive. That assailant was apparently a sailor of some sort, with a fair moustache and foreign accent, Scandinavian or German. He got clean away.

Reid selected a second file marked Annie Milward. He flicked that one open for comparison. This was a case about which he still fretted. He had received a notification from the Workhouse Infirmary in Whitechapel about a woman who was being treated for multiple stab wounds. He had interviewed her and the Infirmary doctor. It was obvious that Annie was a middle-aged prostitute who had been living at 8 White's Row in Spitalfields, though she stubbornly refused to admit her means of making a living. She remained vague about what had happened, not wanting to give away the highly probable fact that she had been soliciting when attacked.

A man, almost certainly a casual customer, had suddenly turned on her with a clasp knife and stabbed her about the thighs, lower torso and along her legs. Reid could see she must have been on her back at the time of the assault. He thought the assailant might well be the same man who had attacked Ada Wilson and wanted more information from Annie. He had left her to be cared for at the Infirmary with the intention of gradually gleaning as much information from her as possible. She recovered enough to be sent to the South Grove Workhouse on the Mile End Road. He then lost track of her for a few days until he received another notification. She had been found dead in a yard at the back of the Workhouse, apparently having been plying her trade when she collapsed. The autopsy said she died of natural causes; another case closed with frustratingly no criminal caught. He now had a bad feeling about Rose Mylett. It would be bad business all around if she ended the same way, more so because he would then have missed his chance to question her about Emma.

The following day, Reid and Detective Sergeant Enright started enquiries specifically aimed at finding Rose Mylett, by now his key witness in the Emma Smith murder investigation. He received very little help from the lodging house records in George Street. She had left owing nothing, so the lodging house had no interest in her. They tried the various pubs in the area until, by chance, they came across Pearly Pol. She was a woman in her fifties, a well-known lady of the night and often a useful source of information for the price of a glass of rum. She was a big woman with a face blotched by years of serious drinking. When she spoke, it was with a voice almost as deep as a man's. Reid put a drink in front of her. She looked him in the eye, she was the same height as the Inspector.

'What name are you going under at the moment, Polly?' he asked politely. He always treated people with civility.

'Polly will do,' she answered cautiously.

'The last time we spoke, you gave your real name as Mary Connolly. However, I'm happy to call you Polly if that is what you like.' He was letting her know he knew all about her.

'Well, Mr. Reid, you ain't here to talk to me about being Pol or Mary. What is it I can do for you kind gentlemen?'

'You know about Emma Smith being murdered. You know that Fingers Freddy is missing. I think that Rose Mylett can help us with information about these two. She started to help but seemed to have lost herself in the alleyways here. I want to know where she is.'

'Oh, Mr. Reid, I never met Fingers, but I did hear about him. I never spoke with him, honestly, I didn't, and I don't know anything about him or what happened to poor Emma. I don't know who did that wicked thing to her. Now you ask about someone called Rose. I don't know a young lady called Rose, but I think the girl you are looking for is called Clara. Fair Clara is who the boys ask for, but she ain't been around for a few days.'

Back at the police station, Reid and Enright went through the files of police arrests, notes and statements covering every arrest or interview over the previous two months. The name Rose Mylett appeared several times in connection with Emma Smith, but what they were really searching for was the alias, Fair Clara.

At last, it was there before them. A uniformed constable had recorded arresting a drunken sailor near the Commercial Road who had been in the company of a young woman called Fair Clara. When she was questioned and threatened with arrest, she gave what she claimed to be her true name, Elizabeth Davis.

They then searched for that name and found it once more in an arrest in Whitechapel, but she was not charged with an offence. The address given was George Street in Spitalfields, so it seemed they might have the right woman but were no further forward in locating her. Enright went off to talk to local beat officers for the east of the division in the hope that someone would recall Fair Clara. It proved to be a shorter task than he feared. A constable immediately recognised the name, and a search of the daily duty logs turned up the name Alice Darley with an address in Poplar. He journeyed the short distance to Poplar, but there the trail went cold.

It seemed that although Fair Clara did work the streets there from time to time, usually being known as Alice or Fair Alice Downey, she had not been around for some weeks, apparently preferring to stay in the Spitalfields area.

Reid was back where he had started. While Rose changing her name so often was common amongst the sisterhood of prostitutes, it made finding her very difficult.

Inspector Reid listened to his sergeant's report on the search for the missing witness. He had one more idea.

'It is just possible that her name, or one of her names, will appear in the 1881 Census. It will give us an address, and though it is very unlikely she will still be there, someone might know her and tell us where she is now. I think we can concentrate on our local Boroughs as she doesn't seem to stray too far. I will arrange for someone to check for us.'

It was the following Monday morning when Reid called Enright into his office.

'We have a smart clerk working at the Records Office in Somerset House. He could not find Rose Mylett under any of the names we have for her, but he has found a Mr. Henry Mylett and a Mrs. Margaret Mylett living at 13 Thomas Street in Whitechapel. They are the right ages to be her parents, so let us pay them a visit. Who knows, Rose might be there.'

They made the visit in the early evening when it was still light. As a precaution, they took a uniformed constable with them. The area was a jumble of builders' yards, warehouses, cobbled streets, tenements, horse-drawn carts and the smell of the nearby river.

Thomas Street was short, running off Whitechapel Road, opposite the London Hospital. The police knew the street well as its main building was the Whitechapel Workhouse which ran along almost the length of the street.

A small, dowdy and thin-face woman answered their knocking on the ill-fitting door to their rooms. The smell of boiled meat and potatoes followed her to the door. On their reluctant admittance, the detectives saw a small but wiry man, bare-footed, moving his boots to the side of the open hearth. They seemed to use the open fire for cooking. Both husband and wife spoke with the clear accents of rural Ireland. Reid knew their histories immediately. The room was furnished and warm. These people were poor but far from destitute and at least one of them, Mr. Mylett, by the looks of things, was in regular employment. Reid spoke:

'We are not here to worry you, and I am not suggesting you have done anything wrong. We are trying to find someone who might be able to help us in a serious matter. Again, she is not in any trouble with us, we simply need to ask her about one or two things. We think the person we are seeking is your daughter. You do have a daughter?'

The two looked at each other. Mr. Mylett seemed too nervous to even speak. His wife, less timid, replied in a hushed, lilting voice.

'We have no daughter living here. We do have a daughter, but she ain't been here for a long time. I don't really know where she is now, but she has been working as a seamstress.' She looked as if she regretted saying anything but was too afraid not to do so.

'Is your daughter named Rose Mylett?' asked Reid.

'No. That is not her name. Our daughter is Catherine, Catherine Davis.'

Enright looked exasperated, but Reid persisted.

'How old is your daughter, Mrs. Mylett?' he asked softly.

'She will be 28, nearly 29. Oh God, please tell me she is safe, she has a little girl.'

'What, she has a little girl living with her?' Reid was concerned for the child.

'No, at least I don't think so. You see, there is some shame in the family, and we have not been told who the father might be. The little one is cared for by a family in Sutton.'

'Could you describe your daughter, Mrs. Mylett, just so the Sergeant and I know we are looking for the right person?' Reid spoke gently to the woman who was shaking and wringing her hands.

Part One: The Nightmare Begins

With a lot of reflection and self-correction, the frightened woman gave a vague description of her daughter which Enright copied into his notebook.

'Well,' said Reid, 'I think that has been very helpful, Mrs. Mylett. I am not sure we have the right person, but let me leave you a florin for your trouble.' With that, he produced a florin, a two-shilling piece, from his pocket and placed it on the table. 'We will leave you in peace.' He had turned to leave when the mute Mr. Mylett unexpectedly spoke in a wheezing, struggling voice.

'Rose, sir, I heard that Catherine calls herself Rose. She's been living up in Spitalfields, somewhere near the Market. But we haven't seen her, sir. True to God, we haven't seen her in nearly twelve months. Please tell me she has come to no harm.'

Reid, smiling a little, turned back to the man.

'Thank you indeed, Mr. Mylett. I can reassure you that she was perfectly well the last time we saw her. As I said, we think she might help us with another matter, that is all.'

Mr. Mylett grew in confidence.

'It must be a serious matter, sir, to bring you to our door at this time.' He remained diffident but was curious.

'Indeed, it is, Mr. Mylett,' said Reid. 'It concerns the death of someone your daughter knew.'

'Not the murder of that poor woman, the one taken by a High Rip gang. Surely not that, sir?'

'I'm afraid so. I repeat that Rose, or Catherine, is not involved, but I do need to see that she is safe, of course.' Reid was taking a gentle, concerned approach rather than trying to bully the couple into talking.

'If I knew where she is, I would tell you, Inspector. All I know is that she was working as a seamstress around Spitalfields.' It was a long passage of words for the broken man.

Mrs. Mylett held a cloth to her face to cover her rising distress. The policemen nodded to her husband and moved back to the door. Mr. Mylett followed them. Once outside, still in bare feet, he spoke quietly to Reid in a thickening Irish accent.

'I know what she is about, sir. I know how she earns her living. I am sad about it and wish it were otherwise, but I pray to Our Lady that no harm befalls her, and that God will forgive her. It is a hard life, sir, a hard life.' Having regained the ability to speak freely, Mr. Mylett was more sure of himself. The father trusted Reid, he spoke

27

man to man, but now, in shame for his daughter's way of life, he stared down at his cold, dirty feet, regretting the truth of what he had said.

A large, brown rat scurried out of the door behind the man and ran across the street. Mr. Mylett paid it no mind. Wherever there was a Workhouse, the rats outnumbered the people.

'Yes, it is hard, Mr. Mylett, and I judge no one,' said Reid, offering his hand in a polite farewell. 'Let us hope that things get better. Thank you for your help, and I wish you both a good night.'

As the trio of police officers walked along the street, many eyes upon them, they heard again the voice of Rose's father call after them,

'Thank you again for your generosity, sir.' He did not look a well man, and it was no surprise to Inspector Reid when he heard a few weeks later that the man had died.

Enright looked at his superior officer.

'Might I ask, Inspector, how do you do it? How do you know when to drop out the florin, win their confidence and get them to talk to you about what they do not say even to each other?'

'Well, Sergeant, it is about knowing people and the good in them. Look at the circumstances in which these people live. Who are the greater criminals, the collapsed souls who sell their bodies for drink or the landlords of the slums and pubs who suck the blood out of them? Compassion sergeant, tempered with reality. However, I take with a pinch of salt the story of her not being there for a while. I doubt she stays away from her mother.'

The two men were both lost in thought. Enright spoke first:

'These women and their men change their names and locations more often than my wife changes her mind. When that sickly chap goes, and it won't be long by the sound of him, his widow will be out on the street. This is not easy. It looks to me as if we are no nearer finding Rose Mylett, Inspector.'

No, Sergeant, we are not. I think maybe we must be patient and wait for her to turn up, but she will turn up again. We can be sure of that.'

CHAPTER FIVE

ROSE AND MARTHA

Rose Mylett moved out of George Street soon after the assault on her friend, Emma Smith. She was keen that no one should associate her with Emma; did not want anyone to think that Emma had confided in her about the blackmail. She had a bad feeling about the place now.

Another friend, Martha Turner, had recently separated from her man, so she found lodgings near her in White's Row. It was always a comfort to be around someone she knew. Martha had also been living on George Street, at number 19, with her man until it all went wrong for her, too. Now, the two women stood at one of the upturned barrels used as tables in The George, drinking beer. Outside, the sun was shining. As the women had eaten a good meal of pie and mash, the only meal either had taken for two days, they were in a relaxed and happy mood and planned to stay in the pub whilst their money lasted and then doze in Itchy Park, next to the great once-white walls of All Saints Church. Both were small in height, though Martha's face was plump, swollen by gin and beer. Both women depended on earning a living on the street to keep them in drink and to buy somewhere to sleep.

'Where was you living before you came down this way, Martha?' Rose asked.

'Well, I'm from over the river, dear. Not one of the Irish from the Borough Rookeries, but nearby, near the Cathedral in Southwark. There's a lot of Irish down there. There was me two older brothers and me two older sisters. Me old dad worked in the warehouses. I think I was about 16 when me old dad left to go off on his own and he died soon after that. When I was about twenty, I met this chap, Henry, he was called. He was alright. Henry Tabram. I married him on Christmas Day in '69 and that's how I ended up being Martha Tabram until I met Mr. Turner and took his name, but me own name is White. When I was first married, we lived just down the street from me old mother.'

'I don't know that area m'self dear, my own parents are also from Ireland somewhere. Do you know Jack McCarthy, who owns all the lodging houses and tenements in Dorset Street? He's a tough one, he is, the whole family is. They think they are proper Cockney Irish now. Well, he is from the Irish, living in Borough by the market, though he claims he was born in France. Always around with that Essex chap, Billy Crossingham. Never apart those two and always up to schemes to rob wretches like you and me, Martha.'

'I know who he is cos I lodged in Dorset Street once, worst billets I ever had,' reflected Martha. 'It stinks down there. But back when I was first married, we wouldn't have anything to do with people like McCarthy. We managed alright back then. I only married him so I would have a man to help take care of me and mother. Anyway, I had two boys in two years, Freddy and Charley. Me husband was working as a foreman in the furniture packing sheds, bringing in decent money, I suppose. He was good to me, but I never really cared for him. I waited for him to go off to work, then I would leave the boys with their Granny and meet up with a jockey or two round the market and have some fun. The trouble was, I got to like the drink and the company a bit too much at times and me old man would find me drunk. I told him I wasn't drunk but having a fit and he sort of believed it cos he wanted to. Anyway, he decided me having fits every night wasn't up to much and he walked out. I left the boys with their granny for a few days and crossed the river for some fun. That was when I met Henry Turner, and we moved down Whitechapel way. Mr. Tabram kept me allowance going otherwise, I would take him to court. I had the boys with me by then, you see, a nice regular 12 shillings a week it was, but then someone told him about me living with Mr. Turner and he reduced me to half a crown a week, the miserable skinflint.'

'You been with Mr. Turner ever since, then?' asked her friend. 'Where are the boys now?' She was interested because she liked Martha, but it was a familiar story, one she could hear from many of the women in any of the pubs she frequented.

'I like to have a little drink and Mr. Turner don't like it, especially when the fits take me. You know how it is. Sometimes, I must earn a little extra and sometimes, I must stay out all night earning what I can. He don't much care for that either. Sometimes, we ended up in the Workhouse on Thomas Street. Well, a couple of times, really. I was there with the boys once.' She tailed off wistfully.

'Fancy. My old folks live down Thomas Street, opposite the infirmary, just off Whitechapel Road. I grew up there,' said Rose.

Martha resumed her story.

'We was only in there a night or two, just casuals, but we hated it and the pig-swill they gave us to eat was just the scraps from the hospital. It's a wonder we weren't all poisoned – then Mr. Turner wanted us back together. He scraped together some pennies to find us a tenancy or failing that a lodging house like we had recently in George Street. I liked it there. He loves me, see. When the boys got older, they got work. I think they are south of the river again. They help me out a bit now and then when I see them, when they come looking for me.'

'So, you are still with him then, your Mr. Turner?' It was genuine curiosity now, Rose warming to the story. She wanted to hear stories of love, if not quite happiness ever after.

'Well, it is just the two of us now, like I say. We used to live down Commercial Road, you'll know the place, Star Chambers, but we were not there more than four months. We got behind with the rent. Henry had lost his job and reckoned all my street and back-alley work was going on drink. He was jealous of the casual men friends I made, but they kept us in food and drink. We tried a bit of street hawking instead but couldn't scratch a living. We did a flit to George Street. Then it all got too much for Henry again and we moved over here. He sulks when he sees me going off to earn our bread. He is trying to get work again in his trade as a carpenter, but nothing much is happening. We live off what I make. I felt bad about not paying the rent at Star Chambers, so I slipped back one afternoon and left the key we still had. I could do that, at least. I made sure they wouldn't find us straight away by changing my name to Emma when we moved up here, but people got me confused with Emma Chapman, so it's Martha again now.'

For Martha, there was no meaning to her life. She simply plodded on day to day, drinking and finding a way to pay for the drink.

'What about you, Rosie? I haven't seen you about with a man of your own. You won't always be young, you know. Get a good one, that's what I say.' There was no irony in Martha's words, no reflection on her own life, and no ambition beyond the next drink.

'Sometimes, Martha, I forget who I am. I was down in Poplar, where I do a lot of trade, and this fellow kept calling out for Alice to join him in the public bar. It took me a while to remember that I am Alice in Poplar. It's a good thing, though, changing your identity from place to place, don't you think? It's like making a fresh start, being someone else. I've a little girl, you know, Flossie; never see her now.' Rose was edging towards self-pity.

'Married in a way was yer?' asked Martha.

'I was proper married in a church,' replied Rose. 'His name was Davis, an upholsterer by day and a wife beater by night. He couldn't cope with me being in the pubs all the time. He got upset because when he came looking for me one night, the barman said, ooh, you mean Drunken Lizzie Davis.'

She laughed a harsh, humourless chuckle as she recalled the memory, then her face hardened, and she continued.

'He gave me a thorough beating for that, so I left him. I don't care what happens to him now as long as little Flossie is looked after. He got to thinking that she was not his; maybe he is right, I can't remember, but he loves her like a daughter anyway.'

She let the matter hang there, leaving her companion to follow a different stream of discussion.

'There's a fight on tonight in the market, Billy Crossingham and Jack McCarthy have set it up, so there will be a big crowd. A lot of toffs from up West will be there, so there should be plenty of trade. I usually work with one or two of Jack's men. I get a punter into the alley, and they knock him over and slit his pockets. The worst I do is make enough for the room and a few drinks and I can do a lot better than that, with luck.'

Rose replied quickly as if already having thought about it. 'No, I don't do the market. I like to go down Limehouse and Poplar, away from here. They know me there and I have a few regulars. It's a safe bet for money.'

'Well, take care getting back to White's Row then,' said the older woman, referring to the lodging houses there. 'But don't stray so far, Rosie, remember what happened to Emma Smith. It will be safer with McCarthy's boys looking out for you around the market, it really would.'

Rosie was gently dismissive of the fear.

'I reckon whoever did for Emma will keep out of the way for a while. I should have a nice few nights anyway. Then I need to go and see Fred Geringher, you know, he owns The City of Norwich in Wentworth Street. Ma says she will be looking for other lodgings soon, Pa is struggling to breathe these days – looks like the police have been round there too, causing bother, looking for me, and my Pa can't work anymore because his chest is so bad. They don't want to end up in the workhouse across the road, so I will find them somewhere to live. Fred owns some places up near Hanbury Street, Pelham Street or Baker's Row, I think, and she wants to move up there. Mr. Geringher knows I am always good to help with the rent.'

She seemed so certain of her ability to arrange things for her parents.

'Geringher is like the rest of them,' said Martha with a good deal of bitterness in her voice, 'he wants to be all respectable with his business friends, but his money comes from you and me, Rosie, from the four-penny fumbling in the alleyways and the two bob from being on your back all night in one of his lodging houses, and he sells the beer to the punters.'

Rosie couldn't remember the last time some sailor had paid her more than four pence. The idea of two shillings was only Martha exaggerating, she thought.

With their money gone, the two women bustled out into the street and, swaying unsteadily, made their way to the open ground next to the great church, now blemished by soot. Like so many, they could doze a while there until they felt like moving on, finding others to be with, and eventually plying their trade. Martha scratched at her ankle, bothered by lice or fleas.

'It's not called Itchy Park for nothing,' she complained.

The Abandoned: *Victims of Jack the Ripper*

Part One: The Nightmare Begins

CHAPTER SIX

POLLY NICHOLS AND DR WALLACE

Polly Nichols listened for the Workhouse bell to clang everyone awake. From the shuffling and wheezing around her she knew that most of the women in the dormitory were awake already; few there managed to get much sleep. All the streets around the Lambeth Workhouse depended on the bell to give them the routine of the day. At six o'clock, everyone in the Workhouse was expected to be awake and getting up for a day's work in exchange for shelter and food. It was a spring morning, and it was still cold.

First came the roll call to see if anyone had run away in Workhouse clothes or died in the night, and then soon, it would be breakfast. True, it was not a meal to dream about, just cold skilly and a brick of bread. The bread was so hard that it had to be softened by dipping it in the skilly before it could be eaten, especially for Polly, as she had lost five of her biting teeth. Being experienced in Workhouse life, she knew a few tricks. First, never sign on as a 'Casual', a single nighter, as their conditions were unimaginably bleak. Some who gained admitance as a casual ran out rather than face the stench and horror of the conditions. She knew that it was always a gamble whether to be arrested for vagrancy and risk three months in prison or seek refuge in the degradation of a 'casual ward'. The decision was often made for them, usually by the porter on the door of the

Workhouse, who decided who to admit and who to turn away. Drunks were always turned away.

She was an inmate, sometimes called 'a patient', though she had only twice been in an infirmary. As an inmate, she was in the newly built Workhouse, which was bigger, more airy and even more anonymous than the old place, which was still used for the casuals. She was one of a thousand poor or elderly, destitute and dying people with nowhere else to go. She had learned the ways to avoid the worst of things as far as possible. She sat at the long bench in the refectory with her bowl of skilly broth in front of her. She looked at it carefully before picking out the small black pellets she knew for rats' droppings. The rats were everywhere, especially in the food stores. She did the same with the small hunks of bread she pulled apart. Along the table was a heap of salt and she dipped her bread into that, too, so at least her food had some taste. Food did not interest her that much, really.

She had been in and out of Workhouses these past six years and liked this one best, not that anyone liked a Workhouse. Perhaps it is more accurate to say she feared the life in this one less than elsewhere. It was security of a sort. She knew the routines and the food menu.

The other women would sometimes ask her what they might get to eat. She knew that their dinner would be at noon today and that the menu was boiled pork with potatoes, some dumplings and suet pudding. It was better than what she got on the outside, where she went days without eating. At least it sounded good. The cooks tried to produce edible food, but it was often cold, greasy and tasteless. The portions were supposed to be unlimited, but no one asked for more. The staff had the same food as the inmates, just better quality and five times as much of the freshly cooked food. Supper would be breakfast all over again, but two or three times a week, they would get cheese, too. The women had a pint of tea to wash it down. They ate in a silence broken only by the scrabbling for salt, the slurping of the gruel, and the subdued sobbing of some of the women pining for their children taken from them, their husbands, and their homes. At seven, they would start their mostly pointless, dreary work.

Trusted to work in the laundry, useful work, the proximity to soapy water helped her to indulge in one defiant scrap of humanity – she kept as clean as she could. All the women wore the same blue striped dresses with a white mop cap and pinafore: she made sure she always kept a clean petticoat aside for herself. Today, though, would be different. She had been told by the Superintendent that as a long-term resident, she had to go up before the Board of Guardians again, which would determine whether she should stay on or leave. She had no thought about it. If they threw her out, she would find her way back to her father's house, and he would take her in. Her oldest son was living with his grandfather, so she would get to see him, too. She thought her son, Eddie, was probably apprenticed to his grandfather as a smithy, but she did not know for sure. Once out, she feared drifting back to her old ways, and once the drink took her, she would sink down again and end up back in the Workhouse. She did not care. Her pride, her self-worth, had long ago crumbled away. At nine-thirty, she was sent for and made to wait in a line of frightened women outside the Superintendent's office, where the Board met.

Inside the office, the Board of Guardians sat to one side of the long table. The table, large as it was, could not accommodate them all, and several spilt out at the sides. Each of the contributing parish councils sent one representative, six others were of the locality – mostly shopkeepers and merchants. They did not share a common understanding of the role. For some, it was to guard the public purse, while for others, it was about social containment and orderliness given that 'the poor are always with us', and it was suspected widely that for one or two, it was about protecting lucrative contracts to supply the needs of the Workhouse; for only one of them, the appointed doctor, it was about the duty of society to care for the individual. The rest of the Board was aware of his non-conformist Christian principles, but each one was uncomfortable with him quoting the critical writing of someone called Frederick Engels, a foreigner, a German philanthropist, some said, who seemed to have an almost religious hold over him. Influenced by this man Engels, the doctor wanted to abolish the Workhouse system completely!

The record-keeping on each inmate was meticulous. Whilst 'casuals' were admitted or rejected relatively quickly, those wanting to stay went through a more thorough assessment, which determined not only whether they would be admitted, whether they could stay, but what work they would do. Lambeth had its own school located at Norwood, so after two or three days, the children were separated from their parents and sent there. No attempt was made to keep families together, although children under the age of two years stayed with their mothers; married couples were separated. Families and couples would only meet again when they chose to leave the Workhouse on giving eight hours' notice of their intention to do so to the Superintendent, though no woman could leave without the permission of her husband if he too was an inmate. Once granted permission to leave, their clothes would be fetched from the store, where everything had become infected with vermin. They would be checked to see that they had no Workhouse clothing with them – though many women smuggled out underskirts, then they were free to do as they wished, a freedom of choice limited for many to starving on the streets.

The Guardians ran through the list of applicants and reviews quite quickly; the recording of information took longer than the interviews. Dr Wallace did his utmost to speak with courtesy to the unfortunate women, an attitude treated with contempt by some of the others. Nevertheless, everyone stayed as close to the rules as possible. Wallace pointed out that sometimes intimate details of the women's circumstances were best given to one of the female attendants and then shared with him as a medical practitioner and the representative of the Board. The others thought this proper. Wallace opined that appointing a woman member to the Board might be of value, but this was so outrageous a suggestion that it was quickly dismissed by all others. Women were not trusted to manage the business of the Board or anything else outside caring for a family at home. The irony that the monarch to whom they swore allegiance was a woman bore no weight in the argument.

The next file presented to the Chairman was of Mary Ann Nichols nee Walker, known as Polly, a destitute woman. She had first come to the Workhouse in April 1882, six years earlier. She stayed for a year, leaving only very briefly to go into the infirmary before returning to the Workhouse. She then left in March 1883, saying she would be living with her father in Camberwell. They noted that by May that year she was back in the Lambeth Workhouse as homeless. Then, surprisingly she left stating she was going to live with a man she intended to marry (overlooking the fact she was already a married woman), a Tom Dew, a blacksmith known to her father, and would live in Walworth. That might have been the last they would see of her, but in October of 1887 she turned up yet again seeking assistance at the St Giles Workhouse for casual vagrants and the following night in Edmonton where she was accommodated for about

Part One: The Nightmare Begins

six weeks. She left there in December only to be arrested for sleeping rough in Trafalgar Square. The police took pity on her and sent her back to Lambeth Workhouse. She stayed for Christmas, then left in the New Year. Records showed her as being a patient at Holborn Workhouse Infirmary on 1st April 1888 - she seemed to have been living in the Spitalfields area. They sent her from the Infirmary back to Lambeth and there she was, home.

'Is this woman a hopeless case?' asked the Chairman. He addressed the question generally but expected a specific answer from the Superintendent.

'We have known her for quite a while, that is certain,' said the Superintendent. 'She is not a woman who copes on the outside of these walls and according to the police reports is given to bouts of drunkenness. Whilst with us she is compliant, generally looked upon by staff in a kindly way. She causes no difficulty and is a good worker. It has been suggested that she has a melancholy nature at times but evokes warmth in those about her; a good-natured woman, but I fear a lost soul. She writes to her father from time to time. We note she is estranged from her husband, and we know nothing of him. As Superintendent, I have no objection to Mrs. Nichols staying here. It is an asylum for her as it is for many.'

'I wonder if we can't help this woman settle back into society,' suggested the Chairman. 'Perhaps she could play a useful role somewhere.' The Board members were always concerned with the cost of charity.

'She is known to be a clean woman who can work in the kitchens and is currently employed in the laundry. I suppose she could work as a domestic servant, but she is not a young girl. She is a woman in her 40s.' The Superintendent seemed to have no real feelings on the matter.

The Chairman was pleased to see a way to rid the rate payers of one more workhouse inmate if work could be found for her.

'Let us consider that a possibility. Very well, Superintendent, bring her in and let us see what we have.'

Yet another woman was brought before them. Another small, mop-capped figure, looking at the floor.

'Mary Anne Nichols. Is that your name?' asked the Chairman.

'It is, sir, but everyone knows me as Polly Nichols, sir.' She was quietly speaking with the familiar south of the river accent, clearly a Londoner. But what surprised the Guardians was how young she looked. Here was a woman who was apparently in her 40s but looked easily ten years younger. It was far more usual to see women who appeared many years older than their years.

'Very well, Polly, you have been with us on and off for quite a few years. For a woman who is not elderly, infirm or suffering from madness, that is unusual. Do you like living in the Workhouse, being supported by the charity of the Parishes?' The tone was critical.

'Nowhere else to go, sir. When I am out on the streets, ain't nothing for me. I ain't seen my husband these three years now, and he don't support me though he has money, sir.'

The Guardians were disquieted by the notion that a man had shuffled off responsibility for his wife, leaving the cost of her care to the Parish ratepayers. The Chairman had the reports in front of him and quickly addressed this.

'Mrs. Nichols, I see here that you left your husband a few months before claiming assistance for the first time, approximately six years ago. You pressed for rightful support, but he successfully contested your claim because you had left him to care for your five children, or is it six, and were living with another man. His claim that you were supporting yourself as a fallen woman was upheld. That is all true, isn't it, Mrs. Nichols?'

'I had to go, sir; I couldn't stay with him. He is a brutal man. My eldest boy had already left to live with his grandfather.' She was close to tears.

'Mrs. Nichols, it says here that you left the family home five or six times before taking up with another man. That is true, is it not?'

'Yes, sir, but it was not like you make it sound. I had nowhere to go. I had to keep going back.' Her expression was that of a desperate, hunted creature.

'Yet your father would take you in. Indeed, he did so, but you left of your own accord to live a dissolute life with a man, not your husband. Is that not so? Isn't it really the case that you are a drunken woman and that your husband could not dissuade you from the liquor? In order to pay for your indulgence, you became a common prostitute to the shame of him, the children, your father and yourself.'

She had been through this before. She knew she had to endure the humiliation. She spoke the words her friend Mary Monk had told her to say.

Part One: The Nightmare Begins

'I'm good in here, sir. I always do as I'm told. I never go out to find drink or a man. I left Mr. Nichols because he had took up with a nurse, sir, the one who attended me with the birth of my fifth child. I know I am sinful, sir, a bad woman, but it weren't all me, sir.' Tears had begun to fall, and despite the experience of the Guardians, there were still one or two there who were softened by her distress.

Dr Wallace spoke up, first clearing his throat and then employing a much calmer and less critical tone than that of the Chairman.

'I think we all agree that the Workhouse is not the place to live out one's days. What this woman needs is support to live out in the community, not to dreary her days away here. We know she is a capable worker. I suggest we take up the offer of a member of my Parish to give a reformed woman a chance in their household. They are in want of a domestic servant and prefer it not to be a young woman. I believe Mrs. Nichols would fit their requirements perfectly as she is most obviously free of the influence of this bad character who once led her astray.' For all his humanity, the doctor gave not a moment's thought to the proposition that the subject of his philanthropy might have a mind and will of her own and want a say in the matter.

There was agreement to this suggestion. It had worked before with other women, at least for a year or so in some cases. The Chairman absorbed the consensus; another person off the register, another sum of money saved.

'The names of these Christian people, Doctor?' asked the Chairman.

'Mr. Samuel Cowdry and his wife, Sarah. They retain me as their physician, and I know them well. There are no children. They are honest Christians; neither touches drink, nor does Mr. Cowdry even as much as smoke a cigar. He has a senior position as Clerk of Works for the Metropolitan Police. They have a well-kept villa home in Wandsworth. There will be no drink in the house to tempt this woman and she will have little cause to leave the premises often. What do you say?'

Dr Wallace had been saving this position for someone like Polly Nichols. He knew the charity of the couple and was sure they would be a good influence on Polly. There was a general grumble of support around the table and the Chairman looked suitably pleased.

'Well, Mrs. Nichols, thanks to the support of these honourable people, you have the chance to lead a decent life outside the

Workhouse. It is our decision that you should leave these premises as soon as can be arranged and take up employment with this family. It is up to you, of course, you can choose to refuse. However, it is my duty to advise you that since an alternative means of earning your living is now available to you, there is no need for the Workhouse to support you. As soon as Mr. and Mrs. Cowdry wish it, you will leave here. Anything to say?'

Polly's head was spinning. In the Workhouse, she did not have to think. She knew she was nothing, just another soulless body to be organised, regimented and kept out of the way. She was worried that as soon as she was outside, she would turn to drink and seek out Tom Dew, the man she still loved. She had hope but no belief in herself.

So it was that on the 12th day of May 1888, Polly Nichols was taken from the Workhouse to Wandsworth, to the home of Mr. and Mrs. Cowdry. They were kind to her, gave her a room of her own, some clothes and quietly showed her around. They told her about Church services on Sunday but did not press her to attend. They explained that she could eat in the kitchen after serving their meals. She did not need to cook for them as they employed another woman to do that. Being used to being told what to do, Polly was quiet and compliant, a little nervous, but it was far from the worst situation she had experienced, and she sensed the compassion of her employers. She wrote to her father:

'I just right to say you will be glad to know that I am settled in my new place and going all right up to now. My people went out yesterday and have not returned, so I am left in charge. It is a grand place inside, with trees and gardens back and front. All has been newly done up. They are teetotalers and religious, so I ought to get on. They are very nice people, and I have not too much to do. I hope you are all right and the boy has work. So goodbye for the present.'

Three weeks later, Mrs. Cowdry returned home from a luncheon appointment and couldn't find Polly there. She looked around the house and discovered Polly's belongings had gone. A few other clothes belonging to Mrs. Cowdry, though nothing of great value, had also gone. Nothing else was missing, and no note was left. The Workhouse and the police were informed. The Cowdrys never saw her again, but tragically, it was not the last they heard of her.

CHAPTER SEVEN

POLLY, MARTHA, DARK ANNIE, AND FAIR ROSIE

For the poorest and most in need, for those who wanted to avoid the Workhouse, there was only begging or crime; both would lead to imprisonment sooner or later.

For women, prostitution and theft were callings many sank to out of desperation. However, very few women relied solely on selling themselves; it was only ever a desperate measure when no other paid activity could support them.

In East London, when a woman was so poor and so in need, when she had no man or family to provide for her, Spitalfields became the only place that provided places to sleep, to eat and to drink whilst carrying out whatever occupations she could. Its Lodging Houses were one step from the Workhouse, prison or death by cold and starvation, whichever way one looked at it.

Once self-respect was surrendered, it also offered a little diversion, the cold hallelujah of drunkenness amongst fellow drunks. Thus, it was when she sought out friends she had met as they passed through Lambeth Workhouse that Polly Nichols eventually made her way there. After all, she could not face her father, having let him down once again. She had come mainly in search of Tommy Dew, but that had not led to anything either.

In the Frying Pan public house, she met up with her old acquaintance, Millie Holland. Having already been forced to risk a night as a casual in the Gray's Inn Temporary Workhouse, she had found her way to the pub Millie had told her was her base. With not a penny in her purse, she found Millie there and was greeted as a long-lost sister.

Millie had become very fond of Polly. Everyone who knew Polly when she was sober or even just tipsy, instantly warmed to her. She was a gentle, harmless soul, and still pretty. Polly meant harm to no one. She never spoke of her children who were lost to her and who existed only as a sad, regretful memory.

When heavily in drink, Polly would struggle along, singing and drawing attention to herself, yet still causing no harm to anyone but herself, not including the heartache to her father.

Millie had a room at Wilmot's Lodging House in Thrawl Street, a few minutes away. She could not always afford the rent herself and shared with two other women to ensure there was always a base, a home to return to but Polly, she decided, would make a fine fourth.

There were only two beds in the room, but there was no shame in sharing a bed to share the cost. The difficulty was that the lodgings Deputy would not extend such an arrangement to the men they found, for that they needed to go elsewhere or, as was usual, provide their services in the streets, alleyways and backyards of the area. Millie gladly provided the money for the first night for her friend, but Polly would have to work the streets and pubs to get her 'doss money' thereafter.

Long after the four women went their separate ways, it was commented on by the Lodging House deputy how clean, neat and tidy the four women kept that room.

Polly needed money straight away and found herself wandering along Whitechapel Road. It was raining again, so she went into one of the pubs along the way. Two sailors were drinking at the bar and, by all appearances, had been doing so for a long time. They had arrived at St Katherine's dock that morning, transporting livestock from Bremerhaven. She did not understand their language, but once she had made it clear they should buy her a drink, the language problem no longer mattered.

After an hour's drinking, she went out into the side alley with both drunken men, sheltering from the rain by pressing against a wooden shed built along the wall. They showed her some pennies, which she took and put in her purse. She lifted her skirts and earned her money. The two left her, and she cleaned herself with a handkerchief. She had sixpence, more than enough for her doss, so she went back into the pub and bought another drink. She was feeling quite drunk by now and looked around for other customers. An hour later, she was penniless again and needing trade. Shortly after 11 p.m., she had meandered back to 18 Thrawl Street and paid her rent, another day done.

In the Frying Pan, her friend Millie Holland was telling a man that despite his pleadings, she could not take him back to her room, so he would have to find them somewhere if they were to spend the night, or part of the night, together. He obviously did not want to take her back to his own lodgings, but as a visiting farmer only in town for the market for a few days, he did not want to pass up his opportunity for some fun. He asked her to suggest somewhere. Millie turned to another woman drinking at a table nearby and spoke to her.

'Any rooms for the night at your place, Martha?' she asked.

Martha Tabram replied easily. 'I'm down White's Row now, dear, with Fair Rosie. We both moved on from George Street, but there will be rooms in White's Row. Oh, thinking of it, as we are so close, try The White House in Flower and Dean Street, you can sign in there as a couple for eight pence.' Martha, Millie thought, looked pale and tired, signs that things were not going well for her.

'Thanks, Martha,' she said, downing the last of her gin. 'Come on then, my lovely, let's head out into the rain, it's only five minutes from here. We can get some ale to take with us. What about your brother?' she said looking across the smoke-filled room to a younger man who stood drinking with a woman at another table. Millie had not seen the woman come in.

'Oh, I think he is managing for himself tonight,' laughed the farmer.

The woman turned around to the noise of the bellowing laughter, showing her face to Millie.

'Dark Annie,' she thought. Dark Annie Chapman from the Ten Bells, from Dorset Street somewhere. 'Well, if you're living on Dorset Street, you deserve a bit of luck, Annie,' she muttered to herself. She smiled at the woman. Annie smiled back. It was a rainy Friday night in what was becoming the wettest summer for years.

Martha finished her drink. She felt tired, worn down and hungry. She had enough money for her bed that night but nothing more. With a great effort of will, she left the pub and trudged through the rain back to her room in White's Row. The lodging house deputy took the last of her pennies from her and let her go to her bed. She collapsed there from exhaustion, not having the strength to go out working the streets that night.

In the morning, when the rain stopped, she would make her way down to Leadenhall Market, where she might scavenge some food or pick up trade. The other bed in the room was empty, so Rosie was probably out working. She lay there, fully clothed except for her battered bonnet, which she put on the chair, and fell into unconsciousness rather than sleep, not noticing the cries and shouts of the rooms around her, not caring for the rain spattering in through the broken glass of the grubby window.

On Saturday, Martha found herself by the Aldgate pump on Leadenhall Street. As she sank against a wall in her weakness, she heard her name spoken. It was Henry Turner, the man she had been living with in an assumed marriage until he could not cope with her drunkenness any longer. He was a fair-haired man, some years younger than Martha.

'Are things going badly for you, gel?' he asked in a kindly, concerned way. He was very fond of his former mistress and loved her in a way, but experience had resigned him to the fact that there was little hope for them together.

'Henry,' she said with a weary surprise. 'How are you doing yourself? I haven't seen you these last few weeks.'

'I'm in the dormitory at the Victoria Working Man's Home down Commercial Street. I'm getting a bit of casual work in my trade, but my lodgings take most of my earnings, and I have to buy new tools. But you don't look well, my gel. Come on, let me buy you something to eat. I'm working today, but you can go over to the pie shop.'

'It is good of you, Henry. I do miss you, you know. If you come back, I can stop the drinking.'

'Here, Martha, I must go back to work, but here is all the money I have with me. It is one and six. You can get yourself a pie and some tea, then buy some trinkets from the market and sell them on the street. Do a bit of hawking. You won't make much, but you should double your money with a pinch of luck.' He handed her two

Part One: The Nightmare Begins

sixpenny pieces, five pennies, a halfpenny and two farthings. 'Go on, gel. If I can get settled, I'll come looking for yer.' So he left her with some money in her purse and the feeling that someone cared about her.

As he walked down the street, Henry Turner felt only sadness. There had been too many times when all their money had been spent by Martha on drink. There were too many nights when he had lain awake, wondering where she was. He didn't know why she had a hold on his affections, but she did. He also knew that she was more in need of drink than ever before and that there was no hope for them. He knew that the money he had just given her, all the money he had, would probably be spent on drink. He was not completely correct in that assumption.

After watching him walk away, Martha went across the street as he had said, bought a pie and drank some tea. Then she bought herself a new straw bonnet for sixpence. She felt better. Her strength had returned a little, Henry had shown her kindness, and he might come back soon. She had money for a few drinks, so Saturday or not, today, she would not be walking the streets looking for trade.

Anyway, Sunday night would be better, and Monday would be a Bank Holiday with a lot of casual trade from men spending all day in the pubs. She felt better than she had for a long time.

By Sunday, Martha was in the Ten Bells on the corner beside the great Church. It had been raining again, and the smell of damp clothing was mixed with the fog of tobacco and the swill of ale in the crowded little bar.

As usual, Pearly Pol was in there and was looking for a companion for her latest plan to make some money. Martha would do as well as anyone.

'I was looking for yer, Martha,' she lied, having been open to meeting with anyone at all. 'Been down Satchels lodging house in George Street, but they said you had moved on. I went down several houses on White's Row and they reckon there is no one of your name been there lately.' That was more or less true.

'Oh, that would be right,' agreed her companion. 'I had to do a flit from a place and thought I might get traced to George Street, so I called myself Emma Chapman when I went down White's Row. I forget what name I'm using,' she laughed.

Pearly Poll was not interested and got to the point.

'Anyway, I've got a bit of a day planned, and I need some companionship. You up for it?'

'What you got in mind, Pol?' asked Martha, unsure of Pol. She was not really all that interested, but she did not want to get on the wrong side of Pearly Pol, or anyone else for that matter.

'I met this soldier from down the barracks just yesterday,' enthused Poll. 'He and his chum are out for the day all day tomorrow. I agreed to meet him and take a friend with me. He's a good 'n Martha, plenty of drink, a bit of supper and not much work if you get me meaning. What do you say?'

'Sounds like a good way to spend a Monday,' said Martha. 'I was planning to go down Whitechapel Road, but just roving about. If you've already got a couple in tow, we might have a fine time of it!'

'You'll have to smarten up a bit though, Martha, you ain't looking so good.' Pearly Pol began to question whether she had chosen the right companion.

'It's just the rain,' said Martha, excusing her appearance. 'I've a new bonnet, and after they've had a few drinks and a laugh, I'll look as good as anyone.' Martha almost convinced herself that she would be fine.

'We are meeting them in the Two Brewers down Whitechapel, so I'll meet you back in here tomorrow, and we can walk down together.'

Pearly Poll was a survivor. She may had been brought low by circumstance, but she made a living of sorts. No one told Pol what to do. Tomorrow would be a good day out; she would make some money and have the soldier-boys paying for everything. In her way, she would make them pay dearly for the five minutes of grunting she would allow one of them in the alleyways. She would decide when and where. Selling her body meant nothing to her anymore. She was free of sin. Men thought they made the rules and made the judgments, but not as far she was concerned.

August Bank Holiday Monday came around. By late afternoon, Martha was waiting for her on the pavement just outside the Ten Bells, opposite the market. Dark Annie was there too, and for a moment, Pearly Pol thought she should have asked her instead because she looked more presentable, and after all, they both lived in Dorset Street.

Part One: The Nightmare Begins

As it was, Pol resigned herself to Martha, linking arms with her as they walked along the side of the great church along Fournier Street, turning right down Brick Lane.

They saw several people they knew along the way and called out greetings to them. Outside the Frying Pan, they were invited in by a couple of young men, possibly no more than twenty years of age. Both of them would usually have been working but instead spent the day idling their time in the pub. This part of the street was fast becoming crowded with Jewish immigrants who spoke no English. 'The Yiddish section', women called it. The two women mocked the strange way of dressing the newcomers adopted. They rarely traded with the poor Jews, but things were finally looking up with the Jews who were well-settled and had some money of their own. Brick Lane ran into Osborn Street, and in no time, they were in Whitechapel High Street, looking out for their customers.

By five o'clock, they had found themselves a corporal and his friend from The Guards inside the Two Brewers. Pearly Pol could not remember if these were the two men she had intended to meet, but they were jolly fellows and generous with their money. The two women, on Pol's lead, would spin this out as much as possible before delivering the services men would want at the end of the evening. They made a night of it, moving from pub to pub along Whitechapel High Street, eating but mostly drinking, laughing, flattering, flirting and being flattered in return. Each one of them knew that this was a commercial arrangement, but they were enjoying themselves along the way, the drink dulling the sorrows of life, the companionship raising their spirits. The men anticipated what was to come, the women anticipated money for their lodgings that night and a little more, maybe.

Well past 11 p.m., obviously drunk, the four of them left whichever pub it was in which they had finished their tour. Pearly Pol was arm in arm with the corporal, and Martha was with his friend. Pol took her Corporal along to Angel Alley where, as she saw it, he took delivery of what had been on offer, and she supplied what she had been paid for.

Meanwhile, Martha led her man into nearby George's Yard, a little way along the alley, a place she had used many times before, a place notorious for its use by prostitutes such as her. There were apartments on three stories above the yard, with plenty of shaded corners and sheltered stairwells where she might not be easily seen.

Having completed the transaction, Pearly Pol and her corporal knew it was time to go their separate ways, but they walked together along the alley up towards Wentworth Street as it was on her way home and was where he had agreed to meet his friend.

With no sign of Martha, she waited a while but was tired and eventually made her way back into the Dorset Street Rookeries, perhaps the most wretched of all the tenements and doss houses, where she would pay for her bed and sleep off the drink. She had no idea what time it was by then.

***

It was about two o'clock in the morning when police constable Barrett saw a man loitering at the top of the alley leading to George's Yard. He was standing on the corner of Wentworth Street. The police officer approached him. The man was calm, though he smelled strongly of drink. When asked what he was doing, the man replied that he was in the Grenadier Guards but currently on leave and waiting for his 'chum' who had gone off with a girl down George's Yard. Barrett made a note of it but did not linger. The man wore an army tunic, and he noticed he had a 'good conduct' award. A soldier or sailor hanging around this area was a very familiar scene to him.

An hour and a half later, a resident of the apartments bordering George's Yard, returning home from a day out of his own, noticed someone apparently sleeping in the stairwell on the first floor. This was a common sight, the homeless or the drunken. Or if neither, then women entertaining their customers. He thought nothing of it and went to bed.

Getting off to work at a quarter to five the next morning, the sky beginning to lighten, John Reeves walked past the same sleeping figure, but then noticed it was in a pool of what looked like blood.

Startled, he ran to find a policeman, returning with Police Constable Barrett. Barrett took in the scene in front of him and knew this was a murder site.

He did not know the victim but, from the attitude of the body, surmised that sexual intercourse had been attempted or had taken place. He noticed that her boots were old and worn down. As he was to be told later, she had suffered 39 stab wounds, many to her breasts and a number to the groin area. The attack looked to the police as if it had followed some sort of sexual rage. As one of the wounds was very deep, it was suggested that the attacker had some form of long knife or bayonet, implements common to sailors.

It took some days for witnesses to come forward and identify the body lying in the morgue as Martha Turner, even then giving her the wrong surname.

The Abandoned: *Victims of Jack the Ripper*

Part One: The Nightmare Begins

CHAPTER EIGHT

MARTHA

Reid was in his office; the report of another murder would occupy him that day and for many days to come.

He was still troubled by the unsolved murder of Emma Smith, his failure to find Rose Mylett, and now the body of an unknown woman had been discovered early that morning. He started the routine: search the area for a murder weapon, speak to the tenants in the rooms around the alley and the yard, ask questions in the local pubs – starting with the nearest, then fanning out, and find out who was missing a wife, a mistress, a mother, a daughter, a friend, a tenant. Pass the description of the victim around the locality. He also waited for the autopsy to see what it could tell him about how this woman was murdered and from that, he had yet to form a theory about why she was killed. He had to gather these facts and see where it took him. As he always did, he sent for the police officer who was first on the scene. This constable might be especially interesting as he had also seen a possible suspect. This was not a good day for Reid, who had been looking forward to a singing engagement that evening, and now he would give himself entirely over to this case.

Constable Barrett was obviously tired. He had finished his night duty some hours ago and had only a short sleep before reporting to the Inspector. Reid was most agreeable with the man and asked him to go through events as he had recorded them but also to build in anything else along the way as it occurred to him. Reid was very taken with the short discussion Barrett had engaged in with the soldier on the corner of Wentworth Street and the alley leading to George's yard as undoubtedly, this must be the main suspect, for now at least.

'Yes, sir, I recall him well, although it was dark being the early hours.'

'Exactly what time do you think it was, Constable?' asked the smaller man.

'It was near to 2 a.m., sir, and I recorded it in my pocketbook. The man was in uniform, and I noticed he had the ribbon of a good conduct award. I estimate his height as being not quite my height, perhaps five foot nine or ten inches. He had light-coloured hair as best as I could make out and a well-trimmed, light brown moustache turned up at the ends. I should say he was a young man, possibly no more than 25? He seemed calm enough, and I took him at his word that he was waiting for a chum. I suppose now he must be a suspect, as must the friend, that is, if he existed.

Anyway, towards the end of my beat, after about two and a half hours had passed, I was called by a man behaving in a very agitated manner. He gave his name as John Reeves, not a man I had noticed before. He directed me to his address in the tenements in George's Yard. People come and go from there all the time, so I was not surprised I did not know him. I accompanied him down to the yard and under the stairs there, I saw the body of a woman. She lay with her clothing disturbed. Her dress, dark green in colour, was pulled up to her waist, and she was exposed as if in the act of copulation, sir. The body was surrounded by a great deal of what I took to be blood. I could see she was dead and that there had been a lot of stab wounds. I walked the short distance to Whitechapel High Street to summon assistance by blowing on my whistle. As soon as I heard answering calls, I returned to the scene and looked around for a possible weapon but found nothing. With the aid of other constables who had joined me, I secured the area.'

'Thank you, Barrett. Did you take the name of the soldier?' Reid hoped rather than expected the Constable to have been thorough.

'I'm sorry, sir, I did not.' The Constable was regretful.

'His regiment or army number?' Reid clung to the hope that something of the man had been recorded.

'No, sir,' was the shameful response.

Part One: The Nightmare Begins

Moving on, encouraging the officer to be as complete in his memory as possible, Reid asked, 'Did you recognise the corpse by any chance?'

At this, the officer picked up a little. 'I've been trying to place her but can't quite get a fit. I know I've seen her around, both in Whitechapel and possibly the Brick Lane area. I can't say that I know her, though. None of us could put a name to her.'

'Right, all very useful, but not as useful as a name, though doubtless, that would be fictitious.' Reid knew this was going to be a slow investigation. He had no further use for the officer, who looked exhausted. 'Now get off home and get some sleep. If I need you before your next duty, I will send for you, otherwise, report back as usual.' Reid spoke more kindly than he felt, but he wouldn't take out his frustration on the officer. He watched the officer depart. He then called for the duty detective sergeant to join him and together with a uniformed sergeant, they made their way to George's Yard.

Other uniformed police were there guarding the scene. The body had been removed and examined by a local doctor. Reid had yet to learn what he had to say, but experience had taught him to await the considerations of the doctor who carried out the actual autopsy. All the residents of the tenements had been asked to remain at home until Reid had questioned them. The first, John Saunders Reeves, lived at number 25. It was he who had come across the body lying in blood and who had run for the police. He might be considered a suspect, having been on the scene of the murder, but Reid had already discounted that likelihood.

Most of the residents had nothing to say, but Albert Crow, a cab driver who lived in room number 37, had reflected on events. He said that it was after 3:30 a.m. when he had finished work and was going up the stairs to his room. It was very dark at that time of the morning, but he remembered seeing what he took for a tramp or vagrant sleeping rough in the stairwell of the first-floor landing. It was common enough to see the homeless on the landings. He now thought that what he had seen was the murdered woman. That was useful to Reid, who could begin to put time around the murder. He was also interested in speaking with the Superintendent of the block, Frank Hewitt. His room was exactly 12 feet from the location of the body. Hewitt was reticent. He stated that neither he nor his wife heard anything until the police arrived. Reid did not believe him. In fact, he found it hard to believe that no one had heard anything, but no one was saying.

Back at the police station, Reid discussed the case with Chief Inspector Swanson.

'We don't know who the victim is. The report from the local doctor suggests that she might have been in her late twenties, that she died from multiple stab wounds, and, very interestingly, he believes that sexual intercourse had not taken place. He thinks the large stab wound to the chest was caused by a large or long blade, though word seems to be out that it was a bayonet. The doctor did not say it was. The other stab wounds were caused by a second knife. This murderer had gone out well-equipped. He may well have had such an attack in mind when he set off. The woman was almost certainly a prostitute. We have issued a description of her, and one name has come up so far. It has been suggested that she might be named Mrs. Withers as no one has seen that woman for a day or two, but I don't have much confidence in that. As for the witnesses – Ah! None will come forward and admit that they heard a fight, a scuffle, a stabbing, or anything at all. It is impossible that someone did not hear something, and I think it is very probable that the superintendent did. I suppose he did not want to get involved or feared being attacked himself.'

The following day, the press was all over the story. Amongst the most searching of reporters was Mr. Best, representing an East End newspaper. He managed to find out from local police constables just who the detectives had been talking to. Like them, he guessed the most likely source of information would be the building superintendent. He flattered and cajoled the Superintendent and his wife into giving an opinion about the murder, which had taken place right outside their door.

First, Mrs. Hewitt let slip that she had heard someone nearby cry 'murder!' It had been so loud because there was an echo along the stairways. Her husband quickly countered that such cries were so common in the area that no one took much notice. It was, at least, the excuse he gave for not looking just outside his door from where the shout undoubtedly emanated. The reporter questioned him about the murder, asking him for his opinion.

'It is my belief that the poor creature crept up the staircase, that she was accompanied by a man, that a quarrel took place, and that he then stabbed her.'

Reid saw the article in the newspaper. He presented it to his superior officer, Swanson.

'This is what we are struggling with in this case. Hewitt was less than twelve feet away from this killing. He obviously heard the cry. How did he work out that the woman had come quietly up the stairs with a man, had a disagreement with him and then was stabbed? He told us he heard nothing and saw nothing. If he and his wife heard the shout of murder, then they would have heard the struggle outside the door. How did he know that a quarrel took place? It's pointless pursuing anyone in the tenement for information, they would rather the murderer got away than help us catch him.'

He was particularly frustrated because he had acted quickly on the notion that the killer might have been the soldier. His detectives had found a mother and daughter who had seen a woman who might have fitted the description of the victim with a Guardsman. That made three people who had seen the suspect. Reid immediately arranged to take Constable Barrett and the two women to the nearest barracks, the Tower, and have all soldiers parade there. The witnesses might then identify the man they had seen.

Meanwhile, word came in that a Mrs. Withers had surfaced, so she was not the victim. The search amongst the soldiers also proved fruitless, another dead-end.

Then, whilst sitting in his office, frustrated and wondering where to turn next, he had his first break in the case. Pearly Pol had sought him out. She had information including the name of the victim – Martha Turner, she said, assuming Martha had been married to Henry. Reid did not know it at the time, but Martha Turner, more properly Tabram, was the first certain victim of a serial killer.

The Abandoned: *Victims of Jack the Ripper*

Part One: The Nightmare Begins

CHAPTER NINE

PEARLY POL

Reid would not be deflected from logical detective work. Having read the medical reports, he decided two things: first, this was not the same killer who had assaulted Emma Smith. Secondly, there was a disturbing similarity between the attack in Mile End, where the victim had escaped, and this one.

In the Mile End case, he was now sure the attacker had been interested not so much in the sex Ada Wilson was probably selling, but in harming her with a knife. He did not know why he would want to harm her. There was the Annie Milward case too, the woman from White's Row who had died eventually from similar injuries.

Was this the same man who, this time, had succeeded in killing and mutilating someone? Was this a killer whose viciousness was escalating? Reid was now less inclined to believe that this was the work of the soldier, whoever he was, but he still needed to find him to eliminate him as a suspect.

Reid had very quickly arranged another parade at the barracks to see if Pearly Pol could pick out the two men she and Martha had been drinking with. She had agreed to be available the following morning. Taking no chances she might drift away, he sent one of his experienced men, Sergeant Caunter, to Dorset Street to escort her. She wasn't there. He didn't give up his quest and started to trace her.

Outside the Ten Bells, he came across two women he knew well: Annie Chapman, who was called 'Dark Annie' on account of her black hair, and Mary 'Polly' Nichols. He told them Pearly Pol might be able to identify the person who had killed Martha. That did not seem to move them, but when he offered sixpence, they pointed him in the direction of the Bell pub down near Whitworth and Gaulston streets. They had seen her going down there to meet someone.

As he made his way down Commercial Street, opposite White's Row, he saw Mary Connolly alias Pearly Pol and stopped her. She feigned forgetfulness. He said he would arrest her and have her sent to prison, but she pleaded for another chance to assist, saying she had already come forward to identify the body and give details of the soldiers, all in good faith. This is what the police were up against. He knew these people would not help the police to protect them. They feared that the police would lock them up. He took her with him to see Inspector Reid. She had to wait at the police station whilst Reid arranged another parade of soldiers for the 13th of August, six days after she had been out with them, so she might identify those she and the victim had been with; who knew how many others she had seen since? Would she recognise them at all?

The visit to the Tower barracks was a washout. In the first few minutes, she looked at the line of troops and boldly told Reid that they would not be there. The soldiers she and Martha had been with had caps with white bands, while none of these did. The uniform she described was that of the Coldstream Guards. Reid had the wrong barracks. He took her back to the police station whilst an inspection could be arranged of the Coldstream Guards who were at the Wellington Barracks, south of the river. That was not done until the 15th of August, over a week after the murder and five days after the formal court inquest was adjourned. Nevertheless, finally, Mary Connelly, 'Pearly Pol,' picked out two men.

She couldn't remember the names of the men she and Martha had been with but was certain one was a corporal. That matched Constable Warren's evidence. Both the men she picked out were Privates. The first had an alibi, which was quickly verified. The second man, Private Skipper, was found to have been logged in to the Wellington barracks on the evening of the murder and so was dropped from the enquiries. Another fruitless search.

At that point, Reid gave up on the identity parades. If the soldiers did not come forward, there was nothing he could do to find them. Like him, Swanson was also thinking that the soldiers were probably not the killers anyway. Nothing in the evening leading to when they went into the alley indicated any problem for Martha. She had been with the soldier all evening, and no one noticed a problem between them. It was perhaps dishonest to let the newspapers think that the killer was a soldier the police could not find, but at least it was something. It showed the police had tried to solve the case. It was just as likely that having left her soldier, she did what so many women in her position did: carried on soliciting until too tired to do so. The number of murders and serious attacks was building up, though, and the Commissioner was calling for a report into what was going on.

Over the next few days, some of the loose ends were tied up. A former landlady came forward and confirmed what the police already knew. Henry Turner was interviewed, to no purpose other than to eliminate him as a suspect. Even Martha's estranged husband turned up, though he was of no help as he had not seen her for thirteen years. On his appearance, her name was officially changed back from Turner to Tabram, the name under which she would be buried.

Reid had a problem with names. The women were known by so many different ones, and it troubled him not only because it made them difficult to trace, difficult for their circumstances and movements to be investigated, but because those who died, like Martha Tabram, might not be properly identified which he believed was a dignity everyone deserved. So he kept a notebook of names. In it, he would record those of the victims of the serial killer, not at first known as the *Ripper*. When he started his list, he had no way of knowing that, alongside Martha, he would add five further names: Polly Nichols, Annie Chapman, Lizzie Stride, Catherine Eddowes, and Mary Kelly.

In a separate column, he listed those who might have been sister victims but were probably not: Ada Wilson, Emma Smith, Annie Milward, Alice Mackenzie, and Frances Coles. The names haunted him.

During his investigations, he would walk the area to clear his head and reflect on life and death all around him. Much was changing in the world, yet the killings in the slums dragged him into a blackness.

The Abandoned: *Victims of Jack the Ripper*

CHAPTER TEN

ANNIE BESANT AND THE MATCH GIRLS

Mile End Road takes its name from the turnpike in Whitechapel, where Cambridge Heath Road meets the Whitechapel Road, standing a mile from the City of London. Traders who came from all the southeast of England, from Essex, Suffolk, and even from further afield like Norfolk and Lincolnshire, brought their goods to the markets of Leadenhall, Spitalfields, Smithfield and others. They passed through this gateway at Mile End to park their wagons along the wide highway and spend the night at one of the taverns in Whitechapel before rising early to arrive in London the next morning.

Like the markets, especially nearby Spitalfields, the influx of traders attracted the attention of rogues, thieves and beggars, as well as women left with nothing other than themselves to sell. To the south of Mile End Road were the docks of the busiest trading site in the world. Inspector Reid was walking westward, towards the city, thinking. This was J Division, his old haunt.

The noise and the smell of the docks lay to his left as the traffic made its way slowly along the congested street, mostly heading west, as was he. Although still early morning, he had already noticed the faces of criminals he knew too well, but these were not exercising his mind so much.

The murders seemed perplexing. As he stopped at the Mile End Waste, a patch of green field where preachers and the newly emerging socialists had taken to congregating, he wondered what was becoming of the world.

To the northeast of where he walked was a curse of slum dwellings stretching all the way up through his current area, H Division, to south Camden.

In front of him was the City, with the Bank of England sitting in Threadneedle Street, the Stock Exchange nearby. All that wealth just a few minutes' walk from the poverty of Spitalfields.

For much of his adult life, he had experienced the optimism of change happening all around him, and he knew unexpected twists and turns were coming. It had been a dynamic time ever since the Great Exhibition back in 1851. What he wanted most of all now was for these slums to be swept away, these dreadful living conditions to improve, the poor to be given the chance of self-respect, and the opportunity to climb out of degradation and crime. That, he thought, was the best way of protecting the women who were otherwise drawn into prostitution.

Meanwhile, the most he could do for them would be to catch the savage killer of Martha Tabram and, thus, prevent others from suffering in the same way. He pondered on how he was spending an increasing amount of time dealing with women, both as victims of the most dreadful crimes and perpetrators of miserable, often petty crimes, especially drunkenness, theft and prostitution.

He was ever more convinced that decent housing and reliable work would end their criminality and drunkenness. Indeed, when he considered the amoral world in which they lived, he marvelled that any who existed in these filthy conditions escaped such a life; not all there were prostitutes and drunks. His anger was with the families who ran the lodging houses and rented out the rooms in the tenements. He was often consulted by worthy groups about what might be done. There were many educated and wealthy women and men who despised what was happening in the east of the metropolis, but with only religion and a sense of moral outrage as their weapons, they struggled to make improvements.

The government did not wish to interfere in commerce. The church congregations sang 'The rich man in his castle, the poor man at his gate', and how this was designed to be so by God, so there was no changing it, according to the church. It was no surprise that he did not believe in God.

Here, on the Mile End Waste, he saw a different sort of change beginning, and if the wealthy, the church and the political masters did not watch out and bend to the coming storm, they would be swept away. He did not think that would mean a better world, but would it be any worse for the people who lived here? He suspected there would be more of the mass insurgencies that had bubbled up here and there over the years, but gradually, resistance to oppression was becoming more organised, purposeful, and galvanised; an air of revolution underpinned it. If the girls and women from the Bryant and May match factory could take on the establishment and win, how long until the male workers became organised to do the same, and then the slum dwellers? He saw the need for change, he wanted change, but he feared the chaos that might be required to bring it about. He opposed any idea of revolution or disloyalty to the Queen. He also worried that the striking women would soon be destitute, and so swell the numbers of those who sold themselves on the streets, creating an even larger pool of potential victims for the deranged killer.

At the Bryant and May factory in Bow, girls and women from the age of 13 were making matches by painting white phosphorous onto matchsticks. Since social campaigners had started looking at the conditions of the poor, especially the working poor, disputes between workers and owners had bubbled up. There had long been disputes between workers and masters. Long before Reid's time, there had been violence around the silk weavers. He knew there had been trouble brewing at the Bryant and May factory, where conditions were harsh, and the women paid very poorly. He knew it because an article had appeared in 'The Link' magazine. It was not a paper he read often, a halfpenny fortnightly publication, but it was brought to his attention by Scotland Yard as a possible cause of unrest. He knew the writer of the article was Annie Besant, co-owner of the magazine and an intelligent, educated woman who seemed to have embraced socialism just as he had embraced Druidism. Whatever their differences, he was strongly in support of what she said. No moral man could oppose the case she put, he thought. However, it troubled him that she was the intellectual and moral equal of any man, superior to most.

Annie Besant had interviewed him more than once about conditions in Whitechapel. He shared her opinion that a major cause of the crime there was the degrading, exploitative housing.

However, he told her that he was not keen on her suggestions on how to handle the matter. He was all for planned change through the law; she was for revolution. Nevertheless, when she published the White Slavery article in 'The Link', he found it hard to disagree with her. She had been to the factory and spoken with a few of the girls there. The article referred to the factory as a prison house, describing the girls as underfed, helpless and oppressed. Their meagre wages of about 4 shillings a week for working 10-12 hours a day standing at a workbench, dealing with dangerous chemicals, was indicative of the contempt the owners had for the workers. Many of the girls developed a painful and disfiguring disease called 'Phossy Jaw' caused by the white phosphorous they had to use.

As Besant found out, many of the girls had to live in the tenements in bad conditions because it was all they could afford. They ate mainly only bread and butter and drank tea. For many, such meagre fare was all that sustained them.

Meanwhile, the shareholders who did no work enjoyed regular high dividend payments. To his knowledge, few, if any, of these women turned to prostitution to supplement their meagre earnings, but with no earnings whilst on strike, he feared it would change.

Annie Besant poured her outrage at the treatment of the match girls into the article. The factory owners tried to dismiss anyone they thought had given inside information to Besant and required the women and mere girls to sign a paper saying the conditions were good. The women and girls, however, had had enough.

Even without anyone to organise or lead them, they collectively went out on strike and elected their own strike committee. They met at Mile End Waste, causing quite a sensation. Mary Besant stepped in at their request to work with them and raise money for their support. Surprising everyone, the well-meaning middle class did indeed support them. Whilst the Times newspaper, the factory owners, major shareholders and bankers deplored the strike, intellectuals rallied to their cause. Mary Besant helped them to plan and organise, others spoke and wrote on their behalf, including the editor of the influential Pall Mall Gazette, William Stead, Catherine Booth of the Salvation Army, and the young firebrand playwright George Bernard

Part One: The Nightmare Begins

Shaw. Joining them and speaking for them was Eleanor, the daughter of the German émigré, Karl Marx.

Eleanor, exceptionally bright and committed to supporting the women, a determined feminist, was probably the first successful trade union organiser. She and Besant were formidable. The secret police watched them, and Reid was put on alert, warned about them, when as far as he was concerned, his time should be taken up not with striking women who had a just cause. He had murders to solve and a disenfranchised public to protect.

The indignation felt across society on behalf of the women was so profound and widespread that within a fortnight, their demands were met. No one knew it, of course, but the Trade Union Movement had just had its first victory in England, one won by uneducated, exploited women from the slums of London. Reid felt ashamed of himself for being grateful that public attention had been diverted from his murder cases. Scotland Yard and the government were more exercised by the fear of the striking women than by the murders. Not for the first time, Reid disagreed with his superiors. He felt sorry for these striking women and admired them for working so hard not to be on the streets themselves. Yet, despite achieving an increase in pay, they were still exposed to the chemicals that would likely deform or kill them. It offended his sense of decency, but their victory was a small step forward.

He reached Whitechapel High Street and crossed the road to the Angel Alley. The world was changing because it needed to change. The strike was over, and that was one less pressure on him.

As he walked into the reeking alley where Martha Tabram had taken her final steps, he heard the noise of the docks behind him echo on the tenement walls, mocking him.

The Abandoned: *Victims of Jack the Ripper*

CHAPTER ELEVEN

MARY-ANNE NICOLS (POLLY), MILLIE, CHARLEY CROSS

Word of Martha's gruesome death got around the pubs and lodging houses of Spitalfields – another woman murdered, again cut up, even worse than poor Emma had been.

At first, there was a general fear the High Rip gangs had been about, but then the story of Pearly Pol and the soldiers became more widely known. There had been a second concern when the Matchgirls went on strike as, without wages, they almost certainly would be destitute and some of them might compete with the street women for trade.

Fearing this, the local street women did not support the strike. The fear of the strikers faded when it was realised that there was a strike fund, an arrangement that kept them free of even worse degradation. Reid, for one, believed it proved the link (if proof were needed) between destitution and prostitution. The Bryant and May strikers avoided the latter gratefully.

Gradually, the street women of the rookeries and lodging houses developed an admiration for the girls, but an admiration soured by resentment that they had got what they wanted, won a victory of sorts against the Masters, and had done so without so much as starving or being thrown out on the street. The women of Spitalfields went back into the routine of their lives just as the Bryant and May workers went back to their struggling lives.

It rained so much that summer that the street women spent more time sheltering in the pubs as trade became harder to come by. It was best to be out later in the evenings when it was darker and when the men would be tipsy or drunk and more easily persuaded to partake of a little excitement for a few pennies.

***

Millie Holland missed her friend, Polly Nichols. The two had shared a bed at the lodging house on Thrawl Street and it was so nice to be with someone who was clean and pleasant, and never had a bad word to say about anyone.

Sadly, Polly had fallen into one of her heavy drinking phases and needed to make more money, so she went out more in search of trade.

As it was so wet in the alleyways and Yards, she had taken herself down to The White House on Flower and Dean Street since, while rather unusually, the deputy there let the women take in men overnight. It made more money for the lodging house, and for Polly, it meant she could be dry all night and have the man pay for the bed, saving her four pence. Of course, any money she saved she spent on drink. She missed her friend, Millie too, and the safe company of the women who shared the two beds in the small room.

She did not know the date, but it was the 30th of August, another rainy day, when Polly spent her evening soliciting in Whitechapel Road. She made some money and wended her way back to Brick Lane, to the Frying Pan pub where she could dry off and spend some of her money on gin.

It was after midnight when she left there and decided that she didn't need to take a man back to a room that night, so she went the short distance to Wilmot's Lodging House in Thrawl Street, back to where Millie was staying. Millie Holland was not in. The deputy could tell straight away that Polly had had a little too much drink and asked for the four-pence bed charge. Giggling, Polly realised she had spent all her money. Refused admission, she didn't argue, just politely asked for a bed to be kept back for her as she would simply go out and earn her 'doss money'; she needed only one customer. She

Part One: The Nightmare Begins

was feeling pleased with herself anyway because she was wearing a new bonnet, and was very proud of it.

Down at the docks, a fire had broken out and it drew a crowd entertained by the efforts of the Fire Brigade and dock workers who tried to extinguish it. It was the most spectacular event in the area for a long time and the police had to keep back the crowd.

Millie Holland was there, watching alongside other women who had abandoned soliciting for the night for the entertainment of the fire. It was probably well after two o'clock in the morning when Millie decided she would not try to find any more business that night and started back for Thrawl Street. She was on Osborn Street, nearly home, when she saw dear Polly, who was staggering a little and then leaning against a wall, clearly very drunk. She went over to her and put her arm around her.

'Polly, my dear, where are you off to?'

Polly's response was to show a broken smile and start to giggle.

'Well, do you like my new bonnet, Millie? You know I went back to the old lodging, Wilmot's, but I had spent my doss money. So, I've been out, and I've made the money three times, but now I've gone and spent it! It doesn't matter, I'll soon have it again.'

'Oh no, Polly, don't do that, come back with me to Thrawl Street. I've got nearly enough for the two of us. How much do you have left?'

'No need, no need, I'll soon have it. They said they would keep a bed for me, but yes, I'll see you back there. I'm going back along the High Street and out a bit. You go on, Millie.'

There was no persuading her. Millie Holland made her way back towards her lodgings, at least pleased that her friend was coming to join her later and not going back to The White House. Outside the Frying Pan, she met dark Annie, who was looking sad and worn.

'I'm a bit short of the doss money tonight, so I'm going out for a walk to see if can stir up any sailors who have been kept awake by the fire. I've got the bed kept for me in Dorset Street, but there is nothing doing up here so it will have to be down Whitechapel High Street to start with, I suppose. I hope it keeps off raining for an hour. I'll do the beat down Whitechapel Road, up by the railway yards and take them along near Bucks Row, because from there, I can walk up Hanbury Street and be back in Dorset Street. It's a bit of a circle, I know, but it suits me.' It seemed she was talking herself into a journey she did not want to make.

Millie Holland did not make the same offer to help Annie as she had done with Polly. She was not a charity.

About an hour or so later, Constable John Neil of J Division was on his beat and walked past Buck's Row, which joined Brady Street at the far end. There was a school along the street, Brown's Stable Yard, and tenements and warehouses, whilst in the distance was a single streetlamp which told him he was near the end of the street. The dim streetlight attracted prostitutes as often as it attracted moths.

A little while after the policeman had gone by, about 3:30 a.m., a man who eventually gave his name as Charley Cross was on his usual route to work when he saw what he later said he thought was an old tarpaulin lying in front of the gates of the stable yard. As he drew closer, he realised it was the body of a woman. He looked around and saw another man walking behind him though some way off and called to him. The second man, who did not know Cross, was Robert Paul. Together, the two men stared in disbelief at the body. The body was that of a woman lying on her back, her skirts pulled up to her waist. One of them touched her hand, which was cold. That she was dead seemed certain. The other then touched her hand and her face. He decided to make her a little more decent and pulled down her skirts; in doing so, he thought he detected some breathing, but it seemed unlikely.

Confused about what to do, they decided to walk on until they saw a policeman and then, as they did not want to be involved, go on to work. Ten minutes later, they came across Constable Mizen in Hanbury Street in Spitalfields. Cross suggested Paul should hang back and he would let the officer know what they had found. He informed the policeman that another officer wanted him down in Bucks Row because he had found a woman who was either dead or dead drunk. Mizen jotted down a few details from the men and thought it odd as Bucks Row was in J Division and he was in H Division, but he set off anyway.

Robert Paul was somewhat overlooked as a witness. As he was second on the scene, it was felt his evidence was less valuable than that of Charley Cross, whose real name was Charles Lechmere, the man who found the body. It was unfortunate that he was forgotten as he had ideas of his own and doubted what Charley Cross was saying. What he recalled seeing in the distance was a man leaning over the body of a woman – Charley Cross, as it turned out. He was nervous and thought at first that he had stumbled upon an assault or had interrupted a murder. He was not totally sure of what had been going on, was uncomfortable walking along with Charley Cross, and was relieved when the two came across a policeman on Hanbury Street.

It was Charley Cross who spoke to the police officer and spun him the line about being wanted. It occurred to no one then, nor after each subsequent attack, that each victim was found in the area where Charley lived, and each had been attacked at a time when he was on his way to work in the dark, early mornings. He blended in well and was never a suspect. That he gave a false name, and a false witness statement was overlooked.

Before Mizen arrived on the scene, Constable Neil was walking his beat through Buck's Row when he, too, discovered the body. He shone his lantern on the figure and realised it was indeed a dead woman. Her bonnet was off her head, lying by her right hand but he didn't at first notice the colour of her hair. Her skirts were disarrayed and her knees visible. He could see that her throat had been cut, her eyes were staring, and there was a lot of blood. Her hands were cold, but he found her upper arms to be warm, so she had not been dead long.

As he took in the dreadful scene, Police Constable Mizen unexpectedly arrived. Neil suggested that Mizen make straight for Bethnal Green Police Station to get assistance and an ambulance. The body would need to be moved to the Workhouse Infirmary mortuary in Old Montague Street. By the time the duty inspector, Spratling, arrived at Buck's Row shortly before 4 a.m., the body had already been moved by ambulance. The neighbours were out looking at what was going on and one of them was washing away the blood into the gutters. A preliminary search of the area found nothing; no one knew the identity of the woman.

At the mortuary, Inspector Spratling found the place still locked up, though the caretaker had been sent for. The body was still in the ambulance, so whilst waiting for the doctor, the Inspector wrote a description to be circulated through the press. He wrote that she was 5 feet two inches tall, probably about 42 years of age. She had delicate features, his way of saying she was pretty, a scar on her forehead, grey eyes, missing front teeth, dark complexion and dark brown hair, greying a little. He listed her clothing, much of it stained with her blood.

Later, when the body was inside the mortuary and undressed, it was noticed that her petticoat had a stencil on it reading 'Lambeth Workhouse PR.' The PR stood for Princes Road.

By mid-morning, Inspector Helson had taken over the investigation and sent an officer to Lambeth workhouse with the description of the dead woman. Whilst waiting for someone to attend, a woman from Spitalfields arrived in an agitated state and gave her name as Mrs. Emily Holland. She thought she might know who the woman was as her friend had not come home that night. She was taken into the mortuary and a sheet covering the body of the murdered woman was drawn back to show only the face. Mrs. Holland broke down in sobs, saying it was indeed her friend, Polly, but she couldn't remember her surname. That mystery was solved when a woman was brought from the workhouse. She gave a witness statement in the name of Mary Ann Monk. In it, she identified with certainty her friend from the Lambeth Workhouse, Mary Ann Nichols.

'She liked to be called Polly,' she said.

***

At the inquest, the details of the death were given. The throat had been cut, and the groin area mutilated so badly that the dead or dying woman had been disembowelled. It had been a savage attack with a long-bladed knife, and yet no one in the surrounding tenements and cottages had heard anything. Perhaps she had been strangled to silent unconsciousness before the knife attack occurred. The press seized on an emerging pattern of attacks on women in H and J Divisions and were equally quick to speak of a lunatic being on the loose.

Polly's father attended the inquest and testified to her drunkenness, but also to her gentle disposition. Her estranged husband gave evidence but would say nothing derogatory against her. Her oldest son, now 21, also attended. He sat with his grandfather and did not speak to his father.

Between them, the three men paid for the funeral and another name was entered into Reid's notebook of victims.

CHAPTER TWELVE

DARK ANNIE CHAPMAN

Dark Annie Chapman, her deep black hair accentuating her pale complexion, found her way back to Crossingham's Lodging House on the night Polly Nichols had been murdered, having herself been in Bucks Row with a paying customer only half an hour before the murder, fifteen minutes' walk away.

When she heard about it the following evening, she knew it could just as easily have been she herself who picked out the lunatic fiend who had killed Polly. It might have been she and not Polly who had been savagely murdered. Still, it was a thought she put aside. She drank her rum in the Britannia Pub and didn't let it bother her. She was coughing again and suffering pain in her chest.

Sooner or later, everyone in the East End coughed and had chest pain. Consumption was part of the legacy of living in the damp, overcrowded properties, not eating well, and, for many, coping with life through drink, which dragged them further down.

Annie had an unusual set-up at her lodgings. She mostly rented a double bed, and although this cost her eight pence a night, she was sometimes able to take a man back there and have him pay for it. Indeed, most weekends, she was joined by a man the other residents referred to as 'The Pensioner.' Depending on how one looks at it, he was either a regular customer or a boyfriend of sorts. When he was with her, he paid the rent and bought her food. He probably did not pay anything additional for other services he might receive. He was not obsessed with her, but he wanted their relationship to be exclusive. He wanted to be her only man. It was well known that he would also pay for the bed of another prostitute, Eliza Cooper, who was a rival for his affections.

Nevertheless, when he spoke with Tim Donovan, the Assistant keeper of the lodging house, it was to ask him not to let any other men sleep with Annie. Donovan, of course, took little notice of the request.

No one could recall how 'the Pensioner' had been given that title other than him mentioning it himself. It might have come from Annie referring to him as her pension because he stayed with her every Saturday and Sunday night, paying her way for her. She called him 'Ted' or 'm'dear', and he certainly was not old.

Some of the residents formed the idea that he might be a retired soldier, again because he implied as much, but there was nothing colourful or glorious about Ted Stanley. He was a labourer who lived in lodgings in Whitechapel and was a part-time militia member. To his mind, Annie worked in the week selling paper flowers on street corners, selling her embroidery, and earning her money in no other way. She certainly engaged in both of those occupations, but it was never enough to earn her keep. Had it not been for prostitution, she would not have afforded to live in the lodging house, eat and indulge her ever-growing need for drink. She had a second regular customer who also used to stay occasionally during the week, a street hawker called Harry. Where most of the residents who came across the Pensioner in the communal kitchen found him to be as inoffensive as Annie herself, no one cared much for Harry. Annie was a downtrodden, pale, deeply sad woman. In her time on Dorset Street, she had only one friend, Amelia Palmer, who cared about her. Only occasionally did Annie care about this woman living with a man who claimed to be her husband. Amelia alone knew Annie's history.

Annie was a Londoner, from Paddington originally. She married John Chapman when she was all of 28 years of age 'almost on the shelf', she laughed. They had three children, two girls and a boy, and had moved away from London to neighbouring Windsor when her oldest daughter was 11. John had a job as a domestic coachman, and everything seemed fine except their youngest, little Johnny, was born with a lot of physical problems. 'A little cripple child,' Annie said.

Part One: The Nightmare Begins

This put the family under a great deal of strain, and eventually, the little boy was taken in by a charitable school.

Annie and her husband loved their little son and experienced a great sense of loss over him and guilt at not coping with him. Then tragedy hit the family again. Their older daughter, Emily, contracted Meningitis and, at the age of 12, died. It was a shock from which neither she nor her husband ever recovered. They both took to drinking heavily, and it was not a habit Annie could cope with or shake off. Her grief overwhelmed her so that only drink suppressed it. Her husband, not so far gone into alcoholism, would come home from work to find their remaining ten-year-old daughter, Annie Georgina, alone, with a message to say a policeman had called and that Mamma was in the police station in Windsor, where she had been taken after being found drunk in the street.

It happened time and again, Annie admitted as much to Amelia. The downward spiral of degradation was in motion. On a later occasion, she told her friend that her remaining daughter had run away and joined a circus and that the last she heard was her living in Paris. The Pensioner claimed he knew Annie from the time she lived in Windsor, but she never said so while he said a lot of things.

Amelia and Annie ate pie and mash in a pie shop near the market. It was not often that the two women ate together, for it was not every day that Annie ate at all. Her favourite pastime was drinking rum, or beer, or even gin, for that matter. Amelia knew that Annie would get upset speaking of her children, but she was surprised that she was also upset when speaking of her husband. She had left him in Windsor, apparently saying she needed to find her sisters and her brother. She never went back.

'When was that, Annie?' her friend gently asked.

'Oh, it must have been three, nearly four years ago now. We were no good for each other anymore, but he did not want to leave Grove Road in Windsor. It was such a nice house we had in a nice, decent road. But I couldn't stay there anymore because the police made it difficult for me. Oh yes, we had a lovely home in Grove Road, not far from the castle where Her Majesty lives, but without the children, it was an unhappy place. So, I came back to London.'

'Was that the last you saw of him, Annie, when you left him for London?'

'It was the last I saw of him, but not the last I heard from him. He never gave up on me, Amy, he always remembered his Annie.

Nearly every week, he sent me ten bob, half his money, and with that and the embroidery and the paper flowers, I kept myself going.'

'So, what happened? How come you have ended up down here with me and my kind?'

'Well, it was the Christmas before last, 'Christmas '86. I had no money from him and no word. I got a bit worried. I was living with a man who had found me selling the flowers. You remember him, the sieve maker. He brought me to Dorset Street. It was all we could afford.'

'Yes. I never took to him, Annie. That's why they called you Annie Sievey then, because of him?'

'Yes, that was why. I used to take the sieves around to market. Anyway, he was getting rattled because we depended on the money coming in from my husband, John. He got angry, so I went down to Oxford Street, you know, down in Whitechapel where John's brother lives. He wasn't that pleased to see me, and he told me that my John had died; his liver gave out, apparently. He couldn't cope with the loss of the children, and then the loss of me, and he just drank himself to death.' With that, her voice choked, and she sobbed, trying to wipe her tears on a bit of paper.

'Don't upset yourself, Annie, it comes to us all, you know,' said her friend in her kindly, caring voice.

Annie continued with her sad history. 'After the children had gone, I didn't have much but misery in my life. Now, John has also gone, well, there is nothing, no hope, no one to care whether I live or die.' She had sunk into feeling very sorry for herself.

'What happened to Sievey? You don't see him anymore, do you?' asked Amelia.

'Oh, when Mr. Chapman's money stopped, he went off. He didn't need me anymore,' Annie said bitterly. 'He is up in Notting Hill, I hear tell. He left me completely destitute and no way to pay the rent. I was put out on the street from number 30, where we had been staying. I went down to my current doss, Crossingham's lodging house, at number 35 and asked for a bed. It was then I had to do it, Amy. I was starving and about to go into the workhouse when the lodging house deputy, Mr. Donovan, got one of the girls to take me out, teach me the trade, to earn the bed money. I thought, well, I have come this low, and I must get some money somehow. The drink got me through it. Then I worked out that if I could keep just a couple of them in tow that might be enough. I've got Ted the

Pensioner most weekends and occasionally, there is the Hawker, Harry, but it doesn't quite stretch. I still need to go out.' Annie started a coughing fit.

'And that cough is not good Annie, have you been to the Infirmary?' asked Amy.

'More than once', she gasped. 'I was up there for three days recently, and they wanted to put me in the workhouse long term, but I wouldn't do it. I'm a bit better now, though sometimes, I do get very weak and shaky.'

'You've got to ease off the drink a bit, Annie and spend money on decent food. You need to build up girl.' This was genuine concern for her friend.

'Too late for that, Amy. It's the drink that keeps me going. I get me one bit of pleasure in the pubs. I tried to find help from my family, but we never got on. Mother and father passed away a long time ago. My brother bumped into me in the street and gave me some money. I went to my sister's house, and she gave me five pence to buy some food and new stockings, but I spent it on drink on the way home. No, we never really got on.'

The two women fell into silence for a while. It was obvious to Amelia that Annie was turning over memories of her time with her husband and children in her mind. Annie looked unwell, though the food was helping. She did not look quite as pale as earlier.

'Do you have your doss money for tonight, Annie?' asked the concerned woman.

'Yes, dear. I'm doing alright today. I have money for food and tea as well as the doss money. But I miss thinking that my husband was looking out for me even though he was suffering himself.' She fell to a whimpering upset this time, and her tears flowed from self-pity. Amelia pitied her, too. A bad winter would see this one back in the infirmary and then into the workhouse whether she liked it or not.

'Another thing, Annie, keep away from Eliza Cooper, she has it in for you,' advised Amelia. 'From what I hear, she has her eye on your pensioner and thinks if she could get you out of the way, she would have her bed paid for every night. She is rough when she is in drink. I've seen her in the Britannia, fighting.'

'Oh, I know about her, Amy. I'm not bothered. Anyway, she has been alright with me up to now, and we sometimes have tea or a bit of supper together in the kitchen.'

Amy cared too much for her friend to show exasperation. 'You are too trusting, Annie, just watch out for her, my dear,' she said quietly. Amelia had a foreboding about the rival prostitute.

Those words of warning came back to Annie Chapman just a few days later. She was in the Britannia pub on the corner of Dorset Street. It was the biggest pub in the area and that night, it was the fullest. Hundreds of people lived on Dorset Street, perhaps well over a thousand and many of them were in the pub that night. Annie was with her paramour, the pensioner who was already quite drunk.

As was usual, Annie had also taken a lot of rum but was only a little tipsy. It was smoky and rowdy in the bar, Harry the Hawker was there grinning at her; Eliza Cooper was there too, joining Annie and her lover.

Annie was inoffensive, even a little timid by nature and relied on drink to give her courage. As the evening went on and the pensioner became ever more drunken, Annie noticed that Eliza moved in a little too closely to him. He had just bought more drink for the three of them when she saw Eliza try the old trick of helping him put his change back in his leather purse, slipping the money into his hand, apparently helpfully, whilst swapping a penny coin for a florin, the two shilling piece he should have had. Annie immediately grabbed at her wrist; the coins fell noisily onto the upturned barrel used as a table.

'Thief!' she exclaimed. 'I saw you palm that florin.'

Eliza was furious and, if the table had not been between them, would have physically attacked Annie. Others stepped in and kept the two women apart. The pensioner did not know what was happening and decided he and Annie should go back to the lodging house, which they did. He paid for the bed as usual and took himself off there. Annie went to the kitchen, a little drunk and shaking from the confrontation in the pub. In the kitchen, amongst a throng of people variously cooking, eating, drinking and talking, was the thwarted Eliza. On seeing Annie, she immediately started shouting at her.

'You cow, where is that soap you borrowed from me so the pensioner could wash himself to get the dirty smell of you off him.' It wasn't a question but an invitation to continue the argument from the Britannia. Annie did not want to get drawn into it.

'Here, buy yourself a new bar,' she said, throwing a half penny onto the table. This infuriated Eliza even more and she jumped at

Annie, fists swinging. She caught a blow just under her left eye, causing the cheek to swell and blacken and the eye to close.

As Annie tried to protect herself, she was struck in the chest, with what she did not know; it might have been a fist, but it felt too heavy for that. The pain of the blows doubled her up. Amidst all the screaming and shouting, Brummy, the large watchman for the house, came in and flung Eliza away. She did not risk fighting back against so large an opponent. Annie staggered off to her room whilst Brummy put Eliza out on the street until she had calmed down. For some time after that, when people avoided or criticised Eliza, she always made out that Annie had attacked her first. All that Brummy knew was that two prostitutes had been arguing over a bar of soap. It did not seem to be anything out of the ordinary to him.

It was the penultimate day of August when Tim Donovan saw Annie in his building on Dorset Street. She had a startling black eye. He asked her about it, but she did not want to speak of it. He wondered at her poor physical condition. A few days later, she again ran into her friend Amelia Palmer on Dorset Street. Amelia was concerned for her friend who told her what had happened with Eliza. Then Annie took her to one side and asked her to look at something. She undid her jacket and her dress. She was black with bruising. Amelia winced when she saw the extent of the injuries and noticed Annie had started coughing again.

'I've been going up to the infirmary for some help,' said Annie.

As she left her there in the street, she saw Annie smile at her with her sad smile and remembered how remarkably good her teeth were, white and strong. Amelia did not see her again for a few days. When they met, Annie was in a low mood and said, 'I've had enough of being around here for a while. I'm going to see my sister and ask her for a pair of boots so I can go down to Kent for the hop picking.'

It was a forlorn comment, and Amelia did not think Annie would have the strength to do it. The following day, the two women met again by chance; Annie's health was worse than ever. She was sitting in the sunshine outside the monumental building that is known as Christ Church.

'How you feeling, Annie?' It was genuine concern.

'I've not been well enough to go out these last few days,' said Annie. 'I am feeling very poorly now, Amy.' Amy was the name she gave to Amelia, one used by close friends. I haven't had any money for food for a while, and I think I might have to get admitted to the workhouse infirmary for a few days again.' This was surely an admission of desperation.

'Here, my darling, here is two pence. Go and get something to eat, and don't spend it on drink,' said Amelia. They parted affectionately but without hope of much in life improving for either of them. They didn't meet again until Friday. Amelia had just enough money for her and her husband to have a bed that night, but Annie did not. They stood in the shadows in Dorset Street and talked for a while. Annie was going out reluctantly that night to earn some money. She hated doing it, but she was getting desperate again. Amelia left her there to go to the shop for a few meagre provisions, and when she came back, Annie was still standing where she had left her. There was no energy or life about her. She rallied a little when her friend came back to talk with her and finally said, 'It's no use my giving way, I must pull myself together and go out and get some money, or I shall have no lodgings.' With that, she refastened her bonnet and walked slowly up Dorset Street towards Commercial Lane.

At 11:30 p.m., Annie returned to Crossingham's Lodging House. She had walked to her sister's house in Vauxhall, south of the river and walked back. Her sister had no boots for her but had given her a few pennies, which she had spent on rum on the way back. Brummy let her go down to the kitchen, where she met some of the residents she had got to know. One of them had some beer with him and invited her to join him. His brother also joined them for a while and noticed that Annie had a small box of pills and that she took one of them. She had them from the workhouse infirmary. The box broke, so she wrapped the remaining pills in paper torn from an old envelope. At about one in the morning, she left the kitchen, and the men thought she had gone to bed when, in fact, she had gone out, having no money yet to pay for a bed.

Annie returned to the lodging house at about half past one. She seemed less miserable and, feeling a little more relaxed, had bought a baked potato, which she was eating. Brummy was waiting for her as Tim Donovan had sent him to collect the money for her bed. As she did not have any money left, she went to see Donovan in the very unlikely hope that he would let her pay another day, but knowing really that this was a forlorn hope, she thought she would just plead for him to keep the bed for her.

'I haven't sufficient money for my bed, Mr. Donovan, but don't let it. I shall not be long before I'm in.'

Part One: The Nightmare Begins

'You can find money for your beer and yet you can't find money for your bed,' he snapped. He had long ago buried any charitable feelings towards the lodgers. In fact, he despised them. His harsh approach ensured he kept his job.

Annie only smiled at him in resignation, it being the response she had expected. She left his office and stood in the doorway as if pondering what to do.

Finally, she said, 'Never mind, Tim, I'll soon be back.'

It was a gracious acceptance of the position. In another time, in another place, Donovan might have been impressed, but right now, he was not. He had told her to go and prostitute herself so the landlord would have his eight pence for a double bed, which would likely have been empty that night anyway.

On the way out, she spoke to Brummy, the watchman, 'I won't be long, Brummy. See that Tim keeps the bed for me.' She was indicating a particular bed, her bed, the one she shared at weekends with the pensioner, though he had been away for over a week now. Her regular bed in the lodging house was number 29. Brummy watched her leave the lodging house and enter Little Paternoster Row, going in the direction of Brushfield Street and then turning towards Spitalfields Market. She never did return.

In the early hours of the following morning, her body was found in a backyard off nearby Hanbury Street. No one heard the killing, not the strangulation, the cutting of her throat, not the terrible mutilation of her body, which was carved open and disembowelled.

The Abandoned: *Victims of Jack the Ripper*

CHAPTER THIRTEEN

INSPECTOR ABERLINE, SERGEANT THICK, AND 'LEATHER APRON'

Frederick Abberline had been a detective constable, a detective sergeant and then a detective inspector in H Division, the Spitalfields section of Whitechapel. He still lived in the East End and had worked there for over fourteen years. If anyone knew their way around the streets, tenements, lodging houses and pubs there, it was him.

At the age of 45, his capacity as a detective was recognised across the Metropolitan Police and so, he had been transferred to Scotland Yard in Westminster, where his skills would be used to improve the Criminal Investigation Department across the vastness of the city. He had enjoyed a farewell dinner given in his honour by fellow police officers. His replacement in H Division was the Detective Inspector from the neighbouring J Division, the flamboyant and nationally famous Inspector Reid. Abberline had been completely unaware on that early September morning that his stay in Scotland Yard was going to be such a short one. Once back in his home area, Chief Inspector Swanson gave him complete day-to-day control of the investigation with every confidence that he would catch the Whitechapel fiend.

At the first briefing meeting with the largest group of detectives he had ever worked with, Abberline set out the procedures they would use to catch their man. First, the uniformed police would increase their patrols and vary the timings of their regular 'beats'. It was thought by some officers that the fiend waited for a policeman to go by, and his local knowledge meant that he knew the officer would not return for a considerable time, giving him the opportunity to do as he liked. Abberline was not totally convinced about this as in the case of Polly Nichols catching him may have been a close-run thing, and the man must only just have slipped away before he could be caught. After all, the body was not cold when Constable Neil came across her. There was no harm in changing the beat times, even doubling the officers on the beat so that more patrols took place, but it was hit and miss and depended on the man striking again and catching him in the act. This did not lessen the risk to potential victims. Someone came up with the idea that as police wore hob-nailed police-issued boots and could be heard coming from quite a distance as their footfall rang on the cobbled streets, noise carrying in the smog, they should deaden the sound.

Consequently, they took to gluing pads of rubber to the sole and heel, making them almost silent. It did not take long for the thick-soled shoes to be referred to as 'brothel creepers'.

Abberline's more realistic plan was to question every prostitute on the street, visit every pub in the area, speak to the watchmen and lodging house deputies and discover any common themes to emerge from their experiences, opinions, memories and observations. Who did they suspect? Who was looking suspicious? Who might be sheltering this man? Ask the bar workers if they noticed anyone hanging around at the official closing time and then following a woman out. Someone, somewhere, knew something. He knew every street and alleyway, and he knew who should be questioned. He also knew which detectives would be reliable and which uniformed officers he needed in different places. They concentrated on the locations where the victims had been known to have frequented on the night they had died. He wanted to know if the victims had worked to a regular pattern, which had made them a planned target, or were they randomly selected? He was thorough. He commanded great loyalty amongst his team of detectives, who had every confidence in him. He knew what he was doing, and he knew what they were doing.

Part One: The Nightmare Begins

The information which came back to him was mainly from the women who worked the streets. Many of them feared the High Rip gangs but noticed that an increased police presence had greatly reduced the times they were bothered by these young thugs. Abberline was already sure that the killer was not a member of a gang. This man was a lone wolf who hunted alone and then scurried back to his den to lie low for a while, his savagery worsening with practice. Surely, someone would see his bloodstained clothing. He sent two men to check all the laundries from Camden to Limehouse, but without anything being found. He understood that given the amount of spilled blood, if clothing was not being professionally laundered, then it was being taken care of in some other way. The *Ripper* might be continually burning his clothing, but this was unlikely.

Could he, or those closest to him, clean away the evidence at home in his lair?

Then, one suspect emerged. A lot of the women spoke of a stocky man in his forties, quite ugly to look at, thick-set, swarthy with close-cropped hair. According to them, he spoke with a heavy accent, but no language was suggested. Another distinguishing feature was that he often wore a leather apron and carried a knife. Some of the women claimed he robbed them.

It was a lead, a main suspect. There was one additional worrying feature: the man was said to be a Jew, and Jews were already unfairly blamed for many of the ills of the area. He might be nothing other than a convenient character to blame. Abberline decided to issue a description of the suspect but deliberately omitted any reference to him being a Jew. He did not want pogroms starting in the East End or his police officers closing their minds to other suspects. In doing so, he may, for the best of reasons, have guided his men away from another suspect, a local, mentally disturbed character whose childhood was spent suffering the violent pogroms of Eastern Europe, a man at least one witness named, a Polish Jew called Aaron Kosminski. Kosminski was not detained or interviewed by police at any time.

After analysing his information, Abberline called a general briefing of all police officers involved in the case. As it proved, it was a good move. In describing the suspect, Sergeant Thick spoke up.

'I think I know this man. At least, the general description fits. The man the women are calling Leather Apron is, I would say, much more likely to be John Pizer, a Polish shoemaker I have known these past 18 years or so. He wears a leather apron for his work, but then so do those who work in the slaughterhouses. I'm not certain of his whereabouts, but I have a good idea where I might find him. I'll go and get him, Inspector. Now I think of it, I haven't seen him around since the murder of Mrs. Chapman.'

'Excellent, Sergeant. Tell me, would you say he is of Hebrew extraction?'

'Certainly, he is. I know him to be a Polish Jew, not one of the Jews to have come here in recent years; very much assimilated, in fact. He has always been around the area. His brother lives a street or two behind the Bell foundry, near to where I live myself. He doesn't spend much time in this area, though. He doesn't work in this area, so he does not always reside with his brother; I will have to track him down. Some of us will know him from the Princess Alice pub on the corner of Wentworth Street and Brick Lane, an unusual-looking little fellow, that is for sure.'

'Thank you. Now, everyone, this is most important,' Abberline's voice conveyed authority. 'As exciting a possibility as this is, this man is only a suspect. We do not yet have any evidence linking him to the crimes. You all know that since the refugees have been coming in from Russia, there has been a lot of resentment towards them from current residents. The Russian Jews have virtually colonised the south End of Brick Lane, and English is a foreign tongue to them. Their presence has pushed the existing people into those sections of Flower and Dean, White's Row, Thrawl Street and Dorset Street, where all the victims lived. I do not want a campaign of blame starting up against the Jews, and it can easily happen because of resentment; the poor turning on the poor. So, no discussions of the Hebrews and most definitely no talking to the press. I will tell you more after Sergeant Thick has arrested Mr. Pizer and I have had a chance to interrogate him. Meanwhile, I want you to assume that this is not the man, so keep searching,' Abberline had the manner of a bank manager, showing a calm authority and a master of clear instructions.

The following day, Abberline's plan for a calm, methodical investigation, carried out quietly and focused, went out of the window. Reporters from the Star newspaper unexpectedly produced a series of sensationalist stories.

According to the Star, at least fifty women described the possible killer as being five feet four inches in height, wearing a dark cap, thick-set, having closely cropped black hair and a small moustache. His age was given as being about 40. The police, it said, had this man

Part One: The Nightmare Begins

as their only suspect, a repellent-looking man with a sardonic grin and small, glittering eyes. The newspaper went on to describe him as always wearing a leather apron and carrying a knife, wearing slippers so no one could hear him coming. Worst of all, the very piece of information Abberline did not want divulged; they claimed the suspect to be Jewish.

The stories which accompanied and followed the newspaper articles created a climate of fear and pointed the finger at Jewish immigrants. No such perverted crimes had been known before these murders before the Jews had moved into the area. Abberline was appalled that Mr. Best of the Star, a sensationalist writer for a sensationalist newspaper, had got hold of this story, presumably by bribing one of the police officers involved, and had now, true to his type, thoroughly sensationalised it. He needed Thick to find his man quickly, for the suspect's sake, before a mob lynched him.

Sergeant Thick made his enquiries. Most people around the area did not like having much to do with the police, having too much to hide. Thick, though, was well-known and respected; he was a tough customer but a fair man. There had been a famous incident in Brick Lane when he attempted to arrest a man carrying a sack with what turned out to be property stolen in a burglary. He overpowered the man only to be assaulted by the man's accomplice. Thick beat off that man who tried to grab the sack of stolen goods, but the sergeant stood on it, so preventing the attempt. The second man ran off, but only to return with a gang who tried to free the first man. Thick lashed out with his truncheon, beating them back and refusing to give up his prisoner. He forced his way into a shop with the man and the swag and was able to hold off the gang until they heard answering police whistles; knowing reinforcements were arriving, they ran off.

In a crisis, he was a man to whom people could turn. He knew the heat was on, and a lot of people, fired up by the press, were looking for Leather Apron to exact retribution and failing him, probably any Jew. He needed to make the arrest quickly.

Early on the morning of 10th September, he went to 22 Mulberry Street and found Pizer there. Pizer's brother had warned him that he was in danger, and he was hiding from any mob which might be about to seize him. He went with Thick to Leman Street police station for interrogation. Thick already knew from speaking to his brother and neighbours that Pizer had an alibi for the night Annie

Chapman was killed, but there were other matters to consider, principally the murder of Polly Nichols.

Pizer was not an easy man to interview. Abberline took a dislike to him but was far too experienced to let that cloud his judgment. Pizer was afraid and would probably lie if he thought it would clear his name. He lied about being known as Leather Apron, but Thick had known him by that name for years. Abberline wanted background information on this man. He was aware that several women found Pizer to be threatening, but whilst that was an indication that the man might be violent, it did not make him the Whitechapel fiend. What Pizer did not know was that Abberline had a witness who claimed he overheard Pizer threaten to kill a woman who might have been Annie Chapman.

Emanuel Delbast Violenia said he was of Spanish and Bulgarian parentage who had been living in Manchester in the north of England. He, his wife and two children had walked from there to London with the intention of finding a ship to take them to Australia, he said. Abberline thought this unlikely as the man might more easily have gone to Liverpool, but then maybe no ships sailed from there to Australia: it didn't really matter.

It seemed when they reached the East End, he found them a place at a common lodging house on Hanbury Street, the street where Annie Chapman was killed.

Early on the previous Saturday morning, walking alone along Hanbury Street, he said he noticed a man and woman quarrelling. Violenia claimed he distinctly heard the man threaten to kill the woman by sticking a knife into her. After hearing of the murder, he contacted the police as he was sure he could recognise the man should he see him again.

Consequently, Abberline asked Inspector Canaby and Sergeant Thick to organise an identity parade in the yard at the back of Leman Street police station. Violenia was then brought into the yard. At once, without any hesitation or any doubt whatever, he went up to Pizer and identified him as the man whom he heard threaten a woman on the night of the murder. Satisfied that Violenia had indeed seen Pizer before, he arranged for the witness to be taken to the mortuary to see if he could identify the body of Annie Chapman as being the woman he saw threatened. He could not identify her. Abberline had him brought back and questioned him in detail. He contradicted himself, became unsure of time and dates and was, the Detective Inspector thought, unreliable; another disappointment.

Meanwhile, Abberline interviewed Pizer about his movements. On the night Polly Nichols was murdered, he said he had been staying at Crossman's Lodging House in the Holloway Road near Highbury, and at 1:30 a.m. that morning of the murder, spoke to a policeman about the fire at London Docks, which he then went to see. The fire had broken out at 8:30 p.m. at one of the warehouses and was so fierce it could be seen for miles. Though brought under control by eleven o'clock, it was not fully extinguished until several hours later. He said he did not watch the fire for long, but returned to Crossman's Lodging House, arriving at about 2:15 a.m. He paid his 4 pence for his bed, then sat in the kitchen and smoked a clay pipe for a while. He slept until 11 a.m., when he was roused by the attendant who told him it was time to leave. He later learned of the murder from a police force placard he saw in the street. The police checked every element of his story only, disappointingly for them, only to confirm it. There was nothing to tie Pizer to any of the murders, and thus, he was formally released.

Sergeant Thick escorted the man home to ensure nothing happened to him. Abberline, on this occasion, informed the press and the inquest that Pizer was not a suspect. For the local press, this was unfortunate as they had whipped up a hatred against this man, describing him in various offensive terms.

Much later, Pizer claimed he had been paid compensation by the press for the harm they did him. However, in Whitechapel, the notion that the stalker and mutilator of women was a Jew took hold. No one leading the investigation made the connection to Aaron Kosminski, the local man who was similar in appearance to Pizer.

On-site investigations continued. In the backyard of 25 Hanbury Street, the next house but one to the scene of the murder, a little girl noticed peculiar marks on the wall and on the ground. She told Detective-Inspector Chandler, who had just called the house to make a plan of the back premises of the three houses for the use of the Coroner at the inquest. The whole of the yard was then examined, with the result that a possible bloody trail was found distinctly marked for five or six feet in the direction of the back door of the house, although Inspector Reid later remarked that it might well have been urine and not blood at all.

Further investigation seemed to show that the trail, if it was blood, could be that of the murderer, who had escaped over the dividing fence between number 29 and 27, and into the garden of number 25.

On the wall of the last house was a stain that looked something between a smear and a sprinkle and had probably been made by the murderer, who, aware of the blood-soaked state of his coat, probably took off that garment and knocked it against the wall.

At the end of the yard of number 25 was Bailey's packing case workshop. In a corner, the police found crumpled paper saturated with blood. It was evident that the murderer had found the paper in the yard of number 25 and had wiped his hands with it, afterwards throwing it over the wall into Bailey's premises. He had not come prepared to clean himself, which seemed odd if this was a planned attack.

Perhaps it was a man who had no control over his murderous actions, who struck out in a sudden frenzy of lust or hatred. The back and front doors of all the premises were always left either on the latch or wide open because tenants came and went at all hours. The general appearance of the bloody trail and other circumstances seem to show that the murderer intended to escape into the street through the house next door but one, not retreating by the way he came, being very alert to his own safety, and not risking being seen. The savage killer was cunning. The victims were probably chosen randomly, but he was alert to his need to escape after the deed was accomplished.

CHAPTER FOURTEEN

THE INQUEST ON ANNIE

All of London, indeed, much of the world took an interest in the events in the East End. Newspapers were selling well on the backs of the stories of different men taken in for questioning, only to be released. Whilst the Star and other alarmist newspapers whipped up feelings, especially fear, others, such as the Times, reported on the details of the adjourned inquests and published letters from its readers. The poor relationship between the police and the press worsened with the press sniping at the Metropolitan Police's inability to locate the killer.

A doctor from his Harley Street practice wrote to the Times to advise the police that they were looking in the wrong place. In his opinion, the killer was insane, but from a middle or upper-class family who could shelter him. The view that the man was insane was not challenged, and similarly, the opinion that someone was sheltering him was thought by police to be highly likely, but shelter could be provided by anyone with a place to do so, not necessarily the well-to-do. The doctor's letter sat alongside the hundreds of letters from all around the country, which suggested how to catch the killer, or even volunteering to take over the investigation as clearly the police were too stupid to manage the case. Within a few weeks, myth was replacing fact and rumour in the public imagination, and it was about to get worse.

Interest in the murders was high, but the police hoped it would tail off once the final day of the inquest was over on the 24th of September.

At the inquest, the police admitted they could not identify the killer and the Coroner was unhappy with that, but it was the details of the autopsy that grabbed the attention of the press and its readers.

The abdomen had been entirely laid open: the intestines, severed from their mesenteric attachments and then lifted out of the body and placed on the shoulder of the corpse, whilst from the pelvis, the uterus and its appendages with the upper portion of the vagina and the posterior two-thirds of the bladder, had been surgically removed.

No trace of these parts could be found, and the incisions were cleanly cut, avoiding the rectum, and dividing the vagina low enough to avoid injury to the cervix uteri. Obviously, the work was that of an expert or at least one who had such knowledge of anatomical or pathological examinations as to be proficient with a scalpel or knife.

The Coroner, also known as the pompous, self-important, self-righteous Mr. Wynne Baxter, did not help the police in his summing up of the case. If anything, he went out of his way to tell the world that the police did not know what they were doing.

In his summary, his prejudice got the better of him as he dismissed what he did not want to hear and added in his own theories as if they were fact. Indeed, for the newspapers, his opinions, however wrong, became fact, and the Whitechapel murders took a sinister turn. With his audience packed before him, the Coroner revelled in unexpected celebrity. His summing up was only partly factual, his conclusions based freely on his own speculations and prejudices, pointing, as the police knew, in entirely the wrong direction.

The newspapers loved the summing up. According to the Coroner, they had an amazing, ghoulish figure to write about. A man possibly from an educated, even privileged background, skilled as a surgeon, yet wanting to harvest organs for money from the fallen women of Whitechapel. It was implied that the police were incompetent, whilst the Coroner himself believed he could and did give a physical description of the wanted man and his motive for murder simply by reviewing the evidence. He praised the doctor who carried out the autopsy for noticing the missing organs but dismissed scientific assertion of the time of death because it did not fit with the

Part One: The Nightmare Begins

recollection of witnesses who, in other circumstances, he would have disregarded as being unreliable. The Coroner chose to believe the local witnesses because they described a suspect. Their versions helped him 'solve' the case for the police, explaining motivation and background, all the police had to do was find the culprit. He suggested that as not many would fit the profile he outlined, it would be an easy task. The image conveyed around the world was of a cunning, chilling figure with surgical skills well able to run rings around the dim-witted police. The Coroner, more than the killer, damaged the reputation of the Metropolitan Police.

Carried away by his own self-importance, the Coroner failed to appreciate that the organs were removed by a different implement to that which caused the mutilation, and probably by a different hand. Had he asked the police, they would have told him as much. The illegal sale of body parts to teaching hospitals from mortuaries was a trade the police knew of, and it was highly likely it had happened here. The missing organs had been removed once the corpse was in the mortuary and not by the murderer.

The inquest into the miserable life and brutal death of a woman had become nothing more than an excuse for the self-glorification of a misguided, opinionated, foolish coroner.

As the newspaper reporters dashed out the views of the coroner, the next twist in the story erupted with a tremendous, shuddering impact. If the sensationalising of the murders simply for the sale of newspapers was not already shameful enough, with the publication the following day of the first of the letters signed *Jack the Ripper*, a letter giving details of the murder, a frenzy took hold of the press and fear spread throughout the city. The murdered women lost not only their lives but their identities, being thereafter known only as victims of *Jack the Ripper*.

The Abandoned: *Victims of Jack the Ripper*

CHAPTER FIFTEEN

THE POLICE, THE PRESS, THE MURDERS

Sir Charles Warren, Commissioner of the Metropolitan Police, was located at 4 Whitehall, the centre of the British Government. It was there that he summoned his team investigating the Whitechapel murders. He had the Home Secretary criticising him in private while not publicly supporting him over the East End reign of terror. The newspapers were making him out to be a fool and were unable to organise the murder investigations, even though they knew he was reliant on his detectives to manage all matters to do with the murders. He did not investigate anything himself.

Now, there was hysteria in the streets. He needed to know everything his detectives knew, a subject he had neglected, having no interest in detective work. He started with his deputy in charge of the detective service, Sir Robert Anderson. Anderson quickly passed the topic to Chief Inspector Swanson, who had full oversight of the case. Swanson made a good fist of summing up the situation.

'As all of us involved in the investigation see it, we are no nearer finding the culprit than at the start of proceedings. Unfortunately, Mr. Wynne Baxter, the Coroner, at the inquest of Mrs. Chapman, has completely muddied the waters. First, the description of the suspect he calls a true one is unlikely to be so because it is based on a man seen by unreliable witnesses at a time that does not accord with the time of death given by the physician. Their descriptions are utterly useless. His intervention means the finger is being pointed by the local populace ever more at any man of Hebrew extraction, a dangerous thing to do when feelings are running high. The police in the East End fear widespread attacks on innocent Jews. Secondly, as Inspectors Reid and Abberline will confirm, there were at least two different types of cuts made to the body; the cuts resulting in disembowelling and throat-cutting were vicious and crude. However, the removal of organs was precise and skilful. This suggests to us that at least two persons were at work here. What Mr. Wynne Baxter claims to be the motive for the murder, the harvesting of organs for sale, is utterly wrong in our view. It is pure conjecture. With certainty, the missing organs were removed once the body was in the mortuary, prior to autopsy. Medical students or a doctor attempting to make money might easily have carried out the careful removal of organs undisturbed as the body waited the autopsy. It is highly improbable that the killer would have had time to accomplish such precise surgery at the time of the killing. Mr. Wynne Baxter asserts the killer is a skilled surgeon – he is not. The killings are vicious and crude. All this inquest has done is raise the level of fear and make us appear incompetent.'

Warren seemed hardly to listen. 'This is not a good situation, gentlemen. Look at the newspapers and the letters from the public they are printing. I am accused even in Parliament of not putting enough police in the area, but you have more than you know what to do with. I am told we should use bloodhounds, but although that is authorised, you wonder what use they would be in such an environment. Today, I read that I am foolishly basing the entire investigation on the use of bloodhounds. I think, gentlemen, nothing short of catching the killer is going to stop these slurs and insults. I see articles written about the refusal to offer a reward for information and letters from vigilance societies wanting that to happen. A member of parliament has offered £100 of his own money because the police have failed to do so. Gentlemen, I agree with the offering of a reward but am prevented by the Home Office from doing so. It is the opinion of the Permanent Secretary that rewards are abused. What can I do? Now we have this letter from a self-styled *Jack the Ripper* that will only stir up more fear and panic once it gets out, which it will.'

Part One: The Nightmare Begins

Warren clearly did not know which way to turn. He continued, his exasperation showing. 'Go on, Mr. Swanson, what else have you to tell me, especially about this letter that has now appeared, where the author chillingly calls himself *Jack the Ripper* and seems to know all about the murders.' With that, he placed the letter on the table in front of them all. 'The postmark shows it was sent on the final day of the Chapman inquest. I received it this morning, thanks to a friend from the Central News Agency. They had held on to it for a couple of days, thinking it a hoax, but then doubted themselves, and it was conveyed to me via the Duty Inspector. You have all seen it. It has not been published, and I pray we keep it that way for fear of the effect it might have on the public. I have already had a letter by another hand from the 24th, which we have dismissed. Well, what do you have to say?' He looked at Swanson.

Swanson remained calm and factual. 'Each of us has looked at it, Sir Charles, and we believe it to be a fabrication. The way it is styled is curious, as if attempting to portray the devil himself. The way of writing is a sort of disguise, too, as it seems to be a clumsy attempt to incorporate American language, the address *'Dear Boss'*, for instance. In our view, it is mischievous and probably written by a journalist. It could be any of many, and my first guess would be someone working for the Star as that newspaper is given to sensationalising everything, but I agree it is well informed so it must be written by someone who is obtaining information from us in some way.' The implication of collusion, bribery even, was left hanging.

The detectives could see that Warren was under great strain and was isolated. They felt they were letting him down. The radical press was rude, even vicious, when referring to him, calling for him to be replaced. No other police commissioner had suffered such pressure. He had no one to speak with apart from friends, one of whom was the trustworthy newspaper man who had passed on this letter. None was able to help. He had no means by which he could give a response to the criticism heaped upon him. As the stories mounted, he became more convinced that senior officers were plotting against him. He now doubted even these men before him today, convinced at least one of them was feeding stories to the press. Sir Charles became blunt.

'What, then, is your collective opinion of these killings? Will this man strike again?'

Abberline spoke up at this point.

'There is no doubt that this man is mad. He may be cunning, but I don't think he is overly so. He doesn't prepare himself particularly well, as far as we can see. He has no system for cleaning himself after a killing, seems to take any avenue of escape, is always at risk of being seen. He avoided being caught by one of our patrolling officers near Buck's Yard by a matter of minutes. No, he has been very lucky. His lair must be close by. Sadly, yes, I am certain he will do this again. Either his luck will change, and we will catch him in an attempt to kill again, or whoever is sheltering him will give him up.' He could see that Warren was not comforted by this reply.

'Should the worst happen, and this man strike again, I must be informed immediately so I might attend. Send for me at any time of day or night.' Warren was letting it be known that whatever his attitude to the investigation had been until that day, he now insisted on being part of it.

The meeting ended with the detectives returning to their duties. It was Saturday afternoon. Warren turned his attention to letters and petitions from vigilante groups. He did not blame local people for banding together, they were afraid. He was beginning to lose faith in his own men to catch the *Ripper*. Some of them, he felt, were prepared to betray him. The legacy of the Trafalgar Square affair hung in the air. He did not regret the actions he had authorised on that day but, rather increasingly, resented having had to make those decisions because the Home Secretary was dithering and indecisive, a career politician. He decided that if anything else occurred, he had to be seen leading his police officers. He did not have long to wait.

Everyone was expecting trouble, and trouble duly arrived. In the early hours of the 30th of September, that very night, the body of a woman was discovered in a yard just off Commercial Road in Whitechapel. Her throat cut.

One hour later, just ten minutes' walk away in gloomy, echoing little Mitre Square, the body of another woman was found, and this one had been savagely mutilated.

Part One: The Nightmare Begins

CHAPTER SIXTEEN

LONG LIZZIE

Not everyone from the East End went hop-picking that September. Lizzie Stride never went. In fact, from the day she arrived in the city, she never went outside London again. Some of the women in the Spitalfields area called her 'Long Lizzie', not because she was tall, she wasn't, but because she appeared to have a long face. She was pale-skinned and spoke with a slight foreign accent as so many did in the East End. She had lived in the area for over 20 years but had been born in Sweden, where she had grown up, been registered by police as a young prostitute, had given birth to a child who had died, where she had been treated for syphilis, then escaped to England to start a new life, working mostly as a domestic cleaner. The police knew her too, both the City of London Police and the Metropolitan Police, because when drunk, which was often, she was a public nuisance, being both voluble and aggressive.

When she was first in London, she worked for a Swedish expatriate as a cleaner, a post supported by the local Swedish Church in London and lived at her employer's establishment in Gower Street in Soho. Within three years, she met and married an Englishman, John Stride, and moved with him to the East India Dock Road in Poplar. According to her, they kept a coffee shop in Chrisp Street in Poplar.

By 1870, they had moved the business to Upper North Street, still in Poplar. So successful were they, she said, that their next move was to the busy Poplar High Street, where they lived on the premises until the business was taken over in 1875. What truly happened thereafter, she never revealed to anyone. Her occasional explanation for her change in fortune was that she was with her family aboard Princess Alice, a river cruise ship, enjoying a day out when it collided with the steamer Bywell Castle in the Thames in 1878 with the loss of over 600 lives. She claimed her husband and children were killed and that her palate was injured by being kicked in the mouth while climbing the mast to escape, which was why she had lost teeth. It was a complete and utter lie as her husband died in 1884, having by then been apart from her for several years. She gave no further information about the children, not even names. It was one of several hard-luck stories she used when seeking the sympathy of charities, such as when asking for financial aid from the Swedish Church. Whatever the cause, by 1882, she had tumbled a long way and found herself in the Whitechapel Workhouse.

People who knew Lizzie tended to like her. She was a person who took pleasure in helping others, but no one could believe much of what she said. That quality did not especially mark her out from so many of her peers; few people in Lodging Houses found any advantage in telling the truth. What a lot of people did say was that she had made a bad choice when she took up with Michael Kidney about three years earlier. He wasn't a man who would say much about his own background. Some told him his surname was a corruption of Kennedy, that he was Irish, or his father was, but he didn't care for that, declaring himself an Englishman and a Londoner. He had lived just off the Commercial Road in Whitechapel for several years before he met Lizzie in a pub nearby. He took up with her, and she went to live with him. From her point of view at the time, her choice was Kidney or the Workhouse; she never pretended it was a love match. Those women who knew her worried about the relationship.

On the one hand, Kidney was a docker and often in work so would have money, but he also had a reputation for being a heavy drinker and known to be violent to women, including Lizzie.

Stories spread about how possessive he was of her; wouldn't let her out of his sight at times, and would even lock her in the room whilst he was out.

Part One: The Nightmare Begins

When they were out together, he fawned over her whilst criticising her in the company of others. Classic domestic control and abuse. Typical of so many under such coercive control, Lizzie denied the truth of it. When asked about being locked in their room, she said that, of course, she had a key, the room being locked only to protect their few belongings.

At other times, Kidney admitted to locking her in, claiming it was for her own good, to stop her looking for drink, a compulsion which necessarily involved her meeting other men if only in social chit-chat. Only the two of them knew the truth of the situation for certain, but despite the probing of others, she was deeply in denial of his controlling behaviour. Like him, she had become an increasingly heavy drinker, coming before the Magistrates for being drunk and disorderly many times.

When drunk, her behaviour became aggressive and her language crude and voluble. The word on the manor was that drink was her only solace for being with a man like Kidney.

Even after moving in with Kidney and his controlling behaviour, Lizzie went missing numerous times, preferring to throw herself on the mercy of the Swedish Church for alms.

The Clerk of the Church got to know her a little and marked how very poor she seemed to be. Somehow, her desperation always drove her back to Kidney, and he would then loudly claim that she preferred him to any other man, saying that when she went off without explanation, he did not have to look for her. He just knew she would be back.

In truth, it seems it was still him or the Workhouse, although there were odd times when she found herself in the Common Lodging Houses, always on her own. She was afraid of him and did not want to go back too soon or without something to show for her absence. Then, in the spring of the previous year, she had had enough of being bullied and beaten, and ran away to Poplar Workhouse, where she summoned enough courage to report him to the police.

The police, who knew of Kidney, were only too happy to arrest him and charge him with assault. Predictably, Lizzie did not turn up to give evidence, so the case was dismissed. Instead, she left the Workhouse and returned to him, knowing he would beat her, and then fuss over her, continuously telling her she was worthless except for her association with him.

Despite his possessiveness, when in dire need of money, he was quite prepared to demand Lizzie go and earn some, knowing full well that the only way she could make any money if there was no cleaning work was by prostitution. Lately, whenever she went out, he taunted her to watch out for Leather Apron, so letting her know he expected her to be soliciting as a prostitute: all the women were by now terrified of the Whitechapel fiend.

On the 25th of September, Kidney went to work at the docks, and she managed to run away again. This time, she had enough money to pay for a bed at a lodging house. Lizzie went to 32 Flower and Dean Street, where she knew the deputy, Mrs. Tanner.

'Well,' said Mrs. Tanner, 'I haven't seen you for a while, Lizzie. Do you have your four pence for the bed?'

'Here it is. I saved it from Mr. Kidney; he won't know I have it. He is going to be in a rage when he gets back, and I am gone, but I have had enough of him.' Lizzie was open about the beatings she took at his hands.

'How are you going to get on, finding your board money, Lizzie?' Mrs. Tanner might pity Lizzie, but money came first.

'I'm looking around for a bit of charring; you know I'm a good cleaner. If you hear of anything, let me know. If it comes to it, I suppose I'll have to take a walk down Poplar.' Her eyes would not meet those of her friend.

Mrs. Tanner knew Lizzie was alluding to prostitution, but that is how most of the women in Flower and Dean Street supplemented their money, a little part-time street walking down where the sailors came in.

By Saturday, the day Sir Charles Warren was informing his detectives how dissatisfied with them he was, Mrs. Tanner did have some cleaning work for Lizzie, who spent an afternoon sorting out two rooms for her, and was paid sixpence for the hard work she did. Lizzie's spirits were lifted by this, and she decided to go for a drink that evening, a more sympathetic Mrs. Tanner joining her in the Queens Head pub.

Although hardened by the lessons of the world, Mrs. Tanner still felt so sorry for Lizzie having to sell herself to drunken strangers. Their little social occasion did not last long, though it left Lizzie in a good mood and looking forward to going out for the evening. Mrs. Tanner thought that Lizzie had an assignation, and certainly not with Michael Kidney. As they walked back, they continued to chat happily together. Lizzie brought up the visit of one of the street missionaries from a couple of nights earlier.

'Oh, don't let that queer chap back in, you know, the missionary,' she said. 'He was down in the kitchen talking to us, and he set off several of the girls crying.' Lizzie was obviously disturbed by the evangelist.

'He means well, dear', explained Mrs. Tanner, 'and he is doing some good hereabouts. He has set up a school for street boys and is trying to take in some of them, better than the workhouse, he says. He reckons saving them from starving means less thieving and giving them a home and teaching them to read will change everything.' She had a lot of sympathy with the man.

'Well, he set us off good and proper; making us cry and such like.' Lizzie was not convinced by Christian do-gooders. When she went to the Swedish church, it was for money, the sort of charity that kept body and soul together.

'Yes,' Mrs. Tanner agreed. 'He told me the women are all afraid of being murdered by the butcher going round at night. He said some of them were owning up to him about prostitution, and he was shocked that their need was so great that they were forced by circumstance to continue in the trade until they were murdered. Indeed, they are terrified by the thought of the killer I told him, but also by the thought of eternal damnation by people like him, yet no matter what he said to them, nothing turned them from their usual course because how else are they going to get enough to pay for a room and food? I didn't mention the drink! I think the poor man was quite shocked enough already without me explaining about that.' She was sympathetic to what he was doing, but her loyalty, such as it was, lay with the women.

'He was nice enough, I suppose, for a preacher,' said Lizzie.

'I'm told he is a doctor lovey, named Barnardo or something like it. Thinks we women might all be beyond his power to help, but he is trying to save the children from sin. Yes, nice enough, a kind man, but I see them come, and I see them go,' she sighed.

The two women parted in the lodging house, Lizzie preparing herself as best she could to go out. It was not quite dark when she left the premises, first chatting with the doorman. He suspected she was off to see someone special because she was dressed up. She smiled at him and seemed to be very pleased with herself. She still had the sixpence Mrs. Tanner had paid her, all in one silver coin and showed it to him.

'Where you off to tonight then, Lizzie? Back down Poplar?' He might not respect her, but he could not help but like her.

'Not tonight, Tommy. I won't be working tonight, if you take my meaning. No, maybe not much beyond Commercial Road tonight,' she winked at him, 'don't you go telling Mr. Kidney if he comes looking. He can look all down Poplar High Street for all I care because I won't be there.' She was pleased with herself.

She was true to her word. Eleven o'clock that evening found her finishing her drinks in The Bricklayer's Arms near Commercial Street. She could not recall the last time she had been there, relaxed and happy. It was not a place where she had ever done business. However, she wasn't alone. With her, from what everyone else in the pub could see, was a man who seemed besotted with her. He was quite well dressed for those parts of the city, wearing a morning suit, a man of middle years who just could not stop hugging and kissing her.

For her part, she seemed to be loving the attention he lavished upon her. For the rest of the world, they were like two young lovers. They made to leave the pub together, but by then, it was pouring with rain, so instead, they hugged and kissed some more, behaviour which to onlookers seemed quite out of character for a man of the social standing they ascribed to him.

As for the woman, no one knew her. Two workmen pushed past them out of the rain and into the pub and ordered their beer. Amused at seeing this middle-aged couple apparently in love, they invited them to come back into the bar and avoid the downpour.

When they declined and obviously decided to suffer a soaking, one of the men called out to her, 'That's Leather Apron getting round you,' a remark they thought witty as the man seemed as far away from the image of the Whitechapel killer as any man might be.

The couple took no notice and, wrapped in a private world, went out into the rain. At last, after years of sadness, degradation and struggle, Lizzie had found a man who not only wanted her, even loved her, but was kind, gentle and respectful. She saw, for the first time in many miserable years, a future that included happiness. She did not pretend to be in love, but she was overwhelmed by the flattery of a decent man who was in love with her.

Part One: The Nightmare Begins

It was not raining at a quarter to one in the dark and overcast early morning when Israel Schwartz, an immigrant from Eastern Europe, turned into Berner Street from Commercial Road. He then saw something he would rather not have seen. A man some distance in front of him had stopped and was speaking with a woman who seemed to be waiting there for someone else.

The two appeared to exchange words angrily, and then the man took hold of the woman and tried to pull her away from the gateway where she was standing, and into the street. She obviously resisted, and he pushed her down onto the public footpath, or maybe she fell when she broke his grip. She screamed or shouted, but not loudly, more in anger than fear, it seemed.

A second man was standing across the street, and was also watching, possibly even waiting for the first man as if he were an acquaintance of the man doing the pushing. The aggressor called to the second man, speaking in a matter-of-fact tone one might expect between friends. Continuing the struggle with the woman, the assailant then turned to the man across the street a second time and, as if referring to Schwartz, who was watching from some way down the street, called out what Schwartz took to be 'Lipski', the name of a Jewish murderer who had been hanged the previous year.

It was a name hurled at Jewish immigrants as a threat or insult. Already alarmed, Schwartz decided to move away as quickly as he could. He did not want to get involved in what seemed to be a domestic argument. His ears heard what was familiar and what he thought would be said. More likely, what was called out was not Lipski but Lizzie, the man across the street being informed of the identity of the woman, perhaps in explanation of the row going on between them. Whatever was said, it was obvious to Schwartz that the man had tried to coerce the woman into leaving with him and to walk down the main street in the general direction of Spitalfields. She had resisted. As he walked away, he felt that the second man was following him and meant him harm, so he hurried all the more.

Lizzie had a lot to say for herself, and it did not include agreeing to leave with the man, whoever he might be. At the same time, she did not want to cause a scene. She was just too well known to police for her record of drunkenness, and this might be viewed as another such occurrence, so she spoke more quietly than usual, keeping her voice down so even her screaming was muted, not wanting to draw attention. Who knows, perhaps her lover of earlier that evening had arranged to meet with her again that night? Now was not the time to get arrested again.

She stepped back into the yard behind her, took out a packet of cachou nuts and began nibbling them, dismissing the attention of the man haranguing her. In the quiet of the yard, she could tell the man exactly what she thought about not leaving with him. Only she and whoever was in that yard would ever know what was said because sometime in the next fifteen minutes, she was killed, her throat slashed.

She was discovered very soon after the attack, her body still warm, by a carter who had turned his horse into the yard. He maintained later that his horse remained nervous as if someone else was hiding in the shadows, someone who slipped away when the carter sought help from the club next to the yard. There was a general commotion as shocked members of the Jewish club looked on the dead body of a woman in the yard. Her clothing was not disarranged, there was no sense of sexual assault, but she had been obviously brutally killed.

If this was the work of the *Ripper*, he had been disturbed in his work by the carter turning into the yard, his lust for mutilation unassuaged. Indeed, if this was so, he needed to find another victim, where he could fulfil his craving.

Thus, about forty minutes later, there was another dreadful, far more gruesome murder in Mitre Square.

Part One: The Nightmare Begins

CHAPTER SEVENTEEN

KATE THE 'COCKNEY SPARROW'

For generations, the poor of London, together with tramps, travellers and gypsies had made their way to the farms and villages of Kent for the harvest at the end of August and throughout September. Like migrating birds, they made their way back to the roosts they knew. Hunton was a small place and not easy to find unless you knew your way around. It was hardly even a village; it was farmland that almost exclusively grew hops for brewing beer.

Jack Kelly had been going there since he was a boy. Most years, he could make a reasonable living at the harvest, but in its own way, the living conditions around the farms could be as harsh as in the slums of London. Very few farms made accommodation available. There were few inns or rooms to be had. Many hoppers slept under canvas or even in the open fields. There were few amenities, and so hedgerows and ditches served as latrines. The way many had to live in the otherwise idyllic Kent countryside was pitiful.

This year, as with the previous five years, Jack attended with a woman who called herself Kate Kelly, though she was not his wife. He had first known of her under the name of Kate Conway, unaware that she had not actually been married to Mr. Conway either, though she had three children from that relationship. Names and families were shifting sands amongst the poor of the industrial towns and cities of England and, especially, in the East End.

Many men changed their names several times. Sometimes, in childhood, they adopted the name of a stepfather, and then, as they grew up, they swapped back to their birth name from time to time, depending on who they were avoiding. Many women adopted the surname of the man they lived with; marriage had little to do with it. Jack and Kate lived together in the lodging houses of Spitalfields and now they huddled together under a makeshift shelter as the rain tumbled from the sky. The wettest summer for years was producing a poor harvest. There was not much money to be made and like many others around them, Jack and Kate decided to walk back to Spitalfields and try to find work there. It was a walk that would take them several days.

Jack loved Kate; there was no doubt about it. He had met her in Spitalfields at one of the common lodging houses and was taken with her looks, her cheerful manner, and her pleasant singing. She had a daughter with her at that time, a pretty thing who soon moved off to be married. He had been about 30 then. He wasn't too sure of her age, and she was obviously older, having a daughter of about 18, but it was ungentlemanly to ask her. She made out that she was a year or two older than him, but he knew it was more than that.

Jack was a hardworking man. He was not overly given to drink and could usually earn them money for food and accommodation by working in Spitalfields market as a porter or carter, sometimes doing better than that by finding work at the docks. Kate was a domestic cleaner, a Char, as she put it. She even cleaned the home of one of the lodging house deputies from time to time for sixpence.

Generally, they got by. Difficulty, when it arose, was with Kate's love of strong drink. Jack would try to keep an eye on her, but her drunkenness was frequent. He heard stories that sometimes Kate would earn her drink money by prostitution, but she always denied this to him. He could not stand the idea of Kate being with another man.

As for her, she was fond of Jack, but he did try to control her, and he would sometimes beat her for coming home drunk or even disappearing for a day or two. Not as bad as Conway, though, she mused as they trudged their way back to London.

Jack thought of Kate as his little Cockney Sparrow, or more properly, a Linnet as she sang so sweetly. He was wrong. Kate was

Part One: The Nightmare Begins

not a Cockney, not even a Londoner by birth. She had been born in the small, grimy, industrial town of Wolverhampton in the 'Black Country' of the English Midlands. Her father had been a tinplate worker, a metal manufacturing trade for which the coal-encrusted industrial little town, skies filled with choking smoke from furnaces, was well known. When the great tinplate strike broke out in 1848, he, his brother and their families left Wolverhampton and walked to London, well over a hundred miles away, to find other work. Catherine, Kate, was about six years old at the time. The factory owners were fierce men who broke the strike and used the law to bankrupt the fledgling union supporting the strikers, there was no wider union with other workers to support them further, no organiser with the ability of Eleanor Marx. His brother eventually returned to the same impoverished conditions he had left, but Kate's father stayed in London. Altogether, her parents had twelve children to care for.

Kate remembered it all so well. She had an education, her father sent her to a Charity School until her mother died when Kate was about eight years old. Then, within a few months, her father also died. She and her brothers and sisters were taken into the Bermondsey Workhouse and then put in the workhouse Industrial School.

Soon afterwards, Kate was sent to live with her aunt in Wolverhampton, living on Bilston Street near the great black stone church of St George that she never attended. Its environs were a centre for prostitution and remained so until late into the following century. St George's was a dark mirror to All Saints church in Spitalfields, the area she came to know all too well.

Once old enough, she worked at the same factory where her father had worked. At the age of 21, having stayed in the care of her aunt, except for a few months when she lived with an uncle in Birmingham and her grandfather back in Wolverhampton, Kate met an older man called Tom Conway. He had once been a soldier with the Royal Irish Regiment, though sometimes, he was known as Tommy Quinn, especially when he drew his army pension. Much to the disapproval of her aunt, she left home to be with this man, living with him as if his wife, and so began her nomadic life.

Conway was an enterprising man who made his living by hawking cheap books, some written by Conway himself. As a couple, they also sold gallows ballads, a business that required them to move around the prisons of the area, anywhere from Birmingham to Stafford, wherever hangings were taking place. They spent most of the

1860s in this shifting, rootless, hand-to-mouth existence. She loved him, and called herself Mrs. Kate Conway, though the couple did not marry, perhaps because somewhere was an earlier Mrs. Quinn who could have caused trouble. For a while, the couple returned to Wolverhampton, where little Annie was born. From there, the family headed to London, where Kate still had family. Two more children were born to them over the next eight years. Kate had the initials TC tattooed on her arm, though she, at one time, told friends that Tom himself had done it at her request.

After her third child, her relationship with Conway deteriorated. He became increasingly violent to her, and she ran away back to her aunt in Wolverhampton, but her aunt had enough of her and her association with Conway and wanted nothing to do with her. Kate went back to London, but by 1881, it was all over with Conway. Kate took her daughter, Annie, with her and headed north of the river; Conway disappeared out of her life forever. She moved to Cooney's Lodging House at 55 Flower and Dean Street, where she met Kelly.

Jack Kelly was not told about any of her history except that she had been married to a man called Conway, who was long gone. By the time he got to know her, her daughter Annie was married to a good man, a craftsman gunsmith, and lived in Bermondsey. Kate went to see her daughter from time to time, but usually only when she was desperately in need of money. She knew that Annie was embarrassed by her, an impoverished mother living in a common lodging house in Spitalfields, and sometimes even in the dreaded, shameful workhouse.

Finally, they reached London Bridge and crossed over the river. It was the end of September, the 28th, they thought. They were totally impoverished, not a penny between them. Jack told her to wait for him and went to see a Mr. Lander, who ran a fruit and vegetable stall in Spitalfields market. Jack had worked for Mr. Lander on and off for years and begged him for some work. By the end of the day, he had sixpence. He met up with Kate, who decided that as he was working, he needed to take four pence and go and get a bed at the lodging house whilst she would take two pence for something to eat and go to the casual ward workhouse in Shoe Lane; he agreed.

The following morning, Kate turned up at the lodging house where Jack had secured a bed. He had no further work for that day, so they were both back at the point of starvation. Jack removed his working boots.

Part One: The Nightmare Begins

'Come on, old girl, nothing for it but to pawn these boots of mine. We ain't anything else worth a penny. Let's go down to Jones' in Church Street and see what he will do.'

'No, Jack, you can't pawn your boots, you'll need them if you get more work at the market.'

'I'll be alright, I'll get by, but meanwhile, we need to get some food inside us.'

So, they tried the pawnbroker and accepted half a crown on the boots. Jack knew he would never see them again. With the money, they bought food, tea and sugar to sweeten it. They went back to the lodging house and cooked themselves a breakfast. They paid for the bed for the night. Having eaten enough, they had a drink and were soon back to having nothing. Jack was confident he could find work the next day at the market and Kate said she would walk over to Bermondsey to find her daughter and scrounge some money from her. They walked together as far as Houndsditch.

'I'll be back in a couple of hours,' she told him.

'Yeah, well, don't be late because of the knife,' he said, reminding her of the fear of the killer on the loose.

It was that evening, not yet dark, when Police Constable Robinson from the City of London Police, a force separate from the Metropolitan Police, came across a disturbance in Aldgate High Street. A woman was lying on the pavement, only semi-conscious, obviously very drunk. He pulled her to her feet, only to see her slip down again. He asked if anyone knew who she was, but no one claimed to know her. Approaching from across the street was his colleague PC Simmons, and he called to him for assistance. The two police officers pulled the woman to her feet and, between them, virtually carried her to Bishopsgate Police Station. She was barely awake.

As she was not able, or willing, to give her name, Sergeant Byfield had her taken to a cell to sleep it off. In accordance with normal practice, she was checked on every half an hour. It was a little after midnight when she was heard singing softly to herself. She asked when she might be released.

About half an hour later, Sergeant Byfield asks which prisoners were sober enough to be turned out. The woman faced the sergeant and gave her name at last. She gave it as Kate Kelly and offered her address, probably false, thought the sergeant, as 6 Fashion Street. Not wanting to have anything more to do with her, and thinking she was by now rational, she was assessed by PC Hutt as being at least sober enough to be released.

'What time is it?' she asked.

'Nearly 1 a.m. and too late for you to get a drink,' says the policeman.

'I shall get a damn fine hiding when I get home,' she said.

'And serve you right, you had no right to get that drunk,' said the unsympathetic PC Hutt. 'This way, and please pull the door shut behind you.' He watched her leave the police station.

'Goodnight, old cock,' she said cheerfully. She turned left out of the doorway, not towards home at all, but back towards the alleyways leading to Aldgate High Street. She would not go home without taking some money to Jack, and there was only one way she could get it now.

Just after half past one in the morning, coming out of the Imperial Club in Duke Street, three companions stood for a while to light cigarettes. On the corner of Duke Street and Church Passage, they saw a man and a woman talking. She was looking into the man's face, and her hand was coquettishly on his chest. The companions saw them both as clearly as was possible to see anything at that time of the night. The man, they later said, was about 30 years of age, five feet seven inches tall, with a loose jacket, grey cap, fair complexion and a fair moustache. He wore a red kerchief about his neck. Each of the men independently formed an opinion that he was a sailor. The men knew what was going on and moved off home.

Fifteen minutes later, PC Watkins, on his beat, which led into Mitre Street and the dingy little Mitre Square, shone his lantern onto the mutilated and disembowelled body of a woman. She lay exposed and gutted, her intestines thrown onto her shoulder, her eyes staring into the blackness of the night. There was no sign of anyone else around. The City of London Police had another undoubtedly *Ripper* murder on their hands. It was the second of two murders that night, although they would not hear of the first, the death of Lizzie Stride, for some time.

CHAPTER EIGHTEEN

LIZZIE AND KATE

Sir Charles Warren was awakened by his valet in the early hours of the morning. It was very dark outside; a drift of light rain fell on the streets. A detective had arrived from The Commercial Road Police station and had a cab waiting with news so much worse than Sir Charles had feared. There had been two murders in the night. He dressed quickly but formally, wanting his clothing to convey the authority of his position. The note from the Superintendent in Whitechapel lay on his table, advising him to attend as a full investigation was underway.

At that time of day, it did not take long to get to Commercial Road police station, where Superintendent Swanson was waiting. Swanson looked tired and concerned.

'Thank you for coming so promptly, sir. We had hoped not to trouble you so soon anyway, but trouble is moving apace, it seems.'

'Yes, quite right to get me here. Now, briefly, what is happening? Who has been killed, and has anyone been apprehended? I do hope the press are not yet interfering in matters.'

'Well, Sir Charles, matters have been developing, as I say. First, we have a murder near Commercial Road, a woman with her throat cut in a dark yard but no mutilation, so we are not sure it is one of the Whitechapel fiend's murders, but if it was, we think he was disturbed too early in proceedings and slipped away unsatisfied, possibly looking for another woman to prey on. We have not identified the victim yet. Then, a major surprise, at almost the same time, just a little later, we were informed by our beat officers of a second murder, more clearly the work of the man we have been seeking, this time in Mitre Square, not far from Leadenhall Street. It is in the City of London police area, I'm afraid, so we cannot get involved.'

'We will see about that! Do we have men at both locations keeping the populace away?'

'Not exactly, sir. As I say, because Mitre Square is in the City of London, the murder site is being controlled by the City of London Police. And I think we have a problem. Their officers have been searching the area for clues, but one of our constables, PC Long, has unearthed a clue in Goulston Street, which is indeed in our jurisdiction. Normally, we would leave the matter to the investigating detectives, but perhaps this time, we should be careful.'

'It is their murder. They can take the lead; we will cooperate. That is the protocol, Swanson, as I am sure you know. However, if they start blundering about, I want you to ignore any boundaries and do whatever is needed to push on with the investigation.'

'There is another problem in this instance, sir, and I think you should make your way to Goulston Street. There is already a dispute between City detectives and our men, the Metropolitan Police as to who is investigating what and meanwhile, we have taken charge of the area. We have found something you must see, sir.'

'Very well, but tell me more of this clue, Superintendent. I want to know everything.'

'It seems that PC Long found clothing taken, we think, from the victim, clothing covered in blood and faeces. We think the killer cleaned his weapons and his hands before throwing the clothing into a stairwell in the street.'

'And the issue with that is precisely what would you say?'

'None with that, although it is the only tangible evidence we have found so far in connection with any of the murders. No, the bloody cloth drew our attention to what is written on the wall in chalk in that stairwell. It is graffiti, which might have been made by the killer, and it seems to be blaming the Jews for the killings. Our sergeant has suggested covering it over in case it enflames opinion and starts a series of assaults on the Jews in the area. You recall that we had to intervene last year when mobs attacked the Jews over this sort of thing. However, the detectives on the scene from the City Police see it as important evidence and want it preserved until it is light enough to photograph it. Unfortunately, by the time it is light enough, all the tenants around the stairwell to the apartments, as well as any passing population, will have seen it.'

'Good God, man! We will have a riot on our hands. Get me over there as quickly as possible.' The Commissioner's fear, looming before him, was the prospect of another riot like that in Trafalgar Square and the press and Members of Parliament calling for his head. There had already been disturbances in Whitechapel, the more established immigrants from Ireland attacking the Polish and Russian Jews, and only a large force of his police had quelled the trouble. It would take very little to inflame another riot; suspicion that the *Ripper* had declared himself a Jew would be all that it would take.

Halfway along Goulston Street, just a few minutes from the police station, Sir Charles Warren, accompanied by duty Detective Inspector Arnold, found a gaggle of police officers disputing who had command. Never, not once since the first day of his appointment, had he doubted that command was his alone. Although he had no authority over the City of London Police, he decided at once that as the location was outside the City of London Police boundary, he would dispute the authority to investigate the matter and take command of all police officers anyway. Everyone recognised him, and no one was about to challenge him.

'Show me the graffiti,' he ordered.

Detective Sergeant Halse of the City Police pointed it out, two of the uniformed constables shining their lamps on the writing. It was in chalk, it was ungrammatical, its meaning was obscure, and it was inflammatory.

The Juwes are the men that will not be blamed for nothing.

On seeing it, Warren immediately ordered that a constable wash it away. The City Police objected to the destruction of possible evidence, but he overruled them. By the time they had conveyed their objections to their own commanding officer, the acting Superintendent of the City Police, Major Smith, the evidence was gone.

Major Smith let everyone know he thought it a blunder and that it was against all police procedure to destroy evidence. In particular, he let Sir Robert Anderson, the head of the Metropolitan Criminal

Investigation Department and the subordinate of Warren, know his opinion forcibly. Sir Robert Anderson put out that the Commissioner was taking a high-handed interest in the work of his detectives and pushing him to one side. He had long been reporting secretly to Monro against Warren, and now the information of breach of normal procedure was quickly, quietly, and critically conveyed to the Home Secretary.

So distracted by the graffiti were the police at the scene that no one, not Warren nor any detective, thought of doing, was searching the apartment buildings around the entrance where the bloody cloth had been discovered. The killer of Catherine Eddowes, the cockney sparrow, had slipped away from Mitre Square, but once in Goulston Street, there were police, including plainclothes detectives approaching from every direction. The apartments in Goulston Street were the first place he could hide; no one thought of it at the time.

A few hours later, he could leave amongst the many anonymous residents who made their way to work. Meanwhile, doctors at the two separate scenes made initial examinations. The bodies were transported to two separate mortuaries to await autopsies by two separate pathologists. There was no coordination between the two police authorities.

Back in his offices in Whitehall, Warren awaited the onslaught from the press; it duly arrived. As expected, the circumstances of the murders were sensationalised, not a difficult task, as the murders were undeniably wicked, gruesome, and shocking.

Accompanying the descriptions of the murders were criticisms of the police and of himself. It was increasingly clear to Warren, that although he usually left detective work to the department run by Macnaughten, all blame from his political enemies was attached only to himself.

Moreover, he was aware of the amount of information leaked to the press from those involved in some way with the on-the-ground investigations: constables, mortuary attendants, witnesses and the like, yet this was less concerning than information being passed without his authority, apparently by disloyal staff, to Monro and to the Home Secretary. No criticism stuck to Sir Robert Anderson who continued to have responsibility for all detectives and to give briefings to the Home Secretary without prior discussion with Warren. Warren needed this investigation to make a breakthrough. An engineer by training, Warren wanted to force the issue to create a change

Part One: The Nightmare Begins

in circumstances, engineer a solution. With that in mind, he reconvened his meeting with the detectives leading the hunt, ordering them to attend his office in Whitehall.

'Sir Robert,' he told his chief detective, 'I have requested Mr. Swanson, together with Inspector Abberline, to join us to review progress on the two most recent murders. As I understand it, we have two Coroner inquests underway. I also appreciate that we have not definitively identified the women, but that is only a matter of time. My first question, gentlemen, is this: were these murders by the same man? My second question concerns the letter we already have because there was a postcard sent to the Central News Agency yesterday, apparently on the day of the double event, which means there was clear knowledge of the situation before it was even in the press. Do we continue to believe these writings to be a hoax? In the latest one, the writer speaks of slicing off the ear of a victim. I understand from the preliminary medical examination that is exactly what happened. Do we need to rethink our opinions?'

Sir Robert Anderson, Assistant Commissioner and head of the Criminal Investigation Department, spoke first.

'We have already circulated the *Dear Boss* letter to local police stations on your instructions, Sir Charles so that the style of writing can be compared with anything known locally. I doubt much will come of that as the literacy of our criminal classes is not high and they do not tend to write many letters to us, or to anyone for that matter. As we can see, the graffiti in Goulston Street has no similarity with the letter, so we can safely assume that it is by another hand entirely. However, today's Daily Telegraph carries a transcript of the *Dear Boss* letter itself. I think we all await the backlash from the public now that the letter is out in the open, hoax or not. I'm not sure what value having the letter circulated to police stations can be, especially as we are all convinced it is a mischievous hoax.' There was no doubt that Anderson was questioning the judgment of the Commissioner.

Abberline took up the discussion quickly, masking the sense of disagreement building in the room. He was very uncomfortable about the tension between his superior officers.

'I understand the concern caused by the second letter stating, gruesomely, that he did not have time to slice off an ear. I think this concern is misplaced, and the mutilation of the ear is entirely coincidental. My guess is that the information about the injury, implying he was about to remove it when disturbed, was, as with the previous

Dear Boss letter, invented from information by someone at the scene, such as a police officer or mortuary assistant, sold on to the hoaxer. I accept the letters are by the same person and I still think it likely he is a reporter. Indeed, he could have even speculated on a type of injury without further information. If I were to guess at an injury to any of the unfortunate, it would be a torn ear, as it is well known that the High Rip gangs snatch earrings from the women as part of their robbery. It is a common injury of such assaults, and the author of the letter, if a reporter, would know that too. As to the ear being cut away, it seems the killer slashed the face of the second victim most dreadfully and, in doing so, sliced away part of the nose and part of one ear, perhaps in an act of rage. According to the police officer in attendance in the mortuary, the ear was not taken away as a morbid souvenir but, once detached, had lodged in the clothing of the victim and has been recovered. The postcard writer doesn't seem to know we have the detached body part. He could have made much more of this.'

Swanson followed on readily, also mindful of keeping Anderson quiet.

'On our way to this meeting, the Inspector and I were subjected to a bombardment of questions from reporters from all over the world. Whatever the printing of the *Dear Boss* letter might accomplish by someone recognising the handwriting, a vain hope it seems, it has certainly increased hysteria in the press and, no doubt, consequently, in the general populace. All we heard was the repeated phrase, *Jack the Ripper*. Now, this second communication will lend credence to the existence of a taunting fiend. I believe our Whitechapel demon has taken on a fearful identity, which I doubt he intended.'

As both Warren and Sir Robert Anderson were absorbing the information and casting glances at each other, Abberline gave a further opinion of the two murders.

'I keep an open mind about the double event, but it is human nature for the general public to now attribute every stabbing to the mysterious *Jack the Ripper,* just as the Chief Inspector says. In my view, although it is possible for one man to have undertaken both attacks, it is not credible. The first attack has some similarity with previous so-called *Ripper* killings as it involved cutting the throat of a woman, probably after first choking her, but no mutilation. There were some stab wounds, but I wonder whether this was to shift the blame to whom we now seem to have to call *Jack the Ripper*. He may, of course, have been disturbed before carrying out his mutilation, but I wonder. The second killing certainly does mirror the earlier work of the man we have been hunting. It seems that his attacks are becoming ever crueller and more macabre. I also think that this is a man in such a frenzy of mutilations that he will not stop until we catch him.'

Warren tried to piece together the information.

'I see, but from the trail following the second killing, he is certainly someone who knows the locality and was heading for the rookeries of Spitalfields where he probably lives?' He looked again at Abberline.

"Even there, we cannot be sure, Sir Charles. Because of the location of the first murder of the evening, there was a lot of activity in and around Commercial Road and the roads which lead back to the docks. So, if the man has a lair there, his escape was cut off. He had to head into Spitalfields, the Whitechapel area, where he could hide in any of the derelict places, gravel pits or tenements. I doubt he would try for a common lodging house because any of the watchmen there would see him. Of course, he could well have a dwelling in the area; we do not know, but it seems to me that he could hide anywhere. Once it was time for men to be about their work, we had no chance of identifying him as he would simply mix with the crowds.'

'And, Inspector, would you say he was responsible for the graffiti to throw blame onto the Jews?'

'It is curious indeed. I am not even sure what the words are meant to convey. It had been raining, so any other graffiti along that street could have been washed away, and this might have been done earlier, surviving because it is in a sheltered doorway. The street is occupied by many Jewish immigrants but is also used by the non-Jewish population as part of the Petticoat Lane market, so there is always tension there. On the other hand, he may have written it, but what a cool-headed thing to do when fleeing from police following at least one murder.'

'So, in effect, you do not know anything at all, do you, Inspector?'

'I think it very important not to leap to conclusions.'

'Well, what of this first murder that night, the one where you think the murderer might be a different man altogether? Do we have witnesses?'

'We have succeeded in gathering some information, Sir Charles. Unfortunately, the witnesses are mostly Russian or Polish Jews with little or no English. Our most important witness did his best in describing two men he saw, but as a foreigner, I am not sure how his evidence would be received by the coroner.'

'Treat the evidence of the Hebrew with the same seriousness you would of an English-born Christian witness. Our experience of the area so far is that few, if any, of the witnesses from the East End are reliable and this man can be no worse than any other.'

He waited for silence to fall before concluding his remarks, 'Very well, very well. That is all, gentlemen. Keep me informed, Chief Inspector.' He looked worried and disappointed. That he had asked Chief Inspector Swanson to keep him informed, so ignoring the chain of command and Anderson's position as Deputy Commissioner, was pointed.

They left the room, each feeling like they were failing in their quest. Anderson was seething with a cold rage. As they reached the outside door, Sir Robert Anderson stopped the other two men. 'All reports will come to me through you, Mr. Swanson. We do not want the Commissioner confusing matters.'

Swanson looked shocked. 'I believe it was a direct order from the Commissioner, sir, given to me to keep him informed.'

'No, Swanson, it was a request only. I oversee detectives, and you will report through me. We will maintain the chain of command. That is an order, Chief Inspector, not a request.' He turned and left them. Swanson looked at Abberline and spoke softly, under his breath.

'Solely so he can carry information from me directly to the Home Secretary. Let us be careful, Abberline. Whilst we are searching for a killer, I fear our masters are playing a different game.' More than ever, he felt they were on their own in investigating the murders.

Abberline was handed a note by a waiting Constable. He read it carefully and spoke to the Chief Inspector, 'A mob has formed up in Berner Street, the site of the first of the most recent murders and is protesting loudly about police incompetence. It will be whipped

Part One: The Nightmare Begins

up by the local Vigilance Committee, no doubt. Inspector Reid has been trying to calm their chairman.'

Swanson looked at him, 'And now they will have the title *Jack the Ripper* around which to centre their ignorance, fear and anger.' He knew what was to come.

Whilst the two men felt an even greater burden pressing upon them, back in H and J Divisions, Inspector Reid had been given the task of identifying the body from Berner Street. Several people had come forward that morning, but he had no positive identification other than the deceased was known as 'Long Liz'.

Somehow, the newspapers reported the victim to be Elizabeth Stride, but the name had not been established. Whilst Reid sought people who might have known her and thought he had discovered the name and identity as being indeed Elizabeth Stride, a Mrs. Malcolm turned up claiming she had a premonition that her sister had been murdered. She was shown the body and, although unsure at first, gave a definitive statement that it was indeed her sister, Elizabeth Watts.

Mrs. Malcolm was summoned to the Inquest on the 1st of October as a star witness. As the only person claiming to be a relative, she was first to give evidence on identification before the coroner and much of what she said matched what became known of Elizabeth Stride, or at least, the story Elizabeth Stride had put out about herself. Mrs. Malcolm said that her sister had lived with a man who kept a coffee house in Poplar, but he had died abroad three and a half years earlier. She told a tale of destitution, an illegitimate birth, a policeman lover and much else. She gave more details of her charitable relationship with her sister and how often they saw each other – at least once a week. She was earnest, but the jury could tell by Reid's questioning he thought she was mistaken, and the victim was not her sister.

On the 3rd of October, the court had the opportunity to hear the testimonies of people who clearly did know the dead woman. Mrs. Elizabeth Tanner of the lodging house in Flower and Dean Street gave evidence that she knew the woman as 'Long Liz' but did not know her surname. She denied that a sister had ever been mentioned and knew of no charity from such a person as Mrs. Malcolm. Mrs. Tanner made a credible witness and was clearly upset at the death of a woman she knew and liked. She was followed by Kate Lane, who also identified her as 'Long Liz'.

Importantly, another lodger at the establishment in Flower and Dean also identified her and this time, he knew her surname. Charles Preston gave her full name, Elizabeth Stride, the name he had given to the police the day after the murder.

The jury waited impatiently for the person they most wanted to see and hear from, her former lover, Michael Kidney, who eventually confirmed she was indeed Elizabeth Stride and had been his companion for over three years.

Thus, Inspector Reid was entirely satisfied he knew the name of the victim and that the police and other witnesses could be called to tell the story of that relationship. The coroner would still not go further with the identification by all her associates, and would still not officially name her as Elizabeth Stride because an apparent relative was saying otherwise. It was not until the 23rd of October that the coroner would formally record the victim indeed as being Elizabeth Stride. He was able to do so then only because Mrs. Elizabeth Stokes from Tottenham in London appeared. She told the court that she, and not the deceased, was the sister of Mrs. Malcolm, and she had not seen her sister for several years. She said that all the lurid information given by Mrs. Malcolm was nothing but lies. The coroner and the jury were moved to indignation on behalf of Mrs. Stokes, but by then, Mrs. Malcolm had dropped out of the picture.

Finally, in the corroboration of Mrs. Stokes, Police Constable Stride, gave evidence. From the mortuary photograph taken on the 1st of October, he identified the woman who had married his uncle, John Stride, in about 1872. At that time, his uncle had worked as a carpenter, he said, and the last he knew of him, he had moved to East India Dock Road.

The problem of names and identities added to the difficulties and frustrations Reid and Abberline had with the investigations. Whilst their investigations continued, Elizabeth Stride was buried on the 6th of October at the East London municipal cemetery in Plaistow. The Swedish Church recorded the death as being murder at the hands of *Jack the Ripper*, so placing that name into official records for the first time.

The inquest into the death of Catherine Eddowes, known as Kate Kelly, was different. It took place in the City Coroner's Court in Golden Lane under the direction of the far less opinionated Mr. Langham. There had been no issue in identifying the victim, though it took a little time to formally register the name as Eddowes as she

Part One: The Nightmare Begins

had not used that name for many years. It had been assumed previously that she was married to a Mr. Conway, but no record of marriage could be found. The jury paid attention to the witnesses with great sympathy, especially to the evidence of Jack Kelly and then of her sisters, Eliza Gold and Elizabeth Fisher. Much sympathy was shown to her daughter, Mrs. Annie Phillips. Annie explained how her mother was mostly avoided by her brothers and herself because of her drunkenness. Her father, she said, was teetotal and it was her mother's drinking that had caused them to separate. She had not seen her father, a hawker, for many months and did not know if he knew of the tragedy.

At the end of the inquest, the entire jury, moved to tears by the testimony of Catherine Eddowes' daughter telling of her heartache in coping with a sad and drunken mother whom she nevertheless loved, handed over their jury fee to her in a gesture of kindness. The outpouring of almost hysterical public sorrow spilled over into the extraordinary funeral of Catherine.

Mr. Hawkes, a local undertaker, arranged the funeral at his own expense, just as he did for Long Liz. Catherine Eddowes, now referred to as Kate Kelly, was placed in an Elm coffin, which was put in an open glass hearse drawn by two black-plumed horses. In the following carriages were John Kelly, Kate's daughter and her sisters. A huge crowd gathered outside the mortuary, and many followed the funeral cortege, escorted by City of London police to Old Street, the boundary of the City of London.

There, the procession was met by the Metropolitan Police, who escorted the funeral to the Little Ilford cemetery at Manor Park. The route was lined with mourners and sympathisers. Once at the cemetery, police kept back the crowd whilst a protestant Church of England burial service took place, Kate being laid to rest in consecrated ground, a remarkable display of acceptance for a woman of her background by a normally class-conscious, priggish and self-righteous church.

The Abandoned: *Victims of Jack the Ripper*

CHAPTER NINETEEN

VIGILANTES

The world went mad with stories of *Jack the Ripper*. Paranoia spread like a fever around the great metropolis and in the Borough of Whitechapel, in the environs of Spitalfields, women lived in fear of being murdered, whilst men feared being a suspect likely to be lynched by a drunken mob. Jews were driven even more into a ghetto mentality for fear of blame and retribution. Persecution from Russia had followed them here, not by those in power but certainly by the poor on the streets.

As the world's press grew to know of Spitalfields, Dorset Street came to be called the worst street in London, marked out for poverty, crime, and hopelessness, where the people clung together as if under siege, yet still fought each other in a brutality of survival. The Horn of Plenty pub at one end of the street, the Blue Boy in the middle and the great Britannia pub at the Commercial Street end of Dorset Street were the only places people felt safe once night fell.

The great church watched over all, but gave no comfort. The watchmen on the street had become extra vigilant, but they did not know who they were looking for. Dorset Street was squeezed to bursting by accommodating ever more of the established population of Whitechapel as increasing shiploads of immigrants from Poland and Russia moved up along Brick Lane and its side streets. The populace of a more recent British and Irish descent resented the newcomers, but London had seen it all before, the rolling tides of immigration.

Nevertheless, the recently established Jewish communities wrote to the rabbis of Poland asking them to counsel against further mass migration to London. Irish immigrants, with recent memories of their own diaspora, felt threatened with further displacement and deeply resented the Jews who were pushing them out of their adopted home territory. As far as all in Dorset Street were concerned, *Jack the Ripper* was a Polish Jew, but then even the poor summer was somehow the fault of the Jews.

The stories in the newspapers and on the streets, the gossip in the pubs, fanned the flames of near panic. The main topic of conversation in the markets, the streets and the pubs was the wraith-like killer, once called Leather Apron, now referred to as *The Ripper* or *Jack the Ripper*. He was thought of as a man with devilish abilities, easily able to outwit the police. The local merchants and the peripheral middle-class professionals of the neighboring areas met to set up their own Vigilance Committee, chaired by a local builder, George Lusk. Meeting in Mile End Road, the group was not at all representative of the social circumstances of the victims or the occupants of the common lodging houses. There was one pub landlord, the only man amongst them likely to have any lawful dealings with the prostitutes; others were shopkeepers and businessmen, about half of them Jewish, who feared for the impact the killings were starting to have on the Jews in the area. Having little faith in the police, they organised their own vigilante force by hiring unemployed labourers from across Whitechapel, setting them on regular patrols in a way very similar to the uniformed police they disparaged. These men were equipped by the Committee with lanterns, police whistles and stout sticks. Apart from the patrols, they also employed two private detectives to track down the killer.

As part of their policy, they petitioned the Prime Minister to offer a reward for information about the killer. He, in turn, passed the demand to Home Secretary, Mr. Matthews, who turned down the idea.

Thus began another avenue of speculation for the newspapers and another headache for the local police. Whilst stories of strange and threatening men began to emerge from the Committee members, some probably invented, and new descriptions of the possible

Part One: The Nightmare Begins

killer were declared and then printed to help obscure the trail to the killer, the patrols themselves sank into farce.

Groups of vigilantes began following men through the streets and alleyways, confronting them only to discover they were plain-clothed detectives.

Similarly, the police arrested suspicious-looking characters only to discover they were from the Vigilance Committee. On different nights, the police and vigilantes were known to be following each other. The women of the area believed themselves no safer than before and complained of being harassed by the vigilantes. Mr. Lusk, meanwhile, enjoyed the status of a celebrity and was constantly quoted in the newspapers, which saw him as an excellent source of copy.

Swanson, Abberline, Reid and the rest of the detective force still had no clear idea who the killer might be. Apart from the reports of how the killings were carried out, first by throttling and then throat-cutting, they knew almost nothing. All the victims were self-selecting in that they almost certainly would have approached the *Ripper* as a potential customer. He did not need to stalk or hunt them.

The police realised that the knife attacks were becoming ever more frenzied as the bodies mounted up, but they still had nowhere to turn for clues. Their only real hope of solving the crimes was to catch him in the act.

Indeed, they flooded the streets around Spitalfields with police officers night after night. If the man attacked on the streets or even in alleyways or yards, they had increased their chances of catching him.

Meanwhile, they looked half-heartedly at the usual suspects, including the partners of the dead women. Jack Kelly, they quickly eliminated from their thoughts. Michael Kidney, though, did trouble them. They had him watched.

On the 12th of October, as much for morale as for anything else, Swanson held a meeting with all senior detectives involved in the investigations. Inspector Abberline undertook most of the summary.

'Gentlemen, yesterday the coroner completed the Inquest into the death of Kate Kelly, properly Catherine Eddowes. As you all know, the finding is yet another murder by a person unknown. I have been back over a series of attacks occurring across the H and J Divisions, which might have relevance to current inquiries and some that do not, going back to the start of the year. Some of you will know all of them, some only the latest events, so this is an opportunity for us all to be at the same place.' He took a sip of water and referred to his notes. The assembled company conveyed a subdued, even depressed attention to his words.

'There was an attack on one Annie Milward from White's Row in February this year. I have also included in my review a thwarted attack on Ada Wilson about a month later, this time in Mile End. The murder of Emma Smith in April, Inspector Reid is convinced, was not the intention of the assault, and he is still seeking witnesses for that matter. I will keep it on our list for now, but agree with Inspector Reid that it is not one of the attacks by the man now referred to as the *Ripper*. However, things then heated up. On the 7th of August, we have the murder of Martha Tabram, also from White's Row; on the 31st of August, Polly Nichols is killed. On the 8th of September is the murder of Annie Chapman. We now come to the double event on 30th September, Catherine Eddowes, or Kate Kelly as we knew her, and Elizabeth Stride. Remember, the Eddowes case is a City of London Police investigation in which we are assisting, although the public does not see any difference between our two police forces as it is all a matter of murder. For the moment, I want to put the case of Elizabeth Stride to one side.'

He took another sip of water, for all the world the picture of a bank manager or rural solicitor. It seemed no coincidence that the two most valued detectives on the case, Abberline and Reid, were the two who took the most pride in their appearance.

'So, what, I ask myself, do we know of these killings? We know that the victims were prostitutes, and this is very significant. The killer can wait to be selected by a potential victim who is willing to go into some hidden place with him, indeed, will find such a place for him. She will be available at any time and in a location that suits his purpose. The victim will know the movement of police officers on their beat, and so will afford inadvertently even greater protection to the killer by choosing a time and place for the liaison least likely to be found by a patrolling policeman.'

He paused again and watched some of the assembled detectives making notes. 'I mentioned that I have put to one side the case of Stride. This is mainly because whilst the Eddowes murder is clearly that of our man, the Stride killing has only some similarity, and the timing makes it doubtful that it would be the work of the same frenzied killer. However, we do not rule it out, and the press, you will

Part One: The Nightmare Begins

know, certainly place it at the door of the killer, wherever that door might be.' Chief Inspector Swanson looked as if he had not slept for several days.

'It appears that our killer is a man who is getting bolder; possibly increasingly reckless. As time has gone on, the attacks have become ever more macabre and vicious. However, do not become distracted by press stories. We do not hold that this man has any medical knowledge or surgical skills. The attacks have been quick and crude. We may have been very close to catching him on those occasions where the body has been found to be still warm, not long dead, meaning he was still in the vicinity. Now, that brings me to location again. He seems to know the area and makes good use of alleyways and the overcrowding of buildings and derelict sites. It is unlikely that he will travel far, say south of the river for instance, but may well live near his victims or have business requiring him to often lodge here. For instance, he may work in the markets and so often stay around Spitalfields but not live here permanently. There are so many lodging houses and pubs, and this could easily be the case. It remains a puzzle as to why we have no consistent description of the man. Indeed, it is irksome that there have been few descriptions of likely suspects. The latest, in the Eddowes case, is given by three reliable gentlemen who describe a sailor. We must not rule out that possibility.' He paused, knowing he had imparted no good news.

'Now, let us consider what we are doing and what we might do. Chief Inspector Swanson will lead.'

He sat down, perfectly calm and collected, with no sign of frustration or panic. Swanson took over, his mild Scottish accent seemed to be returning to him.

'First, some background information you each need to know. Her Majesty the Queen has telephoned the Home Secretary to express her concern that the killer is not caught. In turn, that demand has been passed on to the Commissioner, who has explained our efforts. Do not respond to press taunts that we are criticised by Her Majesty. Meanwhile, the issue of rewards for information, the giving of which is implacably opposed by the Home Secretary, has been taken up by The Financial News with an offer of £300 and the Lord Mayor of London offering a further £500. I am told by the Commissioner that Sir Alfred Kirby has offered a further £100 in addition to making available 50 militia men – no, gentlemen, you will be pleased to know the offer is declined. We already are tripping over policemen and vigilantes. What I do expect is an increase in speculative information as people are attracted by the reward money. I do not think that the offer of a reward is going to help at this stage, but you might disagree with that. You should also know that the Commissioner supports the opinion that the law should grant an amnesty to anyone who has been harbouring the killer in the hope that any such person would give up the man. He has been criticised publicly by the Home Secretary for holding a view that is contrary to the normal execution of the law, and any criticism of him is also a criticism of us all. In my own view, the Home Secretary is misguided, but that opinion stays in this room.'

'Now, the letters. The press are making much of the *Dear Boss* letter and the Postcard which is written by the same hand. It is our opinion that these are not the work of the killer. What is more, we are now being bombarded with hundreds of letters claiming to be from *Jack the Ripper*. I'm afraid we must read them all and it's proving to be a distraction. However, it is the general belief of the man in the street that the two published letters are indeed genuine, even some government officials think so, and I'm afraid the Home Secretary is wavering on this, so refer all enquiries about them to me. Letters purporting to be from the *Ripper* are going to the press, to the Vigilance Committee as well as to us, as I say hundreds of them. It has become a national obsession. I also remind you that we are besieged by reporters from all over the world, and they will twist anything you say to make a good story, so be cautious, gentlemen.' He paused for a moment, like Abberline before him.

'There is something else. Last week, the torso of a woman was discovered in Whitehall, and the press are building up the story that *Jack the Ripper* has struck outside his normal hunting area. I can say from the information I have received that there is no connection whatsoever with our investigations. The victim was not served as those in Whitechapel were. Are there any questions?

Inspector Reid stirred in his seat. He had paid attention throughout, although he knew more than anyone what would be said. He caught the eye of Swanson and spoke up.

'I would like to make one or two points if I may?' Swanson nodded at him and sat down.

'I wonder if we might convey to the Commissioner a problem we have with the latest Criminal Law Amendment Act. It seems that any woman loitering in the street, standing still even, might be suspected of soliciting for the purpose of prostitution. We all know that this has caused difficulty elsewhere in the city, but here about, we tend to know who the prostitutes are and use discretion. The women themselves are less sure of our discretion now, become less trustful of us, and to avoid the risk of arrest, keep moving. It would greatly assist us if the prostitutes did stand still as we could watch over them with some confidence and apprehend any man who approached. As it is, the women are afraid to stay anywhere for long for fear of arrest or even because of harassment by Vigilante men. What we have created by the enactment of the law is the ridiculous spectacle of women parading around known centres for their trade, such as St Botolph Church, walking around and around it, being followed at a distance by detectives in civilian clothes, themselves being followed by employees of the Vigilance Committee who suspect them of being up to no good. I suggest that all this does is provide amusement for the killer.' Swanson raised his hand in acknowledgement of the situation. He replied.

'I'm afraid there is little we can do about the law. The Commissioner has given us every latitude to sail around it, but the Home Secretary is on his back about it. Yes, we shall continue to use as much discretion as possible in applying the law, but the damage is done, and the unfortunates, prostitutes, are reluctant to trust us. As for the vigilantes, I am alarmed that Sir Charles Warren has given them his blessing. That might be a political gesture on his behalf, but it does undermine confidence in the police, I know. Please go on, Inspector, you have a further point to make.'

Reid nodded to his superior officer and resumed his suggestions. 'We have continuing trouble with the press, and I wonder if it would be better if we had formal meetings with those newspapers we can rely on to report facts rather than fictitious stories. As it is, newspapers are inflaming the situation by printing untruths. They are also damaging our attempts to find the killer. For instance, they are reporting stories of the streets being filled with vigilantes and police officers. They are warning the killer about the tactics we are using to try to catch him. That they seem to mock us and undermine the Commissioner has resulted in the populace losing confidence in us. Instead of dealing in facts, we are drowning in hyperbole, morbid fantasy, mischievous letters and misinformation.'

'I sympathise with your views to some extent, Reid, but not totally,' replied Swanson. 'It is the policy of the Metropolitan Police not to brief newspapers. I do take your point that if we met with newspapers formally, we might control or at least ameliorate what is written. Indeed, if any person was suited to hold such a briefing, it would be you as, through your many splendid activities, you have accumulated many admirers in the press. Nevertheless, it is not something I will bother to take up with the Commissioner. It would be a waste of time to try to change his mind.'

He saw Inspector Reid nod in reluctant acceptance of the response.

'Any further questions?' he addressed the room rather than Reid specifically.

'Yes, sir,' one of the senior sergeants spoke up. 'We have pulled in a number of suspects, all sorts of men, and nothing has come of it, but I would like to ask Inspector Reid what the current position in respect of the man Kidney is, the man we are keeping under observation?' There was a general murmuring around the room.

At Swanson's invitation, Reid again rose to his feet.

'This is the case of Elizabeth Stride, a case where Inspector Abberline, myself and others, doubt to be at the hands of the *Ripper* although, of course, we do not rule it out. We have a statement from a witness named Schwartz who described a broad-shouldered man who appeared to be trying to drag Mrs. Stride away from the site of her eventual murder. We have not found that man, but it is very likely she knew him. It might have been Michael Kidney or perhaps one of his friends who was sent looking for her. Equally, it might have been a customer of hers with whom she had spent a little time but of whom she had tired. He may have wanted further attention, but she was strongly resisting him. We know the relationship with Kidney to have been a drunken and violent one. We know that she had previously had him arrested for assaulting her. I think that alone gives us reasonable suspicion about Mr. Kidney. However, if asked how serious a suspect, I have to say that Inspector Abberline, who knows more of him than do I, is of the opinion that if he is implicated in the *Ripper* killings, it is from the edges of the story only. He is a suspect in the murder of Elizabeth Stride, but he is not suspected of being the *Ripper*. I am afraid anything useful we might have learned from him has now been contaminated by the interference of the private detectives hired by the newspapers. He has had plenty of opportunity to cover his tracks.

CHAPTER TWENTY

PRIVATE DETECTIVES

Reid was right, not talking to the press in an organised, strategic way caused the police problems. The press sought out witnesses and bought information from them, adapting their evidence to fit the pre-conceived notions of the reporter. The press tried to get close to individual police officers and court officials too, but it had to be done covertly and none of the information was reliable. All of this meant that criticisms appeared which were unfair and inaccurate, all the time undermining confidence in the police. Sir Charles Warren was constantly having to defend his officers to the Home Secretary who seemed happy to have his lowly view of Sir Charles confirmed by the newspapers. The Evening News took the story to a new level by hiring two detectives to track down the killer. Immediately, the public was informed by the newspaper that its own detectives were more thorough and professional than the police.

In a matter of days, the private detectives claimed to have pieced together a description of the *Ripper*. What the newspaper did not publish was that one of the two detectives it hired was a criminal well-known to the police, a man not to be trusted in any circumstances.

As the police did not give formal briefings, there was really no way Swanson or his team could challenge what was then written about the investigations.

Inspector Abberline had taken his colleagues to one side to warn them about newspapers and the Vigilant Committee bringing in private detectives. This was not a concern about rivalry but more about contamination of evidence. He was worried that in a rush to show results, evidence would be manipulated or manufactured. He also knew the official police could be made to look ever more foolish and incompetent. It took no time at all for his fears to be realised. Indeed, it took only until the Evening News on the 4th of October for events to take yet another nasty turn. The newspaper carried the story of the successes of the private detectives, contrasting it with the incompetence of the police. Abberline had no official way of informing the newspapers that their private detective was a known criminal, a man who had served seven years of an eight-year sentence for dishonesty and theft and was known to carry a threat of violence wherever he went. He called himself Le Grand, but he had a heuristic approach to names.

Once there was daylight following the murder of Lizzie Stride, the police had begun to make house-to-house enquiries. One of the establishments called on was the home of Mr. and Mrs. Packer, a dwelling which was also their fruit and sweet shop, a couple well past middle age. Sergeant White introduced himself and explained that a murder had taken place in the yard across the road from their home in the early hours of that morning. They told him that they usually stayed open to sell fruit and sweets very late, but once the pubs had shut at about midnight, they had gone to bed and had seen nothing. The sergeant did not leave it at that but asked if he might look at the back of the building in case there was any sign of disturbance there. They agreed, he looked around and then left. According to Sergeant White, the statement from Mr. Packer was:

'No. I saw no one standing about, and neither did I see anyone go up the yard. I never saw anything suspicious or heard the slightest noise and knew nothing about the murder until I heard of it in the morning.'

On 4th October, Mr. Packer was extensively quoted in the Evening News as having been subsequently questioned by their two private detectives, Le Grand and his associate, and had given a full

Part One: The Nightmare Begins

description of both Lizzie Stride and a man she was with whom the newspaper claimed to be the only possible suspect.

In the article, Mr. Packer was quoted as saying Sergeant White had asked him nothing about the murder or whether he had witnessed anything suspicious. The article was devastating. The newspaper, through its two detectives, claimed to have unmasked *Jack the Ripper* following just a few hours of proper police work; all they needed was to put a name to the description.

Abberline could not believe what he was reading; he did not want to believe it. The account seemed thorough enough, but it did not accord with police enquiries.

According to the newspaper, the two private detectives had gone to the site of the murder after the body was removed to investigate. The yard had been washed down to clear it of blood, so they claimed they opened the drain to see what clues might have been washed away with the blood. They recovered a stalk, all of which remained from a bunch of grapes. They saw the proximity of the fruit shop to the yard and so approached Mr. Packer. It seems that their highly skilful questioning helped him produce a fuller and totally different recollection of events.

To the private detectives, he was able to recall a woman and a man coming into his shop and buying grapes. The man made a fuss about whether she wanted white or red grapes, and she chose red. The man paid sixpence for them, and the couple left the shop. Mr. Packer noticed them clearly in the environs of the yard and thought it odd they should be standing there so long on what was a miserable night of occasional showery rain. That was not all, for no obvious reason, the detectives asked how the man spoke and bizarrely offered an American accent as an example. Mr. Packer picked up on the American accent.

The Home Secretary was furious. He contacted Sir Charles Warren immediately to ask what on earth was going on, taking the newspaper account at face value as accurate and true. How could two private detectives, operating without preconceived ideas according to the newspaper, have cracked open the case so easily? How could his detectives be so incompetent? Warren had no ready answer for him, and the matter was passed down the line to Abberline. All he could do was dispatch Sergeant White back to interview Mr. Packer, which did not go well either.

Sergeant White, not in the best of moods, returned to 44 Berner Street, the home of Mr. Packer. He was not there. Mrs. Packer happily told him that her husband had willingly gone with the two private detectives to the mortuary to confirm his recognition of Elizabeth Stride. Sergeant White made his way there and en route, saw Packer and the two detectives returning. They had indeed taken Mr. Packer to the mortuary, first to see the body of Eddowes 'to ensure he had seen the right woman'. He had duly confirmed he did not know Eddowes. He was then taken to see the body of Lizzie Stride, and he agreed that this was the same woman who had been in his shop.

As no police official was present, no one could say whether he was influenced or coached when making his observations. They refused to let Sergeant White speak to Packer. As Abberline later opined, they couldn't let Packer speak to the sergeant as first, they had to be sure he had the story straight, their story. Later that day the two private detectives, now confident that Packer had a definitive version of the sightings fixed in his mind, took him in a cab to Whitehall to try and see Sir Charles Warren. They did not manage to pull off that coup but did have their witness give a statement to Assistant Commissioner Bruce.

Abberline and Swanson met in Swanson's office. The days were going by and there was no movement in the case. The City Police had nothing to go on either. Swanson had documents in front of him he wanted to share with Abberline. 'Don't waste any time following up on the Packer evidence. It would not be worth anything in a trial and is probably mostly invented. At least, we cannot pick the truth from the fiction in what he has to say. He probably believes it himself by now. So, look at this. It has been sent over from Westminster police, and it pins our Mr. Le Grand, private detective, nicely.' He passed the documents to Abberline, who read them out aloud.

'A list of known aliases used by Charles Grand, sentenced to seven years imprisonment for offences including theft and dishonesty: Le Grand, Charles Grant, Christian Nielson, Mr. Briscony...' His voice trailed off. 'Does the Commissioner know we are dealing with a rogue?'

'Indeed, he does', smiled Swanson grimly. 'I have told him that because of this, any statement Packer makes would be rendered valueless as evidence.'

'Are the newspapers aware of the background of their tame detective?' It was a logical expectation from Abberline.

'I believe they have been informed, one way or another, and it might be that he falls out of the headlines from now on. Unfortunately, he is not so tame and has done untold damage to our reputation and to this investigation.' Swanson was full of indignation.

'Mud sticks, and we are covered in it,' mused Abberline.

'Yes, we are.' Swanson broadened his concerns. 'The attacks upon us do not come only from the press. As you know, the London Board of Works has been writing to the Prime Minister and Sir Charles criticising every facet of what we do. Sir Charles has responded to them, and I have a copy of his latest response here.' He handed a letter to Abberline. It was a carefully constructed letter, but the calmness and reasonableness Sir Charles was known for was wearing thin; he was biting back and making further political enemies in the process.

In response to a charge of not sufficiently staffing the local police force, he pointed out that the opposite was the case.

Unfortunately, he seemed to place some of the blame for the lack of detection on the women themselves for taking the killer to a place where he could best commit his violence, blaming the victims. He added that the situation was made even worse by the paucity of street lighting in the area, the blame for which he placed squarely on the Board of Works. He returned to the charge of insufficient numbers of police officers assigned to the case by saying that the rest of the metropolis still had to be policed and that Whitechapel had a disproportionate share of the whole police force. He further admonished the Board for wanting to force his hand and declare what the detectives were doing when their work needed to be secret. He told them, in effect, that they did not know what they were talking about.

'What is this all about, Mr. Swanson?' asked Abberline. 'Surely not only about our search for the killer?' he added.

'Ah yes, here we have it. The politics of the matter. Word has spread in Parliament that Sir Charles has badly interfered with the administration of the detective service, preventing us from doing our duty. It is said, for instance, that he stupidly moved experienced officers about and so generally unsettled things. None of it is true, the only transfers were to help our investigations. I believe that behind it is a row between Sir Charles and Mr. Monro, the head of the secret service and nominally below the rank of Sir Charles, though you wouldn't know it. Monro reports only to the Home Secretary. Well, it seems Monro wanted his friend Robert Macnaughten to head up the detective service, but Sir Charles blocked it, having little time for detectives, as we know.

From that day, Monro has been advising the Home Secretary that the Criminal Investigation Department is in turmoil because of Sir Charles' direct handling of it. Sir Charles is isolated. We have both already witnessed the lack of confidence the Commissioner has in his deputy Mr. Anderson, also a friend of Monro, if I am not mistaken.

Sir Charles seems to get the backs of too many people at present. It is politics; it is not our business, but it is bringing pressure and criticism on us, and it is why neither you nor I will rise any further in this service.'

He seemed depressed as well as undermined and defeated by the internal squabbling.

CHAPTER TWENTY-ONE

BLIND ALLEYS

Inspector Reid sat at his desk in the Leman Street police station. He was waiting for Abberline to return from what had proven to be another speculative lead, another which led nowhere. Reid, like all other detectives on the case, was finding it increasingly difficult to separate fact from fiction. Abberline had asked him to review events surrounding the Vigilance Committee, a group of well-meaning citizens who seemed to be forever criticising the police and making life difficult.

It had been three weeks since the double event and much of his time was being taken up with silly press stories, letters claiming to know the *Ripper* or being from the *Ripper*. It all contributed to the low morale of his detectives.

Most recently, the Commissioner, appearing to be ever more desperate, had made a fool of himself over an attempt to test out whether Bloodhounds could be used, an approach which, in theory, might help if the dogs could be put on the scent of the killer within a very short time of a body being discovered; a strategy which was unlikely as the police had no dogs.

Sir Charles had borrowed a couple of the animals for the experiment in which they tracked people, including Sir Charles himself, around Hyde Park. All that had come of it was ridicule for the

Commissioner, who was seen to be ever more flailing about hoping to hit upon an idea to help catch the *Ripper*. It was a gloomy reading.

However, the Commissioner had now added to his order that no one was to enter a scene of a *Ripper* murder until he attended, so undermining himself and Abberline by demanding that he also wanted bloodhounds on the trail straight away. How this would work, the detective did not understand, but knew from what Fred Abberline had told him that it was a measure of the pressure being applied to the Commissioner by the press and the Home Secretary. Whilst waiting for Abberline, Reid turned his attention to the Vigilance Committee.

First, he looked at an incident involving the Chairman of the Committee, George Lusk.

On 4th October, at 4:15 in the afternoon, a man apparently between 30 and 40 years of age, 5ft. 9in. in height, with a florid complexion and bushy brown beard, whiskers and moustache, went Lusk's home in Alderney-street, Mile-End, and asked for him.

Lusk was at a pub nearby and the stranger was directed there. He found Lusk and asked him to go into a private room with him. Lusk was suspicious and found the man's appearance to be odd and refused but offered to talk in the bar area where others were around. They moved to a table. The man started to question him about the timing and layout of the beats the vigilantes were using, information Mr. Lusk was not prepared to divulge. The stranger drew a pencil from his pocket and purposely dropped it over the side of the table, saying, 'Pick that up.'

Just as Mr. Lusk turned to do so, he noticed the stranger make a movement of his right hand towards his side pocket as if searching, he thought, for a knife and seeing that his movement was noticed, suddenly lost interest in the conversation and asked to be directed to the nearest coffee house and dining-rooms.

Mr. Lusk directed him to such a place in the Mile End Road, and the stranger quietly left. Lusk, being suspicious, let the stranger leave and then tried to follow him.

Losing sight of him, he himself went to the coffee house he had recommended to find out more about the stranger. All he discovered was that the man had not been there; he had given him the slip.

This was a story Reid found difficult to swallow. It made for a good story in the press, but either this was another disturbed person trying to engage in the *Ripper* mystery, or it was a fabrication.

Part One: The Nightmare Begins

Again, it went nowhere. It planted the idea in the mind of the public that the *Ripper* was around and was threatening the Vigilance Committee because they were on to him. It was followed by the incident from the 16th of October, which was still being investigated by Abberline: Lusk had been sent what appeared to be a human kidney together with a note saying it was from the victim Eddowes.

Whilst the press again went to town on the story, emphasising possible cannibalism on the part of the *Ripper*, the medical opinion to date made no link of the kidney to Eddowes and it remained the opinion of Reid that although organs were being removed from bodies, from the victims, this was not by the *Ripper*. Most likely, organs were being removed at the morgue as part of the illicit trade in body parts amongst the teaching hospitals.

A constable knocked on his open door and entered with a message. 'I thought you might like to see this. It has been wired to us from the police in Yorkshire, sir. It might save us a bit of time chasing around in the future.' He handed him the note and smiled.

It was nice to see a smile in the police station these days. Reid took the note and read it.

At the Bradford Borough Court on Saturday, one Maria Coroner, 21 years of age, employed in a mantle-maker's establishment, was brought up on the charge of having 'written certain letters intending to cause a breach of the peace.' These letters, as stated by the Chief Constable, purported to be written by 'Jack the Ripper,' whose object in visiting Bradford, as was stated, was to do a little business before starting for some other place on the same errand. She had written two letters of this character, as she admitted when apprehended, one being addressed to the Chief Constable and the other to a local newspaper. On searching the girl's lodging, the police found copies of the letters. The prisoner excused her foolish conduct on the ground by saying that 'she had done it in a joke.' She was stated to be a very respectable young woman. The prisoner was remanded until the next day, the Bench declining to accept bail.

He placed his head in his hands. If this mischief was going on in some distant, northern town, how much more was he in for? He tried not to show his dismay to the constable, who seemed to think he had brought him good news. He turned to the latest problem of Mr. Lusk and the attention this man seemed to engender over the

Ripper case. He had risen from obscurity to a high mark in the national public consciousness and clearly enjoyed his newly acquired celebrity.

It seemed obvious to Abberline and Reid that Lusk now would also attract the attention of malcontents and lunatics and would be stuck with them, just as the detectives were stuck with him. The press loved him. Reid turned over the next report, one he had not been looking forward to, yet another young woman with a tale to tell.

A Miss Emily Marsh was employed in her father's leather shop at 218 Jubilee Street, Mile End, in Whitechapel. It seems that on Monday, 15th October, a man who had been looking at a Vigilance Committee poster in the shop window walked in at around one o'clock in the afternoon and asked for George Lusk's address. He said he saw there was a reward for information leading to the arrest of *Jack the Ripper*.

As Joseph Aarons, the treasurer of the Committee, lived close by, she suggested he should call on him instead, but the man declined, saying he 'had no interest in going there.'

Emily then picked up a newspaper lying on the shop counter, which referred to Lusk's address as Alderney Road, but with no house number. The man asked her to read it out to him which she did, and he wrote it in a pocketbook. He then thanked the girl and left the shop. Emily felt very uneasy about the encounter and the fact that the man dressed like a foreigner, not a local. She sent for young John Cormack, the shop boy, and told him to follow the man a little way and make sure everything was alright. Just as the man was walking from the shop, her father returned and also saw him.

Emily, her father and John Cormack gave full descriptions of the man they saw. Apart from his appearance, they noted he spoke with an Irish accent. The police conveyed the description to George Lusk, but thankfully, he stated that no one of that description had been to see him. It did not match the description of the stranger he himself had encountered.

Nevertheless, the mystery was reported freely in all the newspapers, with the Sunday Times remarking that the matter had not been sufficiently explained, a veiled criticism of the police.

When he was finally able to discuss the matter with Abberline, Reid mused that one of the Vigilance Committee's most prominent members was an actor.

'One might speculate that the Committee has found yet another way to draw the attention of the press,' he suggested.

Abberline looked doubtful.

'Why bother going to any trouble at all? Mysterious goings-on and threatening strangers are coming at us and the Committee from everywhere as it is.'

'Well, whatever the truth of it, this man is probably no more able to help with enquiries than anyone else. I suppose I should make a note of it for the Chief Inspector.' Reid was diligent in his recording.

He went on, 'I have no doubt he will pass the information to the Assistant Commissioner, although whether Sir Charles gets to know about it from anywhere other than the press is doubtful.'

Taking another theme involving the Committee, Abberline added, 'I see that the Vigilance Committee is promulgating the theory that there is not one *Jack the Ripper* but a whole conspiracy of them. Mr. Lusk has briefed Members of Parliament that a gang has determined to rid the streets of prostitution and so has embarked on this campaign of terror and murder. Why should the government have a detective service at all when we have fantasists like Mr. Lusk and his friends?'

It was the first time Reid had heard his colleague express his frustration in such a way.

The Abandoned: *Victims of Jack the Ripper*

Part One: The Nightmare Begins

CHAPTER TWENTY-TWO

FAIR EMMA

The weather in 1888 was extraordinary. It was extraordinary across the entire northern hemisphere.

In England, it was the most unpredictable weather in living memory. One day and night in July, snow fell across the southern counties and even London, with its usually warmer microclimate caused by millions of people concentrated into a small area, burning fires, powering factories, travelling back and forth, warming the streets and atmosphere, had a night of snow. It was an aberration of weather beyond record or memory and not repeated in over a hundred years.

August followed on, cool, dull and wet, weather that the police had vainly hoped would keep murder off the streets. September failed the hops and other crops, with the populace only confounded by October becoming the hottest month of the year, the hottest October since records began.

November began with a weather phenomenon that disturbed man and beast both. A massive cloud, deep and threatening, larger than clouds that bore thunderstorms, passed across part of England.

Over London at 1 p.m., sunlight was blotted out like a total eclipse, it fell dark as night, wild birds and caged linnets stopped singing and strangers on the streets looked to each other for comfort as it seemed the end of the world had arrived.

However, no rain fell, no thunderclaps were heard, and the cloud passed over; the world did not end.

Abberline sat in an office at the Leman Street police station as the great cloud drifted above. Calm and methodical though he was, he too was filled with an instinctive dread as the darkness fell. Lamps had to be lit so he could read the latest reports from detectives and other police officers as they combed the streets, keeping watch in the darkness, in the rain, from street corners, in the public houses, in the hopeless twist of streets and alleyways, deserted yards and derelict ground. Two of his team had drawn up a comparison between the times and dates of the *Ripper* murders with the occasions that cattle ships from the German coast docked in the Thames. The butchers on the ships had long-bladed knives. There was a match in the dates, and it was worth thinking about.

The *Ripper* might not be living in the area after all; perhaps he simply knew it very well. He may have been visiting for years before starting his campaign of violent terror. Abberline wondered if they could match the dates of the murders to drovers or farmers coming to the markets.

In the pubs around the areas, the number of reporters had thinned out. Battalions of them had taken to visiting all the pubs in Whitechapel and then latterly, they had concentrated on the pubs around Spitalfields in particular. They watched the women who watched them back. They scanned the bars for wild-looking, mad-looking foreigners. They even followed some of the women when they left the pubs. It was bad for trade for everyone involved in the vices of Spitalfields.

On the 1st of November, things had gone quiet again and most of the reporters stayed at home while others trailed around with the vigilantes for a while; nothing happened. They tried their usual sources in the police for information, but hardly anything was forthcoming. The *Ripper* was lying low, and they had nothing sensational to write about.

Less than a month after the double murder, women were back walking the streets scared but hoping the worst of fears would not happen to them. None of them had any choice in the matter and for some, the consequences of not going on the streets to earn money

Part One: The Nightmare Begins

was ultimately the same consequence as facing the *Ripper*: it was either death by starvation or death by murder.

In Dorset Street, Jack McCarthy watched over his shop. It was the only shop in the street, and it was rarely closed. Now 35 years of age, a family man, he felt himself to be powerful, important and wealthy. He had no time for those who regarded him as Irish; that had been his birth family. He was an East-End man now, an Englishman. He owned many of the tenements along the street and his biggest earner was Miller's Court, rooms built around an old courtyard halfway down the street and known to everyone as McCarthy's Rents. He employed a couple of thugs to ensure his rent was paid, but he was clever, too. Most landlords would not allow a tenant to owe even one night's rent, but he was more discerning.

Occasionally, very occasionally, a woman he took a fancy to might be staying and need to pay her rent some way other than with pennies.

Recently, he had rediscovered a former tenant of his sister, unusually attractive, already a prostitute and capable of being sent out on the streets to earn money if she was in debt to him.

Unlike the middle-aged, desperate women he usually saw plying their trade for pennies, Fair Emma was young, only in her mid-twenties, very pretty and with a greater earning potential.

McCarthy's sister kept a lodging house near the docks, one almost exclusively rented to prostitutes, women who had fallen as low as they could fall. She, too, had been taken with Fair Emma, though. Here was a young woman who appeared to have had some education, who would amuse people with her skilled drawings and sketches, and who spoke at least one foreign language. She had been with her only a few nights when she heard one of several versions of her history from her.

Emma was a popular name adopted by many prostitutes from time to time, and this one was no different. She gave her real name as Mary, and that was probably true, though no doubt she would change it again as she meandered in a life trapped in the poverty and degradation of the world between the docks and the markets. Her best hope, and the greatest risk to ever escaping this place, was to find a man to support her. It was a favoured if despairing stratagem for any woman, though one with little hope of success in the poverty of the East End. When she spoke to the lodging house owner, Mrs. Carthy, as she called herself, she spoke of a time when her prospects had risen, which seemed to have been promising, but bad luck continually intervened.

Like her landlady, Mary said she was from Ireland, and had been born in a place called Limerick, although she could not remember it at all as the family had left when she was very young.

From Ireland, they went to Carmarthenshire in Wales, where her father had work in local coal mines. It was a place of lovely countryside, miles of nearby coastline but also the poor working conditions of the mines.

In recalling it, she smiled and, giving credence to her history, explained that few people in the town spoke much English, the language of the streets was Welsh, which had become her language too. She would speak Welsh to Mrs. Carthy and to any who wished to hear the beautiful, lilting ancient language of south Wales.

Her early life there had been unremarkable, one of getting by and at the age of 16, she became Mrs. Davies, marrying a local young miner. She had a son, she said, and Mrs. Carthy guessed that the child was the reason for the marriage. When asked about her child, she said he was with her dear mother. Her husband, she explained, was killed in a mining accident, an explosion, when she was barely 18.

As a young widow with a baby, her prospects were of poverty, charity or starvation. She did not stay to suffer but went to the Welsh capital city of Cardiff to stay with her cousin, a slightly older girl who had found other ways of earning a living down near the Cardiff docks.

At first, Mrs. Carthy thought that Mary's journey had simply taken her from the docks of Cardiff to the docks of London, but gradually more emerged. It was a puzzle to Mrs. Carthy as to how this beautiful young woman, with talent and some intelligence and refinement, had ended up there. The story she heard was at first unbelievable, but then circumstances changed so that she did come to believe much of it. She doubted it was the whole truth but thought it truer than not. She later recounted it to her brother, who, though married and not a frequenter of prostitutes, was also taken with Mary when he saw her at his sister's lodging house in Breezers Hill.

Mary's customers in Cardiff would talk of London and flatter her with tales of how well one so young and pretty would do there. She was fresh-faced, had blond hair, and was tall and elegant. She did not hesitate.

Part One: The Nightmare Begins

Cardiff would not be her home for long. She had learned to make a meagre living from selling her body to rough and drunken sailors, how to drown her shame and self-disgust with drink; she could do better. She headed for London, knowing nothing of it.

The train arrived at Paddington Station in the west of a city which throbbed with noise and chaos, a foreign country to her. She found local lodgings and went into the West End, the wealthy part of the city, to walk the streets and the parks to earn her living.

It was there, soon after her arrival, that she was approached by an older woman who noticed her beauty and steered her towards a more lucrative form of prostitution.

According to Mary, she was taken to a fine house in Kensington, the home of a French woman. Mrs. Carthy would often try to remember the details of the establishment and the life Mary said she had there. At first, she thought it was all fantasy. Later, she believed much of it was true.

Mary said that the French woman was a 'Madame' and procured customers for a fee for Mary. In particular, foreign gentlemen liked her for her fair skin and blond hair. She talked of riding about in carriages.

Then, one afternoon, she told her landlady about Paris. It seems she and another girl went to Paris in a carriage where they entertained certain wealthy men. She may have gone there several times. It was afterwards that things went wrong for her. She was very hazy about this, but Mrs. Carthy had read about 'white slavery.'

Putting two and two together, she guessed at Mary being sent to France again but getting only as far as one of the channel ports, probably Calais.

There, she was taken to a house, certainly a brothel, and put to work. She would have been guarded and watched, a sex slave. Stories like these were common. Somehow, Mary escaped from the place and returned to London but did not dare go back to the West End.

Mrs. Carthy thought that if the story were true, there must have been some threat, a fear preventing her from returning to where she seemed to have once made a lot of money. She also wondered if the reason she was sold on to a French brothel if that was true, was because her drinking was out of control and she had become unreliable, too much of an embarrassment for aristocratic and wealthy users of her services. Mrs. Carthy was so taken with the story that she asked Mary if she could remember where the house in Kensington was.

To her surprise, Mary said yes and if Mrs. Carthy would accompany her, she would like to go back there and reclaim her trunk, which contained some fine dresses. They did precisely that. The house did exist, there was a French woman, a trunk and some fine clothes. There was a lot of mystery about this girl. She had arrived at the Breezers Hill lodgings after working as a cleaner and maid in Cleveland Street, having been placed there by the Catholic nuns from the Prudence Row Night Shelter. Like all the women who lodged at Mrs. Carthy's dwellings, there were gaps in her story, but what did seem true was that at one time, she had stayed in that house in Kensington.

Wherever Mary went, there were men around her, seeking her out, wanting to be with her. For a time, she lived with a builder called Morganstone somewhere near the gasworks in Stepney. That did not last long.

For a time, she lived with Johnny Fleming, a stone mason in Bethnal Green, then there was Joe. It never was clear what her relationship with Joe the costermonger was, but he would see her often and give her small amounts of money. He was probably in love with her.

Then, on Good Friday 1887, she met Joseph Barnett, who was born to Irish parents who died when he was young. He was fair like her and the same height as her. He fell in love at first sight with Mary and she saw him as a good man, a working man who would try and take care of her.

They moved in together within days of first going for a drink in a pub on Commercial Street. He took lodgings for them in George Street, near Thrawl Street in Spitalfields and then moved them to Little Paternoster Row in Dorset Street, but he lost the place when they were evicted for not paying the rent having spent his earnings on drink. The manager at the lodgings also objected to their continual drunkenness, which was a common problem on the street.

Still, they stuck together and moved to nearby Brick Lane. By March 1888, they were back in Dorset Street, in McCarthy's Rents, at 13 Miller's Court.

The two became well known around Dorset Street, especially in the pubs at either end of the street and in the Ten Bells by the great church. They were seen to be a couple, and though a heavy drinker, Joe Barnett was able to just about provide for them both because he had a licence to work as a porter in Billingsgate fish market.

Part One: The Nightmare Begins

As long as he worked, Mary did not have to go back on the streets. That all changed when, sometime in July, Joe Barnett lost his job.

It took no time at all for their money to run out.

At first, Joe managed to borrow, but soon there was no money to pay the rent. McCarthy knew what was happening. From his shop, he watched over everything that went on in his properties. He should have sent one of his men to number 13 to collect the rent or throw them out on the street, but he didn't; he waited until a larger debt accrued. Joe went to see him, to plead for more time.

'I'm sorry to have to come to you, Mr. McCarthy, I really am, I really am. I've lost my position in the market and have no money for the rent as yet, as yet, but I'm going to see my brothers to borrow a little and I should be back in employment soon, back soon.' He stumbled with his speech, thanks to his anxiety disorder and, in his nervousness, often repeated part of the sentence he had just spoken.

McCarthy looked at him, weighing up his options.

'It is in my rights, and my usual policy to see you out on the streets, you understand,' he growled at the man.

Joe Barnett trembled a little; he needed a drink. He looked at the floor and fidgeted.

Then McCarthy lightened his tone. 'I am going to be generous in your case, Joe. You go and find work quickly and pay me my money. And I'm going to help you. I have no work for you, but my sister speaks well of Mary, and I might have some skivvy work for her that will at least pay the rent. Tell her I will call on her. It doesn't matter whether you are there, I won't be staying long. Now I suggest you leave the pubs alone for a while and seek work, my generosity has its limits.' McCarthy was scheming.

'Thank you, Mr. McCarthy sir, McCarthy sir,' he gasped in gratitude. He had not expected McCarthy to be so lenient with him. He left the shop, shaking a little and returned the short distance to Miller's Court to tell Mary they had some time. He very much needed a drink, but he first had to seek out his brothers, who both still had work in the fish market.

As he went on his way, Jack McCarthy watched him through the shop window. He was irritated by the man's echoing speech. He did not want him there when he called on Mary, he would be a nuisance, but it did not matter much if he was there or not. It was time Mary became Fair Emma again and started earning some money, this time to pay McCarthy, with interest.

Back at number 13, Joe told Mary that they were safe from eviction for now, but he had to go to his brothers for help. He knew what she was thinking, what was coming, what they both dreaded, and she articulated it.

'We know what we are facing, Joe. I'll try and borrow some money too. I don't have anything left to sell. But then what? If you can't get back at the market, I'll have to do a bit of trading of my own.' She was already facing the certainty that McCarthy would have her back on the streets as the only way she could pay him.

'No, Mary, no, not that. I can't stand the thought of you with other men. I don't want you back in that life. McCarthy is giving us breathing space and I'll find some work somewhere.' He was desperate, in denial of the inevitable.

'You'll do your best, Joe, but we both know this is the only way we are going to survive.' Mary had to take control of the situation as Joe was no match for McCarthy. 'Don't go trusting Jack McCarthy either, he has never done a good turn for anyone, and he isn't going to start with us. He will have something in mind, and it won't be in our best interests.' Her words chilled them both.

'I don't want us ending up in the workhouse Mary, nothing worse than that but death to people like us. All we want is to be together and have a few merry times in the pubs, but please not go street walking again.' He knew his pleas were hopeless.

'Oh Joe, if our debts start mounting, it won't be the workhouse. All those creditors will come after us and McCarthy is the worst of the lot. He doesn't keep those thugs about him for show.' She was the realistic one. If they didn't do as McCarthy wanted, she feared Joe would end up floating in the Thames, his throat cut.

'No, Mary, not back on the streets,' he persisted. 'Give me a few days to find something.'

'I will, Joe,' she soothed. 'You go to your brothers and see if we can have money for food. I'll see what this job is that McCarthy is talking about. It might bring us sixpence a day or more, depending on what it is.' She was reassuring him, but in her own mind, she was steeling herself to go back on the streets. She had no faith in McCarthy, she knew what he would want her to do.

Joe left for Billingsgate, where his brothers would be finishing work for the day. If they had already gone, he would go round to their lodgings, south of the river. Jack McCarthy was watching from his shop window. He saw Joe Barnett leave Miller's Court and let him get out of sight. He called his shop girl to stand behind the counter. 'I'm going out on business for quite a short while. Mind the shop.' He took his bowler hat and a stout cane and strode out into his empire.

Number 13 was at ground level. It was a single room with sparse furnishings and a fireplace on which the occupants did their cooking. He glanced through the window, paned glass too dirty to let in much light, and knocked on the door with his cane. She opened it slowly, then stepped aside to let him in. He did not wait to be asked before sitting on one of the two wooden chairs in the room. His first action surprised her and took her off guard.

'Mrs. Barnett, I have something for you, delivered to the shop yesterday. I didn't want to give it to you whilst Joe was around as I'm not sure what it might contain. You know me, I don't like trouble between couples – bad for business.' He reached into his coat and withdrew an envelope. 'The name on the envelope is Mary Kelly, and I know that is a name you go by. It's from Dublin and there is an address on the back. From a Mrs. Kelly.'

Mary gasped. She was flustered. Without meaning to say so, she blurted out, 'It's from mother. She must have gone back to Ireland like she always said she would. My brother is in the army, and I heard he had been sent to barracks in Dublin.' She was speaking more to herself than to him.

'Is she able to help you from back in the old country where all I hear of is rain, poverty and ignorance?'

'She won't have anything, I suppose, but it's no business of yours.'

'I think it is, Mary. You have no money; you have been borrowing from people, I hear. You owe me over a week's rent, and I want paying. I can't afford a reputation of being a soft touch for a pretty face.' He was stern, uncompromising.

'What is it you want, Mr. McCarthy? Apart from the money you know we don't have, what is it you are after? You want me to work for you, or is it payment in kind you are after?'

McCarthy remained calm. He was impressed that he was dealing with an intelligent woman for a change. He almost liked Mary, but what he really saw was a business opportunity. 'It's like this, Mary, you'll soon be owing me more than I can expect to be paid, even if

Joe does find work. I am not going to let the debt go and your debt to me comes before anything owed to anyone else. You know that whatever Joe gets, you will both spend on drink, anyway. I want my money back, but I'm realistic. I am going to invest in you. I'm going to lend you some money for food and to brighten yourself up a bit. When I say money for food, I mean you can come to my shop, and I'll extend a little credit. After all, if I give you money now, you will spend it on drink, eh? I'll add it to the rent you already owe me. Then, if it is not paid back by, say, the end of next week, we will have to come to terms, my girl.' His tone became menacing.

He stood up. 'You had better make up your mind quickly, I could let this place out tomorrow if I decide to throw you on the streets.' He paused for a moment, then openly reflected on her situation.

'You could have done a lot better for yourself than all of this,' he said, his hand sweeping the air. 'Why Joe Barnett? Is it so you can have someone to boss around? The man is a nothing, hardly a man at all, in my book. What are you about, woman?' He left her, crying with anger and with fear of him, of the workhouse, of prison even, and of what she had to do. She clutched her letter and, despite her trembling fingers, gently opened it.

Joe Bennett returned shortly after eight o'clock that evening. Even though it was by then the end of August, it was cold. The light was already fading as he reached number 13. Mary was waiting for him and looked as if she had washed her face, combed her hair and put on a clean apron. She had lost the pinched look she had when she hadn't eaten for a day or so. She had bread and cheese waiting for him on a board on the table. He looked at her with his tired eyes.

'Where did this come from, did it come from?' He gave away his agitation by his repetitions, once endearing to her but now, in stressful times, annoying.

'We have a little credit at McCarthy's, Joe. It's not much, but we have a bit of time for you to get work and it looks like I have a bit of skivvying starting so we can pay him back.' She did not sound convincing.

'I've borrowed nearly two shillings from my brothers and my sister. I ate a pie on the way back.'

He hesitated, 'I still don't have a job, Mary and I don't know how we are going to pay our debts.'

'It's not something we have to worry about tonight, Joe,' she said softly. 'We will find a way out of all of this. Come on, let's go to the Horn and see if any of our friends are there. They might know if there is any work going.'

It was a strange relationship. They were a comfort to each other at times, which was better than being alone, but Joe's value to Mary had diminished greatly.

He was a passive man and did not beat her, but apart from that, if he could not provide for her, she wondered what the point of him was.

She preferred his predecessor, also called Joe, but he did beat her. She knew that her current paramour was outliving his usefulness. He would not be able to protect her from McCarthy's brutes. He also didn't know the full extent of her debts, which made their position even worse than he thought it was. It seemed that McCarthy hadn't told him, something else McCarthy held over her. No, it was better to go out and have a night where the company and the drink would take away the worry; she needed a drink.

The Abandoned: *Victims of Jack the Ripper*

CHAPTER TWENTY-THREE

MARY KELLY

That weekend was momentous for Mary. She and Joe were over a week behind with the rent and had no money. She was in debt to the shop and Joe seemed not to care. He wouldn't tell her why he had lost his job at Billingsgate, but whatever the reason, he seemed in no hurry to get another. He said he was waiting for his old job to be available to him again, but when that might be, no one knew.

She was putting off what she knew she had to do, but she would not do it until absolutely forced to do so. She suspected either Jack McCarthy, hunger, or a need for drink would decide when she would be Fair Emma, Ginger, or Blackie again.

The last name might depend on whether she could colour her hair. Avoiding the rain and not wanting to be at home, she crept into the great All Saints church, somewhere quiet where she could hide a while, where the doors were normally kept locked to keep out the homeless and couples indulging in the services the women offered. She sat on a long bench at the back, where the Verger did not see her. He was working away quietly, making a repair to something near the high altar.

It was something she never mentioned, for it was not anything of great importance to her, but she was raised a Protestant, not a

Catholic, as her name and Irishness implied. It was a distinction that once had marked her out.

Still, she couldn't stay hidden for long, so she rose to leave before she might be evicted, pondering that in all her days in Spitalfields, this was the only time she had been inside the church.

***

By the middle of September, three weeks or so since Jack McCarthy had sent her back on the streets, the wet summer plodded its disappointing path. She had no money but went into the nearby Ten Bells pub anyway in case there was someone there she knew. Standing just inside the doorway was a man she would have preferred to avoid, Joe Fleming, her former lover; he was drunk.

'Why, it's my fair Emma, my ginger beauty,' he laughed, 'come on over here, Mary and keep me company.' His use of her street names was intentionally insulting.

She made no excuse, ignored the reference to her past, knowing he would buy her a drink. She smiled at him and knew what to expect. He gave her sixpence to get a drink, and she bought a tot of rum for four pence. She dropped the change into her own purse.

Fleming grinned. 'Still up to your tricks, I see, my girl. Keep it. I'm thinking I might be calling on you a little later anyway. I miss you, Mary. Why don't you cast off from that wastrel and come back to me?'

'You know my Joe is not so bad. He looks after me when he is at work. It's just that he's a bit unlucky at the moment.' She knew as she spoke he wouldn't believe a word of it.

'You don't fool me, Mary. I can see why you took up with him. His wages might be useful when he is working, I grant you that, but that isn't what it's about now, well, is it?' He had a malicious look about him. 'I bet he leaves you alone, eh? I bet you don't let him touch you unless the drink addles your brain. I was the man for you.' He was smirking now.

She stood up to him.

'Not like you touched me, Joe Fleming. No, he is not like you at all. He is respectful of me. You were the man who knocked out one of my teeth, as I recall. Is it any wonder I left you?' There was anger in her voice.

Part One: The Nightmare Begins

'Now then, my Mary, I know things went a little too far at times, but you can be fair argumentative when the drink is in you. I provided for you alright, didn't I? You never went hungry or in need of a shawl when you lived with me now, did you?' He had a smirk in his voice.

'I recall it differently, Joe. I remember times when I had to walk the street to bring *you* money. I've never had to do that with my Joe.' She was satisfied that was at least partly true.

'You are harsh, Mary. It wasn't often I sent you out.' His voice was falsely apologetic, still sneering. You know that you are the only one for me. I've always loved you, Mary, but I reckon you don't have much time for men in your heart, do you?' There was by now a dark insinuation in his tone.

She did not like the direction this discussion was taking. He had accused her before of having passions for other women. She had escaped him, but not entirely. How could she be rid of him when she relied on his occasional small gifts of money, even now taking drinks and pennies from him? She could smile at him, still flirt with him a little, but only for the money; she hated him. She hated him for beating her, she hated him for saying what she secretly knew about herself, that the only desire she ever felt for another was the ache she felt for other women. Her best approach to his hostility was to show servility.

'Don't let's fall out, Joe. Buy us another drink and let's be happy.' She wanted to distract him, and anyway, having more drink paid for by him suited her.

He laughed out loud and pulled out some coins from his pocket. 'I think I will get these, Mary – it works out cheaper than sending you to the bar!' and he laughed aloud at his own joke. They stayed for two more drinks, and then Mary left, tipsy, for home.

Joe Fleming went home, too, determined to call and see her the next day. Who was to say when she would have enough of Barnett and be back with him? She was pretty, a catch, in a way.

Mary stepped outside into Commercial Street. Suddenly, she didn't feel like going home just yet. She didn't want to share her money with Joe Barnett. She had taken two pennies from Fleming when she fetched the drinks from the bar and then taken advantage of his drunkenness and swapped one of the pennies for a florin when she helped put his change in his pocket. It was such an old trick that it only worked on drunks. She smiled to herself when she left because he had given her a shilling to buy food.

'What a nice, kind man,' she said to herself. 'Nice enough to beat me and send me out on the street when it suited him. Only nice when it suits him; all about himself and what he wants from me.' Now, she had three shillings and a penny. She hid the florin in a garter purse as she would need that later. Then she walked purposefully down the street, determined to have a good time whilst she could.

Something, though, told her she should make a plan to get away from all of this. In a sudden contradiction of intentions, she turned and hurried home. Joe was not there. She let herself in and raising a broken floorboard near the fireplace, hid the florin. She would put away anything she could get.

If she had to go back on the streets, then she must, but she would hide her money, maybe save enough to run away. If only she could be sure Jack McCarthy couldn't track her down. He knew all the landlords in the borough, and beyond.

She could hear people coming and going outside. She went out and locked the door behind her. She had a distant feeling of purpose, of hope. In her purse was a shilling and a penny. She was going to buy a penny pie and then a shilling's worth of gin. She needed to get out of Spitalfields to enjoy herself in safety though, needed to be sure she wouldn't run into Joe.

She walked down towards Whitechapel High Street, taking the long way round, crossing Houndsditch and wandering down Creekchurch Alley, over Mitre Street and along to Leadenhall. There, she turned left and walked past the Aldgate pump and into the first pub she came to.

Two or three hours later, singing and staggering, she meandered her way back towards home, fended off an enquiry from two sailors, then took to screaming and shouting at the next man who approached her.

A small crowd gathered to watch the drunken woman shout abuse at anyone who crossed her path until a heavy hand fell on her shoulder and her eyes looked up to see the stern glare of a policeman. He gripped her arm and said the words that chilled her – 'I think you had better come along with me.'

Mary spent the night in a police cell and the next day was up before the Magistrate, a man thoroughly sick of drunks accosting people in the street. She was too afraid to invent another name and anyway, Detective Constable Dew was in the station, and he knew her.

The Magistrate fined her two shillings and sixpence, a full half-crown, and accepted an offer from her to pay it off at five pence a week as she had not a penny with her.

The Magistrate was not convinced she would pay and so also imposed a sentence of three days imprisonment should she default. This was a bitter pill to swallow. The police had almost not bothered to take her to court as there was a huge investigation going on, with detectives everywhere, so she had been unlucky.

It was only from the announcement in court that she knew the date, the 19th of September.

The Abandoned: *Victims of Jack the Ripper*

CHAPTER TWENTY-FOUR

IN DORSET STREET

She arrived back at her hovel of a home later that morning. There had been many times in her life when she had felt despair, and this was another. The familiar feelings of hopelessness and wretchedness welled up inside her.

Her life, she decided, was a long catalogue of struggle, desperate decisions and always being close to drowning in poverty. She had nothing, not even self-respect. She sat on one of the two wooden chairs in her room, which she pathetically kept clean and tidy. She felt nothing but sadness, putting her head in her hands and weeping.

Her problems were insurmountable and now she faced the prospect of prison and then the workhouse. She tried to think through her situation, but her reasoning was fogged with fear. Her rent was four shillings and sixpence each week, and she was falling ever deeper into arrears. She could think of no way of getting that amount of money without Joe working and her returning to prostitution.

Even then, they would be paying off one set of debts whilst building up others. She wondered about going back to Joe Fleming. She knew that he loved her, even if he did bash her about now and then, sometimes out of jealousy, but he lived hand to mouth too, and he could not shelter her from the debt to McCarthy.

She knew that even worse, within a week, she would default on her debt to the Court and that a warrant for her arrest would be issued; she might be taken off to prison at any time.

Then, she remembered George Hutchinson. She shuddered. George had availed himself of her services and had then given her money which he now wanted back. Either she paid him his money, or he would keep on harassing her.

As he saw it, he could have her for free until what he was owed was paid back. She couldn't even remember what the sum was. George was a tough customer, a former soldier who worked in the markets and she was afraid of him; she was afraid of everything.

There was one more thing, something she knew was the biggest worry of all: she was pregnant. This time, there was no money for an abortionist and drinking gin had not worked. She wished she were dead.

As she sat there, she remembered she had two shillings hidden under the floorboard. She hurried over to the right spot to check it was still there.

She eased up the loose planking, and found it to be where she had left it. She had to think about her next steps.

She could pay some of her fine, but even if she didn't, she might get away with it as long as she was not arrested for some other offence. She knew the police would not be bothered to come looking for a fine defaulter especially as they were so busy chasing the *Ripper*.

She wanted to save the money and anything else she could get. This way, she might raise enough to pay off her creditors or enough to move out of the ugliness of Dorset Street.

Maybe she could start a small business of some sort? It was a big decision to leave the money there, but it was the one she fixed upon. She replaced the cover and tried to compose herself. There was a jug of water in the room, and she washed her hands and face. She let down her dirty blond hair and combed it out. She felt her clothes pressing a little tighter against her abdomen and knew the baby was growing inside her. Her strength was returning. One good thing about being locked up by the police was that they had given her a mug of tea and some bread and cheese for breakfast.

She stepped out into Miller's Court, then into Dorset Street. She had not gone more than a few steps when one of McCarthy's men took her by the arm.

'Glad I caught you. Mr. McCarthy wants a word with you.'

Part One: The Nightmare Begins

She didn't resist, there would be no point in struggling. He looked at her and knew she would be compliant.

'Tell you what. He wants a private conversation so not in his shop. Just go back inside your place for five minutes and I'll fetch him.'

'There's no need. Tell him I know what he wants me to do and I'm making a start on it tonight.' She smiled up at him.

'Not so fast, Missy. You don't think the boss is going to take you at your word, do you? No, go and wait for him. He won't be long.'

There was no point in doing otherwise. She returned to her room and waited. True to the word of the bully, she did not have to wait long. He did not even knock on the door, simply walked in accompanied by another of his thugs, Indian Harry, so-called for his years spent in the army in India. He had a box under his arm.

'Now, Mary, you are in debt and it's getting deeper. I'm not going to let it go by, so here is what we are going to do. This is our business arrangement; I won't beat about the bush. You are a good-looking woman and should have no difficulty pulling in the trade. You are a lot younger than the other 'unfortunates' around here. Get yourself up west, move on from the docks, pick up casual trade around here by all means, but get earning. This little device is going to help you pay your way.'

With that, he placed a heavy wooden box on the table. It was padlocked but had a slot in the top.

'Each time you have a customer, you are going to put half of the fee in this box. You won't be able to get at it once it is in there. And don't think I won't know about how many men you will be servicing. My people keep watch on the Rents, and I will know exactly how many men you bring down here. You can charge above the odds, but I will expect three pennies for every man I know has come down here. As it is unusually warm at last, I expect you can get away with a lot of trade in alleyways but just in case you think you can get away with not paying me, I'm having you watched. You might give us the slip, of course, so every time I know you are out on your beat, I am going to charge you a shilling anyway, which I think is generous of me. One of my men will collect the box each week when he calls for the rent. You will still pay the rent, Mary. Come November, it will be cold, and you will be doing more trade back here, so you had better get Joe out of the way. I don't want him putting off business.'

'What if I won't do it? What if I can't do it anymore?' She heard herself say the words, but even as she spoke them, she knew there would be no pity for her.

He glared at her, then nodded to Indian Harry, who spoke up on his behalf.

'Oh, you *can* do it, Missy, and you will do it unless you want to find out how the *Ripper* goes about his business. Understand?'

She nodded. She knew exactly what he meant. He may not carve her up as the *Ripper* would, but he would hurt her very badly, probably finish her off and throw the body in the Thames.

McCarthy stood up. This was not a negotiation; she was working for him now. She was no longer an occasional prostitute staving off starvation or paying for a night out in the pubs, this was full-time prostitution, working for someone else, a violent pimp. It was total humiliation and servitude. He left; Indian Harry grunted. Tragedy was closing in on her.

She was thinking now and had to act quickly. She could not run away as she had no money and nowhere to go. She needed to make money.

First, there would be no paying of rent. McCarthy would think he would be getting that one way or another through her work. She needed to keep out of the pubs unless a man was paying for the drinks.

Joe had to go.

She would throw herself into the work and make what she could as quickly as she could.

What else, what else? She needed to secretly sublet her room. She could have a 'friend' stay there with her.

More importantly, she could tell some of the other women they could use her room for a small fee, say two pence a night to bring back several men if they wanted, or maybe just a penny. She needed every penny she could get. Going out on a regular beat would be no good because McCarthy would know. She needed to change the times and places, not bring many back, but still put money in the box.

She stood up and squared her shoulders. The time to start was right away. It might be too early to find customers, but she could start spreading the word discretely that her room is open for business.

Part One: The Nightmare Begins

She went to the Horn of Plenty, where Mrs. Ringer, the landlady, knew lots of the women. She would ask who was around.

Mary had to play Joe carefully. While she did not want him around, she still needed him to find work and give her some money. She needed to keep up a good relationship with Fleming, too.

When Joe Barnett came in from looking for work, she told him straight that she had to go out on the streets. He pleaded with her not to do it, promising to find work somewhere, but it was a forlorn promise. She ignored his pleading and told him they had to put the rent money and additional money towards the arrears in the box McCarthy had brought around. She didn't tell him the rest of the history behind the box. He grumbled and whined about it.

She pressed him to go back to Billingsgate to beg for his old job, but when he fell silent on the matter, she knew he had been sacked from there. About the only reason a reliable porter was sacked from the market was for theft, and that made sense. She and Joe had been steady for money for a time because he must have been stealing goods and selling them off. It would take a while for his brothers to get him back in there.

Two nights later, he came home to find they had a guest staying for a couple of nights, a woman he did not know. It was quite clear to him that this woman and his Mary were working the streets together. He complained and he told Mary he couldn't stomach it.

After two weeks of it, he had taken all he could of different women staying, and when she was unmoved by his pleading, he moved out, saying he would not come back until she gave up the street life. He warned her about the *Ripper* and feared for her safety.

However, he did promise to give her some rent money so she could keep their place ready for his return and somehow, he managed to do that a few days later.

What he did not know was that his money, like that of her temporary tenants, went under the floorboard, not into the box. Even before he left, although increasingly out of the way, Fleming had taken to calling more openly. He provided another trickle of income.

At the end of the first week, McCarthy had called for his money. He had opened the box and counted out the coins in there. It did not cover the rent but did pay off most of her debt to his shop for that week. This was only what he expected, and it did not bother him too much. He had collected about four shillings, which was four shillings more than the previous week and more than if he had thrown her out. He was satisfied that as she got into her job, she would make him a lot more than this. He pocketed the money and relocked the box.

'You've got to do a lot better than this, Mary, very much better. A pretty, clever girl like you should be making this much every night. Let us see if you can at least double this for next week because if it is not worth it to me, I'll have to decide what to do with you.' It was a threat he could carry out without any conscience.

'I've arranged a fight night next week and have some friends coming to watch the bouts and do a little gambling. I want you to entertain one or two of them, so be available. I'll let you know when and where – and no stealing from them, or you know what you'll get.' He left, placing the box back on the table. She moved it under the bed.

The following week, there was a little more in the box, but he was suspicious. He knew she was out working the streets, but this was not much of a return. Then, she did not go out at all for a few days, saying she was ill, so he had almost nothing in the box.

He let her know that her arrears were now about 25 shillings. Still, his friends at the fight, staged in the market, had paid him for her services and wanted to have their pleasure with her again next time, so he had no need to put on any more pressure. Yet.

He heard there had been a row and Joe had gone the night before, but he saw him visiting the next day anyway, no doubt trying to get back with her. He did not know he was bringing her money.

When Fleming visited, his spies told him he was courting Mary behind the back of Barnett and trying to get her to go and live with him. He would keep an eye open for her moving on and find out where Fleming was living. He did not know that Fleming, too, was bringing small gifts of money. The more McCarthy watched for her comings and goings, the less he noticed other women from the area wandering with their men friends into Miller's Court. They could be going anywhere; he did not know they were using number 13 for a small fee.

The autumn days of October ticked by into the start of November. With Joe having moved out, Mary was uneasy. She had expanded her money-making ventures a little further by befriending Maria Harvey.

Maria was an unfortunate, like herself, but had an income as a laundress. As a little sideline, Maria would steal some of the clothes

Part One: The Nightmare Begins

she should be laundering. Mary let her store them at number 13 and then began to sell them for her, sharing the profit. She also let Maria move in and bring her customers back. Mary would find other places to stay for free if Maria and the other women she befriended were working and using the bed. She would return in the early morning so she could sleep for a few hours and hide away her meagre earnings from the rent she was receiving.

Increasingly, Mary found herself drawn to Maria and enjoyed her company.

Life on the street, meanwhile, was as nasty as ever she remembered it to be. It was degrading, unpleasant and, with High Rip gangs and the *Ripper* at large, it was dangerous.

However, she had some protection even though she had not sought it. There was less fear of a customer turning on her or a gang robbing her because although she did not like him, George Hutchinson was around again. She had been on the streets only a few days when he had approached her. He started with threats, of course, wanting back a few pennies she still owed him and was not deterred when she countered by saying she was working for McCarthy.

He did, however, modify his position.

It was a familiar proposition. He would forget the debt, shadow her when she was working, offering 'protection'.

When she found a client who might be a class above the drunken sailors who formed most of her users, she would service him and send him out into the darkness where Hutchinson was waiting to attack and rob him. She hated the trade but was afraid of Hutchinson.

For his part, he treated her with contempt. He pushed her more into working the areas where the middle-class Jews might be likely to visit when searching for a woman, as he had decided they had more he could steal, he hated Jews anyway. Mary made a fuss about his work, she despised it, and when she objected openly about it, he thought of beating her but changed his mind and instead gave her a few pennies from the robberies now and then to keep her co-operation.

The protection Hutchinson was supposed to offer, keeping away the *Ripper* from being a part of it, escalated her problems when his ready violence turned a calamity into a disaster.

It was in the first few nights of November, working away from Dorset Street, at the Mile End, when she picked up a smartly dressed young man in a pub. The two left together and he steered her into an alleyway on the side of a warehouse.

From the corner of her eye, she saw a shadow and hoped it was only Hutchinson and not someone even more dangerous, like the *Ripper*.

The young man spoke to her, cheeky and urgent.

'Are you going to show me the goods then?'

'Well, I don't know. You are a nice young man, very attractive and all, but I am a penniless girl you know.' She smiled at him.

'How much to let me go all the way to paradise then, girl?' his excitement was obvious.

'Have you got sixpence, Billy?' she asked. She thought he would have.

'I thought four pence was the going rate with most of the tarts around here. Why are you so different?'

For someone, up until the discussion of the fee so keen, his attitude had become harsh and unflattering. It conveyed she was nothing more to him than a common prostitute, unworthy of respect or civility.

'I am young and pretty, if I say so myself, and I will give you a really good time.' She kept her equilibrium. She was used to being ill-used.

'What did you say your name is?' he asked again curtly.

'Call me Emma. I will call you Billy. If you want me to lift my skirts, first give me sixpence, Billy.' She continued to be as coquettish as she could, hoping her apparent refinement would show him how lucky he was to have her for sixpence.

The man changed his tone. He spoke steadily and sternly, becoming official and threatening.

'You don't remember me, but I know you. No, don't call me Billy and I don't think I will call you Emma. Your name is Mary Kelly. I am Detective Constable Dicks and I was in the court when you were fined for being drunk and disorderly. There is a prison cell waiting for you, Kelly, if I'm not mistaken, especially as I can also arrest you now for soliciting prostitution.' He smirked. All the power in this exchange was his alone.

Mary went cold. She didn't recognise him. He was looking down into her face, enjoying the terror he caused her. He felt powerful, and with this power came cruelty. She did not doubt anything he said either and knew he would happily arrest her. She felt panic rise inside her.

'Please, I was desperate. I don't do this normally. I was sent out by my old man, and he will kill me if I go home without money, but I'll do you for nothing if you let me go home.' She was close to tears.

'And just where is home, Miss Kelly? I'll bet it is not the address you gave the custody sergeant.' He glowed in the anguish he caused her.

He gripped her wrist very tightly, so tightly it hurt, and she winced. 'I can make it hurt a lot more than this unless you want to be very nice to me,' he sneered.

She could see now that he was flushed, getting excited. He could arrest her if he wanted to, but first, he was going to taunt her and use her if it pleased him.

She sensed that frightening her, dominating her, and being violent to her excited him. He was not on duty, he was using his position to bully her, probably beat her, rape her and rob her.

She must have squealed with the pain as he twisted her arm, she could not remember. Everything happened quickly, but she felt as if she was watching a play as it slowly unfolded in front of her.

A bulky shadow appeared behind the plain-clothed policeman, and she heard the heavy thud of the pacifier as it struck his head. His eyes turned upwards, he released his grip and fell to his knees.

The shadow raised his hand, clutching the sand and lead-filled leather cosh to strike again when Mary heard her own voice, shrill and shaking, 'No, he's a Peeler!'

The assailant stopped, hesitated, then turned and fled, leaving her standing over the policeman, who was sinking into unconsciousness.

She saw the retreating form of George Hutchinson in the light of a streetlamp.

She had to get away.

Mary stepped past the man and tried not to run; she must not draw attention to herself. She heard the man groaning and then her survival instinct took over and she ran anyway.

She was implicated in the attack on a policeman; if he died, she might even hang for this.

If he didn't, he would come looking for her.

The Abandoned: *Victims of Jack the Ripper*

Part One: The Nightmare Begins

CHAPTER TWENTY-FIVE

MARIA HARVEY, LITTLE LIZZIE, AND MARY

Mary was shaken. Along the streets, there were a few stragglers, mostly drunks, who didn't seem to take any notice of her. Even so, she kept away from the streetlights, although there were not many. She wanted to take the shortest route home, but her fear was so acute, she would not risk the alleyways and any street in complete darkness.

For some reason, a sudden dread of the *Ripper* formed in her imagination; the main streets were her best protection, but the main roads were also where she would most likely be seen by passing policemen or vigilantes, so either way was a risk to her. Already, one policeman had recognised and remembered her, so she did not want to be seen now so close to where he had been attacked. She had to be as far away from the assault as possible.

The fear stayed with her all the way to Dorset Street, that dank little road smelling of sewage and misery. There were only a few lights showing from the windows and McCarthy's shop was closed. Her hands trembled so much she could hardly turn the key to her rented room, but she got in and closed the door as quietly as she could. She sat on the edge of the bed and wept.

Outside, she heard the rain starting to fall again. She had curtained the window after a rough fashion to keep out prying eyes, but one drunken night, when arguing with Joe, she had broken one of the small windowpanes, something she needed to keep from McCarthy before he charged her for it. Joe had stuffed rags into the broken pane to keep out the draught and the cold. She tried to compose herself, lit the fire and meagre though it was, it warmed her. She felt vulnerable and alone. All of life was conspiring against her.

As she knelt in front of the glowing fire, feeling its warmth, there was a tapping at her door. She knew it would be a woman because a man's knock would have been harder. She half thought she should be cautious and not respond, but as she hesitated, she heard a voice, a woman's voice, ask for her, 'Mary, it's me, it's Lizzie.'

Mary opened the door and let in her young friend; the only friend she had who was younger than herself. Lizzie was small and lost, pale-skinned and doe-eyed, wet from the rain and cold. 'I've nowhere to go tonight, Mary, can I stay here a while, just until I've warmed up?' The girl was about 19 or 20 years old but looked much younger. She had managed to find work in Crossingham's Lodging House, a room included, but often found herself out on the street if additional rooms were needed or if the deputy wanted her out of the way for a while. Mary had befriended her, a waif, and was fond of her. Having someone else to care for seemed to lift the weight from Mary's shoulders.

'Come in quickly, Lizzie, kneel by the fire and warm yourself. I'll make us some tea.'

Mary had a kettle filled with water ready for use and she hung it on a bar over the fire. She took the wet shawl from Lizzie, draped it over the back of a chair and placed it near the fire to dry. Then she knelt behind Lizzie and put her arms around her, drawing her tight to herself, rubbing her thin arms to warm her. Lizzie leaned her head into the breast of her friend and let herself be comforted. Mary gently rocked the girl, keeping her close, feeling her slowly relax as the cold left her. Hugging the girl was comforting for Mary, too.

'Are you still a good girl, Lizzie, not a whore like me?' she almost whispered.

'Don't speak badly of yourself, Mary. You are the kindest and best person I know.' Lizzie admired and loved her friend.

'Well, learn from me, girl. I don't want you getting into the deep water that is drowning me. Don't ever go on the streets, it is the worst path you could take. If I could get just enough money for the fare, I would be on my way to Ireland, to my Ma and Pa. I hate this life, hate it.' She spoke the words softly, reflecting on the sadness of her life.

'You still have a Ma and Pa, then Mary? Do you ever see them?' Lizzie wanted Mary to be happy.

'I grew up in Wales, Lizzie, and I don't really remember Ireland where I was born, not at all, but my brother is in the Scots Guards and is barracked in Dublin. I don't know why he is in a Scottish regiment, though, or why they are in Dublin, seems all at odds, doesn't it? Anyway, my Ma and Pa have gone there to be near him, to be a family again. My Pa came to London searching for me, but I was so ashamed of this life that I hid away until he gave up the search. My brother tried to find me too. I should have swallowed my pride, but what if my Pa found out I am a whore? He might have disowned me.'

'No, Mary, you are lovely. I love you. You are the only one who is kind to me.' Lizzie raised her head to look innocently into Mary's face.

'I would be happy if it could be just like this, Lizzie, warm by the fire, but it can't be. Come on, the kettle is boiling. I'll make us some tea, and then we had better get some sleep. I'm not going out working the streets tonight. You can stay with me. We can share the bed and keep each other warm. It can be our little bit of comfort.'

When morning greyed into the room, the two women rose and dressed. Mary had no food put aside for breakfast, not that she felt like eating anyway. The fear of the events of the previous night flooded back into her mind. Not only that, but she also suffered bouts of morning sickness.

Lizzie could see the worry in her and asked what was wrong, but Mary only shook her head and stroked the girl's face sorrowfully. Lizzie assumed Mary was thinking of her family in Ireland and the misery of being trapped here, working as a prostitute, an unfortunate. The girl could do nothing to help and had to hurry off to her work, so she took her shawl and wrapped it around her, kissed Mary on the cheek, and left her there, promising to return later that day. Mary watched her go.

She could not hide away in her room all day, she had to go out. Even so, she delayed leaving her room as long as she could, and it was almost midday when she ventured outside. There were lots of people around, and she looked anxiously amongst them all, afraid of seeing a passing policeman and nervous of seeing the very one who had been sent crashing to the ground by Hutchinson. The world was closing in on her. Despite her resolve not to, she found herself drawn to Ma Ringer's, the pub at the end of the street. She had a beer there to steady her and almost immediately bumped into her new friend, Maria Harvey.

'Oh Mary, I've just been to your room looking for you. I wonder, am I able to stay with you for a couple of days? I'm doing a bit of business, and I can't take anyone back to the lodgings I am in. I'm waiting to get a room in The Rents.'

'You are welcome to use it, but it means I will have to be out a lot whilst you are working, and I have been not too well lately.' Mary wanted to help but was still afraid to be away from home.

'I'll make sure there is something in it for you, Mary, and we can have some food together too.' Maria Harvey had set her mind on using Mary's room.

'Yes, well, let's go and get some breakfast now over at the market and go back to my place for a sleep if we are both working tonight. It's a miserable day to be out anyway.' Mary was again thinking of getting out of sight.

'Better than that, Mary, I have acquired some clothes you might want to take to the pawn shop. You are welcome to keep anything you can get. I don't want anyone to see me going down there in case they put two and two together. I don't want to be pinched for stealing from the laundry.' Maria had managed to steal clothing from one of the laundries.

The two women left, arm in arm, and Maria noticed how jumpy her friend seemed to be.

'Are you in trouble, Mary? You are jumping at shadows,' she asked.

'Oh, it's like I said, I've not been well just lately. Joe has not been working; he's been a bit of a nuisance and has gone at last, but he has left me with the rent to pay.' She was not going to tell anyone about the Detective Constable who would be out looking for her, nor about Hutchinson's part in it. She must avoid Hutchinson, too. He would be afraid she would give him away if she were taken, so he would be threatening towards her now. She did not want to give him any excuse to turn on her.'

That evening, the two women went out together to the Britannia pub. Maria had left more clothes for Mary to dispose of, so there was money to be made the following day.

Part One: The Nightmare Begins

In the pub, they drank little, for Mary's anxiety was such that she could not settle. She was afraid of what might come out of the darkness of the streets, yet the darkness afforded her the greatest anonymity. She feared the police, the High Rip gangs, Hutchinson and, like everyone else, had a dread of the *Ripper*. The two returned briefly to number 13 as it was too cold and too early to go out searching for trade.

Mary was determined to take no one back to her room but to work the alleyways. She would let Maria use the room and receive some reward for that. She reckoned she would make more money that way.

Back in the room, sitting around the small fire with a single candle in a bottle burning on the table, they were interrupted by Lizzie, who was unhappy at seeing another woman sitting in the room. She stayed only a short while, Mary trying to tell her that she would be out for the next few nights, working. She really did not want Lizzie mixed up in any of this.

At about ten in the evening, the two women left again, heading in slightly different directions. Within an hour, Maria Harvey was back in the room, entertaining a sailor she had met in the pub. He did not stay long, soon being replaced by another and then another. Twice, Mary returned to the room but, seeing the agreed signal of a candle burning, wandered away again into the cold night. She stuck hard by Spitalfields, not daring to go near Mile End.

Mary needed to keep warm. She had no sight of Hutchinson, who was probably keeping well out of the way and had heard nothing about a policeman being attacked. The less she heard, the more anxious she became. She went back to the Horn of Plenty, where she saw Joe with a drinking friend of theirs. Maurice Lewis was a tailor who lived nearby. Maurice had his wife with him. The woman was always pleasant enough, but Mary knew she didn't like mixing with unfortunates.

Mary joined them for a drink and Joe was affectionate to her but asked her quietly if she was still on the streets. She looked at him with contempt; how could he think she wouldn't be? She did not stay long, leaving them, saying she was going home to bed.

Joe knew she would not be going home. Joe said he would call round the next evening and bring her something towards the rent. She headed down towards Leman Street where, despite it being the location of the local police station, she felt reasonably certain of herself.

She knew all the policemen from Leman Street and the one who had accosted her was not from there. If anything, he would be from Whitechapel, and she was avoiding that area. If he were searching for her when on duty, he would be searching around Mile End, where he had picked her up that night. Once he was off duty, he could look anywhere and that would be when she was most at risk of being found.

It was nearly 4 in the morning when she returned to find the candle was out. She entered the room cautiously and by the glow of the coals in the fireplace, she could see Maria alone on the bed, sleeping. Mary took off her shawl and a bonnet she had been wearing, she did not often bother to wear one as she liked to show off her long hair but had only done so because the rain was unrelenting. She undressed to her petticoat and washed her hands and face in the cold water in the basin. She added some warm water from the kettle and washed herself more intimately, drying herself on a piece of rough hessian sacking, which she kept on a rail by the fire. She folded her clothes as normal, then climbed onto the bed beside the sleeping Maria. She pulled the bedclothes around them both and put her arm around the woman both on their left sides, close together for warmth. She felt safer having someone with her.

Maria spent only two nights with Mary, as she found a room nearby. Folded into a corner of the room, she had left a small pile of clothing stolen from the laundry for Mary to sell or pawn for her and that was it.

As soon as she knew Maria had moved out, young Lizzie was back visiting. She would have stayed as long as she was allowed, but that night, she was told again that Mary would be working and that Mary or Maria, or any of a number of women now, might be using the room right through the early hours of the morning. Lizzie looked glum at this news. She was sitting by the fire drinking tea with Mary when Joe arrived. He obviously had hoped to find Mary alone and was cool when speaking to Lizzie whom he assumed was another unfortunate using the room for bringing back men.

Lizzie felt uncomfortable with him around and left soon afterwards. At the corner of the yard, where it met Dorset Street, she bumped into Maria Harvey and told her that Joe was with Mary. On hearing that, Maria thought better of her visit and went away. Lizzie

Part One: The Nightmare Begins

was pleased that Mrs. Harvey was not going to be with Mary. As it was, Joe did not stay long. As good as his word he gave Mary some money for the rent and told her that he would soon have his job back and he would take care of her.

As soon as he had gone, she locked the door behind him and added the coins he had given her to her treasure chest under the floorboards. She looked resentfully at the box McCarthy had left and shook it. There was quite a lot of money in there and she dared not touch it. He would be around to collect it the next day. She hoped there was enough to keep him satisfied for a while longer yet.

She went out and left the door unlocked. The usual signal applied, but she intended to use the place herself that night as it was getting just too cold and wet to work outside. On Commercial Street, she met with Lizzie Foster and another woman she knew only as Julia. Julia was much older than Foster, who herself was middle-aged. The three went across the road to the Ten Bells, where they started a night of drinking. Mary found that she could not face life anymore without a lot of drink inside her. It calmed both her distaste for the work and the ever-increasing fear of being taken by the forces of the law, or what was more likely, by the forces of evil.

The three spoke of the *Ripper* and what he was doing to women like themselves: carving them open, stealing their organs and eating them. Julia thought he was a ghost, an evil spirit; Lizzie Foster said he was a mad Jew.

Gradually, they became so hysterical with a fear they could not sustain that they began laughing about him. Mary proposed that he was *Jill the Ripper*, the abortionist, and they all laughed. That led Julia to suggest it was either Sergeant Thick or Inspector Abberline, which led them into even more shrieks of mirth.

Eventually, Julia said she had to go on the beat to earn some money to redeem some shoes from the pawnbroker and asked Mary if she had the room free. Mary told her of the arrangement – light the candle so no one else would come in and leave some money or something of value, even if she stole it from her customer. Julia nodded in agreement and set off towards Whitechapel High Street. Mary and her new best friend decided to go to the Britannia pub and see who might be there. The weather had changed for the worse again and it was such a cold and damp night; neither wanted to be walking too far. They would be working close to home.

As it was, Mary did not have to wander very far that evening. She left the Britannia at about eleven o'clock, feeling more drunk than sober. The drink gave her bravado and gaiety whilst all the time underneath, she was crying out for someone to help her. A few minutes along Commercial Street, someone did exactly that.

A middle-aged man followed her out of the pub and called to her. He had a European accent and spoke English in a broken, un-tutored way. He was blunt.

'How much, lady?' he asked.

She turned and looked at him. He was clean enough, not a sailor, but he didn't appear to be dressed like the immigrant Polish and Russian Jews she recognised from the area.

'Well, that depends on what you want, deary. If you want to step over into Itch Park or around the back here, I would want sixpence for my trouble. But, if you want to have a good time and come back to my place, well, then you will have to be a little more generous.'

'I like you,' he smiled, 'I will buy some beer from the public house here and we go back to your place. I wish I could spend the night with you, but no, I must not. In the early hours, I need to meet people who wait for me on the corner by this pub and do business away from here. So come, let us not waste time.'

He seemed an odd sort of customer. He knew the form alright, buying a pale of beer, going back to her room, not risking staying all night in case he was robbed. He had even let her know he had friends waiting for him. He was careful. Still, it suited her to get him out of the way quickly and get back to work.

So, she went with him to collect the beer and took him on the short walk down Dorset Street to her room. She drank most of the beer, he indulged himself with her and being reasonably pleased with events, was happy about the shilling he had paid the bright young lady and left. He was a perfect customer for her. After he had gone, feeling rather drunk, she put his shilling into her collection and nothing into the box. The drink was getting to her, and she began singing loudly to herself. She sang the Irish songs her mother had taught her. She was becoming a little reckless. She straightened her clothing, still singing, she doused the candle flame in case some other woman saw the signal and rent came her way and set off again.

In the back of her mind was the fear of being spotted by the police, yet somehow, the fear of being taken by the *Ripper* no longer worried her. She had already decided that her life was so dreadful she would rather be dead anyway. The cold night air cured her of the singing. It was long past midnight.

Mary Cox, a neighbour from across the yard, kept an eye open for the candle in Kelly's room. Cox also worked the streets but had to keep returning to her own room to get warm. She couldn't take anyone back there because of her 'old man' and wondered if she dared risk taking someone into Mary Kelly's without her old man knowing about it. She was so cold and needed somewhere to go. It was probably one o'clock in the morning when Cox went back out, the light still burning in Kelly's room. She could hear her singing those sad Irish songs again, waiting to go out herself, no doubt.

***

A youngish man, perhaps about 30 years of age, well-dressed, clean and well-mannered, approached her. He appeared to be a little uncertain of himself and begged her pardon, but he had seen her in the pub with other ladies earlier and wondered if he might spend a little time with her.

Mary Kelly was charmed. She placed her hand on his chest and smiled at him. He was too well-spoken to be from around this area of town. She guessed he was unmarried and, in all likelihood, was a Jew.

He was so charming and gentle in appearance that it was a relief to be accosted by such a man. It must have been nearly two o'clock in the morning by then, so there was no doubting his purpose.

'Tell you what, my fine gentleman, take me back into the Britannia and buy a pale of beer. Then it's just a short walk round to my place where we can be comfortable.'

'Of course, and if there is anything else I should purchase to make ourselves comfortable for an hour or so, please do say. It feels awfully cold tonight after all the warm days we have been having.'

'Well, you know a girl like me is not any old common tart. I expect you to treat me properly and give a little gift, like a shilling?' She spoke to him gently, coaxing him.

'I was thinking of a little gift somewhat smaller than that, Miss. What would you say to sixpence?' He was young and not from the area, but he seemed to know the going rate for a woman in Spitalfields was probably about four pence, so by suggesting six, he was being generous.

'I say we should not be haggling in the street on a cold night like this. Come on, let us buy the beer and go and get nice and cosy. I haven't seen you around here before.'

'No, I don't live here. I am doing some work for my uncle, who has a clothing business near Brick Lane. I told him I would be back tomorrow as I was seeing friends and going to a Music Hall. He did not approve.' The man was smiling at her with a friendly, even kindly smile.

'You been with a lady like me before, my boy?'

'I'm afraid so. I admit I have taken the opportunity each time I have been down here near the market, but not with any as beautiful as you. They have been older, I think, and not nearly as nice as you are. I couldn't believe my eyes when I saw you amongst those other women. I mean, you really are quite remarkable, you know.' He was completely genuine in his assessment of her, flattering her.

'Well, my boy, a lady likes to be appreciated. Yes, I am a cut above what you've been used to - it's why it's a shilling.' She smiled happily back at him. 'Now come on, it is freezing out here.'

As they walked back towards the pub, she saw Hutchinson approaching, taking in every detail about the young man. She knew what this was about.

Hutchinson would wait for the man to leave her place, follow him and then roll him. He would cosh him and steal everything of value the young man had.

She wondered if she could let that happen. There was something about this one she liked. She put her arm through his, protectively. Hutchinson studied them both carefully and skilfully. He weighed up what he could take from the man and how much effort it might take to knock him down. He smiled to himself. Kelly would have him drunk, befuddle his head with her services and send him out unprepared for what would greet him.

He followed them, just out of earshot and watched as they stopped at the corner of Miller's Court, where the man kissed her.

'Good,' thought Hutchinson, 'This should not take long. She doesn't normally keep them more than 20 minutes if they are that needy; any longer than that and he is probably staying the night, and I don't see that happening with a toff like him. Easy pickings, George old boy.' He took a position in the darkness at the end of the courtyard.

CHAPTER TWENTY-SIX

A TWIST OF FATE

Hutchinson was correct in his assessment of the young man with Kelly. Once in the room with her, watching her remove her outer garments, he was overcome with passion and happy to pay his shilling to get what he wanted. Five minutes later, he lay on his back panting, with Mary smiling beside him.

'I think someone was very much in need of that trip to paradise. If you want a return trip, it will still be another shilling, though.' She kissed him on the cheek.

He looked at her, her long blond hair spread on the uncovered pillow.

'Well, you are a very attractive and commodious young woman, and I thank you. Perhaps when I am back here next month we might enjoy this arrangement again? I think I ought to make myself a little presentable and leave you to your leisure now.' He had achieved what he had paid for and for the first time in several encounters with unfortunates, he had lain with a young and an almost cultured woman. He knew he would keep thinking of her, but he had to get home, ready for an early start.

She watched him get up from the bed and rearrange his clothing. She poured some water from the jug into the basin. 'Come, wash yourself and don't be in such a hurry. We still have the beer.'

'Thank you, but you have it. I have had enough.'

'Wait'. Her command was serious. 'I saw a man follow us along the street. He will still be there. I think he may mean you some harm, so just wait a while.'

He was alarmed. 'Oh my God. I've heard of this sort of thing. Tell me you have nothing to do with this!'

In his alarm, he looked even more youthful, and certainly no match for a brute like Hutchinson.

'Of course not,' she reassured him. 'It's just that I have learned to keep my eyes open and my wits about me. I know how these robbers work. How long have we been in here, would you say?' her tone was serious and filled him with trust.

Nevertheless, the man was worried, confused, 'I don't know.' He looked at his watch, 'about twenty minutes at most.'

'Right, he won't stand out there more than half an hour. By then, he will assume you are spending the night with me so I will blow out the candle and that will convince him we are sleeping together for the remainder of the night. I'll check in ten minutes, but he will be gone.' She was so certain, so protective of him, that he felt she was the most wonderful woman he had ever met, as well as the most beautiful.

He looked at her. He saw her and the life she led for the first time and pity and shame flooded his emotions. It would not take much for his pity and gratitude to become confused with love. 'Thank you. I don't even know your name, your real name that is.'

'It's Mary'. She did not ask for his name.

As they sat together on the bed, in the glow of the fire which supplemented the candlelight, he saw a tired, troubled, but beautiful young woman. Her blue eyes looked straight into his and he felt, for the first time in his life, the self-loathing for indulging in his weakness for women being displaced by new feelings he didn't understand.

There was something about this young woman. She was familiar and easy with him. She was not coarse and lowly like the others.

Of course, he reasoned, she was with him only for his money and at first, he had wanted only a physical need to be fulfilled by her, but was that any different to the arranged marriage awaiting him, he asked himself?

Part One: The Nightmare Begins

Now, new feelings were bursting to the fore. He was shocked at what he had started to feel for this woman, and he wanted to see her again.

He *must* see her again.

He felt ambushed by a new emotion, but he would not name it, not yet, even though he could. He was already forming a fantasy of taking her away from this life. He could set her up in a room somewhere to be his mistress, but in his deeper self, he knew it could not be so.

Ordinary young men like him, making their way in the world, could not afford mistresses. He tried to think of something to say to her, but his courage failed him. Her eyes looking into his told him she had experienced his hopelessness many times, in the tired, doomed dreams of previous lovers. She did not want to give him hope of a romantic relationship with her.

From experience, Mary knew his feelings would deepen for a while but not last. He would recover himself and see her for the wanton, degraded woman she thought herself to be.

When he did, he would resent her and hate her; she didn't want that. She, in turn, thought of him as only another customer, albeit one of her more pleasant ones. She expected nothing from him and would be surprised if she ever saw him again. And so they sat and waited, Mary dousing the candle. He put out his hand to hold hers tenderly. She let him.

Despite herself, she enjoyed this unexpected moment of tenderness though she had no deep feeling for the young man; gentleness always caught her unprepared. Because it felt the right thing to do, she sang quietly to him to pass the time and to calm him and in listening to her, his heart was lost.

They waited until Mary at last suggested it should be safe for him to leave. They heard people coming and going, probably Mary Cox, for one, going home to get warm before going out again. The man pulled his coat about him and fixed his hat. She could see he was nervous and, in a moment of tenderness, decided she might as well go out with him. She was confident Hutchinson would have gone, cursing his luck, but she would make sure.

After her guest was on his way, she thought she might as well try nearer the docks to see if there was any passing trade. Her guest took comfort from her leaving with him. She shut the door very quietly and did not lock it: there was still a chance another woman would want to use her room and would pay her a small fee. She still had to make every penny she could. At the entrance of Miller's Court, there was no sign of Hutchinson.

'Where do you want to try, my dear? Is it back to Commercial Street or somewhere else?' she asked him.

'I need to be at my lodgings near Bishopsgate tonight. Where should I best go, do you think?' He trusted her completely.

'Come on, we can turn right here, then go through the alleys and come out by the railway station. You are only a step from Bishopsgate there, but the alleyways can be risky, so I will walk with you to the station and leave you there. You should be safe with me.' She smiled at him, feeling good about herself.

She put her arm through his, and the two huddled together against the cold night air of early November.

Opposite Liverpool Street Station, she let him go. He turned to her and did not know what to say, so seeing his discomfort, she kissed him on the cheek one last time and turned towards Houndsditch.

He raised his hat to her and mumbled his gratitude; she did not hear him and did not look back. He walked on down Bishopsgate, in love with a pretty, blue-eyed, blond unfortunate named Mary. He knew that even if he never found her again, he would not forget her. Throughout the years of his pending loveless marriage, he would think of her whenever he needed to comfort himself with the knowledge that once, as a young man, he had known love. He would never allow himself to face the reality she knew so well, that any man could have her for just a few pennies.

Mary hugged herself against the cold, felt a little unsteady from too much drink and were it not for what was about to happen, would never have thought of him or that night ever again.

She had decided to go closer to the Mile End Road, a risk if the rogue policeman was searching for her, she knew, but she wanted business and there would be sailors there from the cattle boats.

As so often had been the case, she was found by several drover sailors from the German ships. Typically, they paid her a few pennies, taking her into an alleyway or doorway, up against a wall or under a stairway; she no longer cared.

As she meandered her way back towards Spitalfields, she thought she was being followed. Her head was still muzzy from drink, but she was sure someone was watching her, waiting for her to be isolated somewhere. She decided that any more work would be a risk, so she walked as steadily as she could along the main roads.

Near Angel Alley, she saw him under a streetlight, a policeman in uniform, not a detective, but a police constable: the same police constable Hutchinson had coshed.

Before he could see her, she fled through the alley and ran all the way to Flower and Dean. Her mind was spinning, she was panting, her heart thumping.

Hiding in a doorway, she looked all around. She listened for every sound, but there was no sign that she was being followed. Whoever had been watching her might have been frightened away by the policeman, whilst the officer himself had not seen her. It was her lucky night. If she could only get home now and sleep away the morning in her usual way, she would be alright for at least another few days.

She made her way to the moon shadow of the great Church of All Saints, then crossed the road to the stinking stretch of buildings along Dorset Street. She saw no one. It must have been about half past four in the morning by then. She walked as quietly as she could into Miller's Court and went into her small room, locking the door behind her. She couldn't light the candle because it had burned right down: someone must have used the room over the last couple of hours. The fire, too, was nothing but a few red embers. She was very tired and looked on the mantle for the spare candle she had bought on credit from McCarthy's shop.

All the time, she was aware of a horrible stench that seemed to be invading the room. It was worse than the usual smell of rot and sewage that lingered about the street. She found a spill in the hearth and, lit her spare candle and looked behind her.

'Oh murder, murder,' she shouted out and pushed herself against the wall as far as she could go, her hand to her mouth. Her legs gave way, and she dropped to the floor as she stared in horror at what lay before her on the bed – the butchered remains of a woman.

The Abandoned: *Victims of Jack the Ripper*

Part One: The Nightmare Begins

CHAPTER TWENTY-SEVEN

ESCAPE

Mary did not know how long she sat trembling on the floor. She grew cold and tried to stir herself. The horror that lay on her bed was surrounded by a pool of drying blood on the floor.

Mary had stepped into it; it soaked into her skirt and underskirt. What was even worse was some of the gore had also stuck to her clothing. She tried to make sense of the scene and knew she had stumbled across a victim of the *Ripper*, a victim who could have been her.

At the foot of the bed, on a small chair, the victim had left her outer clothing. Shaking with fear and disgust, Mary struggled to her feet and tore away her own stained and despoiled clothes, not screwing them up and placing them in the fireplace as she might have done, but folding them away in a dream of habit. She was not thinking of what she was doing, she simply needed to rid herself of the death splashed onto her clothes. She had dropped her bonnet into the gore too, and she did throw that onto the fire, having to stagger back when the straw and pitch in the hat burst into a fierce flame.

What was she to do? The police would come, she would be arrested for non-payment of her fines, the injured constable would find her and charge her with attempting to kill him, Jack McCarthy would be furious, and even should she escape prison, he would never let her set foot in one of his rooms again.

She was in turmoil. Next to her, piled on the floor were the clothes Mary Harvey had stolen and left for her to sell. She could not have them found there so added them to the fire.

Slowly, a manic sense of what she must do was coming to her. She must remove any evidence that might incriminate her. She could not do anything about the body. How would she explain what that woman was doing in her room? Her sub-letting would be out, and McCarthy would want his money. She had to run away. She felt she was standing in the waiting room to hell.

There was no avoiding it, Mary had to get the pay-box from under the bed. She used her broom to locate it and pull it towards her. It was intact but had a layer of filth over it. She had no means of breaking it open to steal its contents, the money she had worked for, so she tipped the box to one side, hearing the coins shift over. Then she placed the empty side in the corner of the fire: she would weaken the wall of the box or even burn it through and hope the coins did not melt. She would have to keep an eye on it.

Then she lifted her loose floorboard and scrabbled around for her savings, tying the coins in the red handkerchief her last decent client had given to her.

Where was that young man now? Would he have helped her?

The heat from the fire made the stench worse, but she couldn't go yet. She took off the remainder of her clothing and as before and out of habit, folded them onto the chair at the bottom of the bed. She picked up the victim's clothes which were clean and serviceable, she must have undressed for her killer and dressed herself in the dead woman's clothes. She was alternately hot then cold as the trauma before her took hold of her. She waited and waited for the box to burn. She pulled it from the fire and cracked it open on the floor. The money poured out, too hot to touch, but in good condition. She let it cool then added it to her parcel. She now had more money than she had seen in several years.

Outside was a grey light. It was time to go, but the shock was taking hold of her. She had been in that awful room for over three hours, and nothing seemed real to her.

Clutching her few belongings, Mary left the room and stepped into the courtyard, only to have to re-enter to check that she had left nothing.

Part One: The Nightmare Begins

Then again, she struggled outside in her unfamiliar clothing, not daring to look at the hacked-about corpse and locked the door behind her. She vaguely heard a group of men in the yard playing pitch and toss: everything was so unreal. She managed to take a few steps when the cold, fresh air hit her, and she threw up.

Engaged as he was in his game, Maurice Lewis, her occasional drinking partner from nights in the Britannia pub, saw her in the corner of his eye, noticing she had left her room, returned almost immediately and then left again; he didn't take much notice of her at the time. He knew it to be her from her hair as she did not often wear a bonnet and, indeed, had no bonnet that morning.

Mrs. Caroline Maxwell, the wife of a nearby lodging house deputy, also saw Mary and noticed straight away that she was looking dreadfully pale and unwell, leaning against the wall near to where she had just vomited. Mrs. Maxwell knew Mary by sight though they were not friends as such, but she had never seen her in such a state. Her clothing seemed wrong; she did not normally dress that way; she was usually smarter, cleaner.

'Mary, my love, what brings you up so early? Are you unwell? You look like you have seen a ghost,' she said to the stumbling woman.

Mary recovered herself as best she could. She had hoped she would not be seen by anyone who knew her. 'Oh, Carrie, I do feel so bad. I have the horrors of drink upon me. I've had a glass of beer, and I've brought it up again,' she said in reply and walked as best she could past the woman.

Suddenly, unexpectedly, Mary started to laugh, then cry, then both laugh and cry at the same time as she walked in a staggering fashion down Dorset Street. Any capacity to think clearly had now left her.

Mrs. Maxwell watched her go and thought the whole scene very strange indeed, so unusual that it stuck in her mind. She would think the whole episode even more confusing when she heard the news which broke out later that morning.

Meanwhile, Mrs. Maxwell went on her errand to buy her husband's breakfast. On the way back she saw Mary again, this time outside the Britannia public house. She thought Mary might have gone in there briefly but could then have been leaving for elsewhere.

'Such lovely hair, no wonder she does not wear a bonnet,' she thought.

Mary had been gone from the grisly room for a couple of hours when Indian Harry turned up to collect the rent on behalf of his boss, McCarthy. He banged on the door but had no response. He tried again, knowing that Kelly had been instructed to be there, but still, there was no response. He tried to see through the window though the curtains were drawn across.

Not wanting to give up, he noticed that one of the panes of glass was broken and the space filled with rags. He pushed the rags out so enabling him to pull the curtain aside a little and see into the room.

What he saw, in the dimness, was a corpse lying on the bed, a bloody and mutilated body. He pulled away and then ran to the shop where his boss was waiting for the rent and other debts. The sight of him as he entered the shop convinced McCarthy that some tragedy had struck.

'What is it, Harry? What has happened?' he already feared the worst. Only what he feared was not nearly as terrible as what he was about to discover. Harry could hardly manage to speak.

'She is dead, boss. I looked through the window and could see a sight I never want to witness again. She is chopped up on the bed!'

'Hold hard there, Harry, I'll come and look.' He had never seen his strong-arm man shake like this.

The two men walked the short distance to 13 Miller's Court. Harry lifted aside the curtain as before and McCarthy looked in.

Like Indian Harry, he was shaken by the sight, but he regained control quickly. He noticed that the yard was empty of people even though the water pump was close by number 13. People often disappeared when he or Harry turned up. It was strangely quiet. He was shocked but had to act.

'Harry, this is what I want you to do. Get down to the police station and tell them that he has struck again. Tell them we have a *Ripper* murder. Can you do that, Harry?'

The former soldier immediately sprang into action. He responded well to instructions and orders.

'Right, boss, I'll get down there. Five minutes,' and he set off.

McCarthy looked around. He was a strong-minded man, even though he had never seen anything like this scene before. He looked around once more to make sure no-one was watching. Before the police arrived, he had to get in there and get his box with the money.

From his pocket, he took a bunch of spare keys, selected one and let himself into the room. He hardly dared to look around and the smell nearly made him wretch. He squatted to look under the bed where he knew the box was kept, but it was gone.

'So,' he muttered to himself, 'The *Ripper* took my money too.'

It was what he had feared. The women were usually robbed and this time it was *his* money that had been taken. Then he saw the broken, charred box by the fireplace. He picked it up and put it under his arm.

'The devil even broke into it here rather than risk drawing attention to himself,' he thought.

He left the room and locked the door. He had been inside less than a minute and had not looked at the corpse once. He walked as fast as he could to his shop and dropped the remains of the box and the padlock into an old barrel, then he ran to the police station to join Harry.

When he got there, Indian Harry had already roused duty Inspector Beck and Detective Constable Dew. It was eleven o'clock on a cold November morning. He added to Harry's description of the discovery briefly, then returned with the police officers to Miller's Court, where the stream of contradictions, confusion and panic started its course, swelling by the end of the day to a flood of press hysteria and police bafflement.

The police officers looked through the window and saw the tableau the others had witnessed. There was no doubt this was a *Ripper* murder.

Inspector Beck was now in difficulty. He had a standing order that no officer was to enter any scene of crime associated with the *Ripper* until Sir Charles Warren, the Commissioner, was present. He did not know that Warren had resigned the previous evening, effective from that very day. He also had to wait for the bloodhounds Sir Charles had commissioned, in anticipation of further murders, to be brought to the scene.

Meanwhile, the presence of police attracted attention, a small crowd gathered; word spread that the *Ripper* had struck again. It would be only half an hour or so until the press arrived, interfering with the investigation, taking witnesses to the pubs to elicit information and, no doubt, turning their scorn on the police. Inspector Abberline had been sent for. Beck made a note of what he could, knowing that his notes would be scrutinised by Inspector Reid. Word came to him that Superintendent Arnold was on his way.

Unaware of the drama unfolding in the place where he had been playing pitch and toss, Maurice Lewis had gone to the Horn of Plenty pub with his friends. He was drinking, laughing and joking with them and saw Mary Kelly out and about, for the second time that morning. She was with a couple of other women, but he did not recognise them, so she went away in a corner. He thought nothing of it at the time.

He only noticed her because she seemed to be laughing unusually loudly and wildly for her. When he next glanced in her direction, she and her companions had gone. There would have been little point in him going home then, even if he had wanted to, because from mid-day, the police had sealed off Miller's Court and were questioning everyone in Dorset Street.

He was still in the pub an hour later when the first of the press corps arrived. One of the reporters looked around the bar and called out 'Anyone here know who lived at 13 Miller's Court?'

'Yes', said Lewis, 'I live in Miller's Court and number 13 is occupied by young Mary Kelly and her man, Dan or Joe something. Why are you asking?'

The reporter took stock of him, weighing him up to see if he might be useful. 'Sorry, old man, it looks like *Jack the Ripper* paid a visit there last night and your neighbour Mary Kelly is his latest victim. The police have just taken her man over there to formally identify what is left of the body.'

'No, it can't be,' exclaimed Lewis, 'it's not possible.'

'Sorry, old man. Was she a friend of yours?' The reporter feigned sincerity.

'No, you don't get my meaning,' gasped out Lewis. 'It can't have been Mary Kelly because I saw her here not half an hour since and it was certainly not a ghost either!'

Now it was the turn of the reporter and those around him to be taken off guard.

'I think I had better buy you a drink, sir, just whilst we have a bit of an interview for the papers.' The reporter could smell a story.

Back in Miller's Court, Superintendent Arnold had arrived. He ensured the press were cleared out from the yard and from much of Dorset Street. It was now early in the afternoon, and he had been informed that the Commissioner would not be coming, but not why that was so. He rightly assumed that if the Commissioner was not attending, the dogs would not either and anyway, it was probably far

Part One: The Nightmare Begins

too late after the event for them to pick up a trail. He turned to his gathered officers.

'Right, enough of this. Get the landlord to open the door.'

Jack McCarthy was summoned from his shop. He arrived, apparently willing to do anything asked of him.

'Unlock the door, Mr. McCarthy, and then step to one side if you please.'

'I can't do that, I'm afraid, I don't keep spare keys for the rooms in case the tenants accuse me of going in whilst they are away and stealing from them.' McCarthy lied fluently but unconvincingly.

Arnold looked at the man with measured disbelief. 'Then open it some other way,' ordered the exasperated officer.

McCarthy went back to his shop and returned with tools which enabled him to force the lock. The door splintered open and Superintendent Arnold went in to witness the worst crime he would ever experience.

There was no doubting what had happened or that the body on the bed was long dead. He turned to his sergeant and, in almost a whisper, said, 'Bring Mr. Barnett here so he might formally identify the victim and have a couple of officers stand near him in case he should faint at what he sees. Warn him that it will be a distressing sight.'

Joe Barnett, who loved Mary and who had been waiting out on the street for over an hour, shaking with anxiety, was brought forward between a uniformed constable and a Detective. The Superintendent asked him to look at the face of the deceased and state whether or not it was Mary Kelly. He knew this would be a grim and crushing ordeal for the man. Barnett was already trembling before he had even entered the room, his former home. He was directed to look at the face of the corpse.

All he saw was disfigurement; the face had been slashed and hacked about, and the hair was matted. From the blooded and wounded head, two open, glassy blue eyes stared without seeing. He could not help but take in the whole scene, his eyes fixing on the neatly folded set of clothes on the chair at the foot of the bed. She had always been so clean, so neat. Her boots were in front of the fireplace.

'Oh mercy, oh my God,' was what he uttered when he looked upon the work of the *Ripper*.

'Is that to the best of your knowledge, Mary Kelly?' asked the Superintendent.

Barnett saw only the staring blue eyes, nothing else was recognisable.

'Yes,' he said and was led from the room into the darkening afternoon. He leaned against the wall, an officer supporting him, his head back against the brickwork stained black by the smoke of the city. He stared up beyond the buildings at the clearing November sky.

Apart from giving evidence for the inquest and in those first few days when he was cornered and plied with drink by the press, he never spoke again for all his life of what he had seen in that room.

He moved away from Spitalfields, found work, and eventually married, but never again spoke of his Mary.

That night, there was a strange November sunset so all over London, it seemed as if the sky was on fire.

CHAPTER TWENTY-EIGHT

WHO WAS THE VICTIM?

It was on the following Tuesday, the 13th of November, that Superintendent Arnold hosted an informal meeting in his office. It was the usual lead detectives, Abberline and Reid, as well as Inspector Nairn, who had represented the police at the inquest on Mary Kelly on Monday and Inspector Beck, who had been first on the scene of the killing. The men smoked and the fog of the room matched the fog polluting the world outside. It was not a happy gathering. Rather, the mood was sombre, if not a little depressed. Arnold offered coffee to his guests and one or two joined him in that.

'Well, gentlemen, what do we have to say about the inquest? Inspector Nairn, you were the non-participatory representative, so you make a start.' Arnold was trying to be enthusiastic, but it felt flat and forced, which indeed it was.

'Straight to the point then, it was a farce from start to finish.' He looked to his colleagues who had been present for agreement. Reid chipped in.

'I was not there, of course, but I read in this morning's Daily Telegraph that the event started with a row between the coroner and the jury. Is that correct, Inspector Nairn?'

Nairn responded to the question.

'Yes, the whole event was almost derailed in the first five minutes. It was the usual dispute about where jurisdiction for the inquest should reside. The coroner, our rather pompous Dr Macdonald, was challenged by the jury, who obviously did not want to be there. One of them pointed out that the inquest was being held in Shoreditch when the victim had lived in and been murdered in Spitalfields, so there was no jurisdiction. Macdonald was not going to have that; he was not about to miss out on his part in the sorry story of *Jack the Ripper*, no by Jove. He pointed out that as the body had been removed to the morgue in Shoreditch, and as he held the position of coroner for North-East Middlesex, which included both Shoreditch and Spitalfields, it was legally constituted. The jury again challenged his ruling by not disputing *his* right to be coroner but claiming *they* had no duty as Shoreditch or Whitechapel people to hear a Spitalfields inquest. Any inquest they were summoned to should be in Whitechapel only and presided over by their local Borough of Whitechapel coroner. Dr Macdonald overruled everyone and threatened to have anyone who further questioned his authority thrown in the slammer, presumably by me.' The company smiled at his retelling of the events, but no one was feeling particularly cheerful.

'Once he had the reluctant jury in harness, he sent them off with Fred Abberline to visit the victim, greatly cleaned-up, who lay next door in the morgue and then visit Miller's Court, a trip which set off the argument over responsibility for the inquest all over again. Perhaps Fred can pick it up from there.' All attention switched to Abberline.

'Well, not much to say about the little trip out. The body had been carefully covered as far as possible and cleaned, but no one really wanted to look. The trip out to Dorset Street was far from welcomed by the group and they argued about it all the way there and back again. I suppose it set the scene for them, but it carried the case no further.' He looked at Arnold to see how he wanted to proceed. Arnold himself then spoke.

'Well, I found the evidence disturbing in two regards. First, I found only one witness to be compelling, and that was the one piece of evidence I did not wish to hear. Secondly, the medical report was the most blatant attempt at obfuscation I have ever read from the medical profession. I'll expand on my views and perhaps you each might comment.'

Part One: The Nightmare Begins

'The various witnesses we paraded before the court mostly told the same story: Kelly was a prostitute who was seen out and about with several different men that evening, or perhaps one man who kept changing his appearance! We know there was a cry in the night, possibly about 4 a.m. We know that her lover, Barnett, pulled himself together long enough to identify what was left of the body as being Mary Kelly. His was the only evidence of identification and it was not questioned. What really stirred me, and the coroner, of course, was the evidence of the Maxwell woman. She was unshakeable in her belief that she saw Kelly twice, both times well after the time she is thought to have been murdered. How was that possible? It was not explained, and we were left to assume that the woman had mixed up the days: I have to say she did not strike me as a woman who would confuse the time and the day. Dr Macdonald was at pains to point out that hers was an 'idiosyncratic viewpoint'. So, having left that situation hanging, we were moved on to the medical autopsy, or rather, we were not because the autopsy was not presented. Instead, we had a medical statement, which I could have pieced together myself from reading the evening newspaper, and although the coroner was unhappy about it, he let it go by as he was not likely to take matters anywhere useful. It seems to me, gentlemen, that the medical profession had avoided airing in public an internal dispute about the time of death. Any comments?'

Abberline stirred again. He was about to say something possibly controversial and before doing so, he adopted his bank manager persona.

'Let us start then with the Maxwell woman. She was spoken with by several of us and I agree that her view was forcefully put. I accept that she honestly believes what she said but let us assume her to be mistaken with the day. Now, and it stays in this room, she was not the only person to claim to have seen Mary Kelly alive well after any approximate time of the killing, so maybe our assumption that she is mistaken is itself mistaken. The papers have carried an interview with a Maurice Lewis, who also supports Mrs. Maxwell's story, and he knew her better than did Mrs. Maxwell. Inspector Reid and I have been through lots of statements and these two stand out, but they were not the only sightings. Our men found many others who 'thought' they saw Mary Kelly throughout the whole of the afternoon that the body lay in that wretched place. We have collated the description, and I am leaning toward the opinion that if Maxwell and

Lewis are both wrong, it is because someone who looked like Kelly was around that day. That does not explain away the alleged conversation Maxwell might have had, of course. Nevertheless, what every witness said was that the woman was not dressed as Kelly usually did, so I think it might well be mistaken identity.' At that point, Inspector Reid spoke.

'The mistaken day, the explanation for Mrs. Maxwell's evidence of a conversation with Kelly seems logical. The parallel recollections of Lewis are a little troubling, but as the press got to him first, we do not know if the idea was planted in him by those unscrupulous people. He was not called to the inquest to give evidence because of that association. However, although everyone noted the clothing on the woman thought to be Kelly seemed unfamiliar, I looked at other common factors in the description each gave of the woman they claimed to be Kelly. I did this first by speaking with Detective Constable Walter Dew, who knew Kelly and has a detective's eye for detail. He said that young men will flourish in this profession, and I asked him to describe Kelly. He said that unlike every other unfortunate in the area, Kelly almost never wore a bonnet. She would show her hair. Maxwell, Lewis and every other potential sighting of the mystery woman points out that she was not wearing a bonnet and that her hair was fair. This does concern me. How far do we stretch a coincidence?'

Abberline replied, 'Maxwell and Lewis, in fact, all the sightings refer to the woman as wearing the wrong clothing and, so it probably was not Kelly. The confusion arises only because the stranger had no bonnet. As everyone spoken to is regarded by the police as unreliable, I do not think we can pursue this. If the body in Kelly's room, with Kelly's blue eyes, with Kelly's neatly folded clothes on her chair as was her custom, and Kelly's boots by the fire is not Kelly, then who was she? No one else has been reported as missing.'

Reid smiled his friendly, doubting smile.

'There have been any number of women reported missing. It happens all the time. Often, they turn up again under a different name. Sometimes, we never hear of them again. Yes, the body was identified as Kelly, but is that evidence any more reliable than the evidence of the many who claim to have seen her alive?'

Arnold then intervened.

'I take some comfort from this, if comfort is the appropriate expression, that there have been no further sightings of the

Part One: The Nightmare Begins

doppelganger. I know that Fred has had our men watching out for her, but as she no longer seems to exist, I think we might assume she never did exist. As far as I know, no further sightings are reported from amongst her regular associates either.'

'Yes,' said Reid, 'that makes a strong case for mistaken identity or confusion over the date. I would have expected her to have shown up by now. For although these people of the lodging houses do disappear and change their names, we hear of them or catch sight of them all the time. For instance, I had an interest in speaking to a prostitute and potential witness called Rose Mylett, but she vanished. Yet reliable sightings of her emerge now and then and I am confident she is still in the area. I will pick her up when it suits me. I do not get the same feeling with the Kelly case. My instinct tells me it is mistaken identity, and it is indeed Kelly who was butchered by the *Ripper*.'

Arnold resumed with, 'What of the medical evidence?' He looked again to Abberline.

'As far as detection is concerned, the evidence most likely to be of help to us would be time of death. As the doctors cannot agree amongst themselves when this might have been, I have taken the claimed hearing of the exclamation of *murder* as being around 4 in the morning as one reference point, but that it is not at all certain; it could have been earlier or later. However, as a police officer, I have always experienced rigor mortis in any corpse to begin in about 3 hours after the death of the victim and peak in about 12 hours after death. According to Dr Bond, who performed the autopsy on Kelly at 2 p.m., rigor mortis had started to set in by then and continued to progress during the examination.' He broke off to pick up a statement and read from it. 'Dr Bond's annexed report of the autopsy states *Rigor Mortis had set in but increased during the process of the examination. From this, it is difficult to say with any degree of certainty the exact time that had elapsed since death.* So, if the autopsy started at 2 p.m. and rigor mortis was already setting into Kelly's body, I am estimating that rigor mortis would probably have peaked between 3 and 4 p.m. Therefore, I believe Kelly probably died sometime after 3 or 3:30 a.m. that morning.'

There was a silence in the room, indicating a lot of thinking. Reid spoke first.

'I see two main implications from the timing Inspector Abberline has outlined. The first, almost too horrible to contemplate, is that Kelly was rendered unconscious by 3:30 in the morning but was not dead when the *Ripper* started his work if indeed he did start at about 3:30. She could have regained consciousness whilst he was slashing her body and cried out at about 4 a.m., as witnesses said. However, I am not sure this is credible as she would surely have lost too much blood to have regained consciousness, and her throat was deeply cut. I believe the *Ripper* cut the throats of his victims to prevent them from calling out. The second possibility is given that in all previous cases, the *Ripper* accomplished his business very quickly, and although this time he was even more savage, he may have satisfied his sadism in a little over half an hour. Now, if that is the case, he may have left the scene before even four o'clock and a second person could have entered, seen the carnage, cried out *murder*, and then run away.'

'Yes,' said Abberline, 'but that does not explain the locked door and the missing key. Why did the *Ripper* take the key? Why did he bother to lock the door at all? The same applies to any hypothetical third party who walked in on the site.'

'Well, all of this leads me back to a worrying thought,' said Reid. 'Could it possibly have been another woman lying on that bed? Did Kelly return to find the body, cry out *murder* in her horror, but then gather up her belongings and flee? She alone could have locked that door, though, as Inspector Abberline says, I can't think why she should do so. I know that Barnett said the key was lost, but it is likely it was only withheld from him, and that Kelly had the key.'

'No,' said Arnold, 'her clothes were found at the scene. She must have been the victim.'

'It is possible she could have changed her clothing, say if she had gore from the body splashed on her when she entered the room. Not likely, but possible,' mused Reid.

'Well then,' said Abberline, 'time will tell. If Kelly turns up, as she surely will if she is alive and in this part of London, we will have an unknown corpse to match our unknown killer.'

'And that brings me to the real problem,' said Arnold. 'We still have no idea who the *Ripper* might be'.

Abberline shook his head in apparent disagreement. 'There is a suspect, as we all know. We choose not to acknowledge it openly because until we are completely sure, perhaps by catching him in the act, his identity would enrage the local population; we would have a war on our hands.'

Part One: The Nightmare Begins

Reid looked doubtful. It was not something he wanted to acknowledge.

Whilst the detectives pondered the latest tragedy of that grisly year, elsewhere in London, another person was on the move. At Paddington station, with a third-class ticket, a young woman boarded the train for the long journey to Fishguard, the harbour town in Pembrokeshire from where the ferry to Ireland sailed. Her knowledge of Welsh might prove useful were she to need lodgings for one or two nights in the little coastal town. She would pass by Carmarthen where, a lifetime ago, she had been a child. She had only one bag with her and, from time to time, felt the butterfly movements inside her where her unborn child innocently rested. She could not say who the father might be, and it did not matter. Mrs. Mary Davies, once Mary Kelly, was going home.

***

In London, the *Ripper* murders stopped, and no one knew why. Reid continued in his belief that no Jew could be responsible, and in doing so, he and others missed the possibility that it was the incarceration in an asylum for the insane by his family of the violent Aaron Kosminski that ended it. Once Kosminski was locked away, the killings stopped. He had lived within the killing fields, a man apparently deranged by a childhood which witnessed the brutality of the pogroms in Poland. He was protected from the Metropolitan police by a disbelieving, frightened immigrant refugee family, most of whom spoke little English until he attempted to murder his own sister with a knife.

Thus, the year of terror passed. Poverty and prostitution continued. The lives of women were even more miserable than the lives of men. As if a traumatised population could not let go of him, a legend that the *Ripper* had escaped the country emerged. He would be free to carry on his wickedness elsewhere.

The Abandoned: *Victims of Jack the Ripper*

PART TWO

PANIC IN NEW YORK

The Abandoned: *Victims of Jack the Ripper*

Part Two: Panic in New York

CHAPTER TWENTY-NINE

NEW YORK CITY - 1891

Two years as a Unionist soldier in the Civil War, then fireman, tough guy, and New York City policeman, Thomas Francis Byrnes rose to be a police captain and the inspector of detectives in a force full of immigrant Irishmen like himself. The spores of famine had slipped into Ireland when he was a child, failing the crops year on year and though his parents did not think so at the time, they were the lucky ones who made it from Dublin to America before starvation could add them to its victims.

Their son grew big and strong, gloried in his physicality, and prospered in the Land of the Free as a man of action. Respected and feared, he had become famous across America as 'The Great Detective'.

This day, in the sunshine of late April, he stood on the Brooklyn Bridge and caught the stench from the docks on the Lower East Side. He was uneasy.

The Lower Manhattan waterfront was no place for decent people. Passenger liners, newly in from Europe, were segregated from the common merchant ships; the wealthy and other non-immigrants were hurried away into the smarter parts of the city. They didn't come here, where the detective stood.

Here, Byrne's police wrestled with every sort of base criminality. The docks brought in itinerant labourers jostling for work, corrupt waterfront gang-masters, merchant seamen seeking drink and loose women, smugglers and gangsters, prostitutes, pimps, pickpockets, and penniless immigrants from Europe via Ellis Island—most with nowhere to go, and all trying to make money any way they could.

The desperate, the feckless and the lonely found their way to the bars and cheap hotels to exploit and be exploited. Landlords offered little other than slum dwellings. Some streets in the city were home to ethnic groups: the Chinese controlled the opium dens crouched in cellars alongside the rising tide of Italians around Mulberry Street, the Italians themselves jostling with the established Irish for gang supremacy. Ethnicity, though, mattered little to Byrnes; he treated all with equal contempt, even the Irish like himself.

Here on the Lower East Side was the worst of it: the most over-crowded slums in the Western world readily absorbed anyone with nothing more to lose. Here, the London landscape of Whitechapel and Spitalfields was transplanted. Perhaps it took a man as ruthless as Byrnes to give at least the appearance of imposing law and order in such a place.

From the bridge, he tried to make out the East River Hotel, which squatted on the corner of Water Street and Catherine Street Slip, right on the docks. He hated the place.

Byrnes preferred working the criminal areas of the West side. He could identify from memory every minor gang leader and petty criminal from amongst the ragged and vicious street criminals there. Mulberry Street, right down to Five Points, was the centre of his operations; slums were as stinking and intense as anywhere in the city, the mirror of the East side, but packed into a tighter area. It was there, not here in the shifting population of the East side, that his thoroughness in getting arrests and convictions had made him famous.

The West side was also where he had his political alliances in Tammany Hall. There, the Irish were organising the local wards to ensure they had political and economic control of everything, and they needed him and his detectives to back them up. Byrnes readily supported them, unconcerned by, or unable to appreciate their corruption as, after all, their patronage made him the most important and celebrated police officer in the city, perhaps in the whole of the United States. But the waterfront, this swamp of broken humanity on the East side, was far less influenced by those who occupied Tammany Hall. Neither did he have reliable sources of information amongst the felons on the East side. Monk Eastman, who ran most things here, as much as crime could be organised in a shifting population, seemed to know nothing of it, neither who had committed it nor why it had been done. This was the trouble with the dockland slums of the East side, it was too easy for offenders to slip ashore from ships and barges and ghost away again. So, not a gang member, according to Eastman, but a lone wolf. Byrnes would need to bully the prostitutes, drunks, and petty criminals who crawled like lice over the fetid streets. They must know something. They always had something to hide.

It worried him that this was a murder like no other he had dealt with, and he had inadvertently put himself under pressure to solve it. His career and reputation now depended on catching the devil who had done this and he knew that the whole world was watching. Given to boasting of his many triumphs, he was now faced with a case so extraordinary, so gruesome, he dared not fail. He must solve it quickly and before panic hit the streets. He turned it over in his mind. The Press, though, was at his heels. This crime was a sensation and would sell papers.

Down there, in the East River Hotel, a woman's body, a prostitute, had been found in a locked bedroom. Her throat had been cut, she had been disembowelled and her body savagely disfigured. He knew what the press would print, that *Jack the Ripper* had escaped London and was here in New York City. He, too, feared it might be so.

The Abandoned: *Victims of Jack the Ripper*

CHAPTER THIRTY

OLD SHAKESPEARE

Bella and Maisie, two middle-aged, poorly dressed women, full-skirted, cracked and leaking boots, battered bonnets covering greying unwashed hair, sat in a badly lit bar somewhere along the lower East Side of grubby Manhattan. The room was awash with up-town reporters and some from further away than that, the noise of their conversations deafening. The women looked older than their years. They were sallow and thin, had long ago abandoned respectability, and openly looked over the men in the room only to dismiss them as potential customers.

These were not the sort of men who would stoop to what the women could offer. These men, if they wanted such services, would find cleaner, better dressed and younger women elsewhere in the city.

No, what these were after was the story. The two had done well so far by selling stories for the price of a glass of whisky, but that well was running dry as it became clear that they knew no more than anyone else about the murder.

No one seemed interested in the victim, though, other than to establish that, like them, she was a prostitute. Just like them, she used to live in the flop houses in the Bowery district, somewhere around Bleecker Street maybe, but as she and they got older, and as the

Bowery these days mostly attracted men looking for the company and custom only of other men, women looking only for women too for that matter, they found trade elsewhere.

The older the women got, the less physically appealing, the more alcoholic they became, the greater their need to work down near the docks where the trade was more desperate, less choosey, more likely to be drunk and where the street gas lights were too feeble to disadvantage the women.

It occurred to them that they had not discussed the victim much, even among themselves.

'In the papers, they are saying it was Carrie, poor old Carrie,' said Bella.

'If it was going to be anyone, it would be someone like her,' added her companion sagely. They batted the conversation back and forth.

'Poor old Carrie,' went on Bella. 'I've known her for about two years, ever since I came down to the Bowery. I think she was one of the first people I noticed. I thought that if someone her age could still turn a trick, then I could find enough trade to keep body and soul together and still manage a drink or two and a room in a flop house.'

'Same for me', said her companion. 'I used to see her down here. I think she didn't search too far anymore for her Johns. She had one or two regulars, which is strange when you think how old she was, but some men were just comfortable with her that way, I guess. She didn't care much who she picked up so long as drink was involved and sometimes a free bed for the night. That is why she went to the hotel on the Slip so much; no one asked questions and there were always rooms available there. I've used it myself often enough, but I won't be going back, no, not me. It gives me the creeps now.'

'Yeah,' agreed Maisie. 'Look at the state of Mary Miniter, the drudge there. She is who all of these hacks are trying to get hold of because she reckons she saw him, the killer, and now she is scared half to death herself.'

'Mary? She is a half-wit and a liar. When did anyone believe anything *she* said? Bella was incredulous.

'Well, whilst one of these up-town boys was buying me a drink,' went on Maisie, proud she knew something her companion did not, 'he kept asking about Mary. They can't get hold of her because the cops have locked her up—just in case the killer comes back for her, they said.'

'Not if I know old Byrnes,' grumbled Bella, knowingly. 'They've locked her up so he can wheedle the truth out of her, and how come she saw the killer anyway in the first place?'

'Ah,' said Maisie, keen to add to the story. 'The Star-Journal man says Eddie, the clerk, was busy serving drinks, so didn't have time to check in Carrie and her John and told Mary to do it. She works there, you know. She had him sign in and that's how she saw him.'

'A likely story, I should say. Since when did anyone check in and sign a register at the East River Hotel? I never do. Have you ever signed it?' Bella was scornful.

'Maybe once or twice, but hardly ever. It's the law, Eddie says. Anyway, you hardly ever see Eddie except to hand over the money and get the key. That takes less than a minute. With me, John usually hangs back a bit, out of sight, not that Eddie ever cares.' Maisie was vaguely aware that she was defending a version of events she didn't believe.

'So, Mary reckons she saw Carrie that night with the killer, does she? I suppose that much might be true.' The scorn and the sarcasm lay heavy in Bella's responses.

'But you know how it is,' Maisie went on appeasingly. 'Carrie might have been in there two or three times with a different man each time, so Mary could well have seen her. She definitely had a regular she would see down there, and I know for a fact she asked for the same room with him each time.'

Bella snapped her response, 'Mary couldn't walk a straight line. She will say anything to the cops if she thinks she is in trouble or there is a reward in it.'

The two fell to silence for a while, the debate about Mary and the drudge at the hotel having played out. Bella was staring into space as if searching her memory for something she could not quite recall. Then she spoke up as if suddenly uncovering a rare gem of information.

'Now I think about it, someone told me Carrie was an actress once.'

'We are all actresses dear, one way or another,' smiled Maisie sadly.

'No, I mean a real one,' said Bella. 'She was on the stage. She did proper acting, not just Vaudeville. Don't you remember when she was well into the whisky how she would make those long speeches with lots of strange words? And then she would finish by saying *that is Shakespeare, you know.*' Bella was animated, pleased with herself for remembering it.

'Is that why she was called Shakespeare, then?' It was all a bit beyond Maisie.

'I guess so, or maybe because she was English, like Shakespeare,' said Bella.

'Never knew she was English. She always sounded American to me,' added Maisie.

'Well, she did say that she had folk in Maryland or Michigan, somewhere.' Bella was recalling more and more. 'She had children who must be all grown up by now. She left them with her husband when she went on the stage, but like it is in this life, once the drink gets to you, it's all you really want.'

'So just how old was old Carrie, *Shakespeare,* do you reckon?' asked Maisie.

'Couldn't say, sixty maybe?' Bella had no idea but was happy to make a guess.

'Well, if it was *Jack the Ripper* like these press boys say, do you think he found her out because she was English?' Maisie's brain, a little slower than her friend's, was catching up.

'No, she sounded American like us,' said Bella, 'but the guy on the end of the bar there, in the bowler hat, yes him, he says that the *Ripper* specialised in killing older turns, down in the London docks, just like here and he has come to New York to taunt Byrnes because Byrnes had said he would have caught the *Ripper* as quick as anything.'

'Now's his chance then,' said Maisie. 'Come on. I don't fancy working down here tonight and these reporters are scaring off trade anyway.' Maisie had suddenly had enough of the conversation and was uncomfortable in the noisy atmosphere being created by the swelling number of strangers.

The two women clutched their shabby cloth bags and waved to the barman, who half smirked as he pretended to ignore them. One of the reporters at the bar looked at them for a while, turning over something in his mind. Then he called out to them, leaning away from the bar and his companions.

'Ladies, do you think we might have a short conversation? About the terrible happenings that have occurred?' he said.

They looked at each other and shrugged an agreement.

'Not here though, somewhere a little more private, a coffee shop perhaps,' he said.

The women were of one mind.

'We could get a little breakfast across the street if you're buying,' said Bella.

'Of course,' he said, raising his hat. He had a notebook in his pocket. He wasn't a cop, but at least he looked like a reporter. He handed over a card with an unpronounceable name and the logo of the Chicago Sun. This certainly must be a big story to attract staff reporters from distant cities.

They walked across the street to a small coffee shop where the women ordered bacon. He asked for 'just a coffee'. It was not quite noon, and both women smelled distinctly of alcohol, but the waiter seemed unbothered by this, judging the man with them to be one who could afford to pay for two women if that was what took his fancy. A few minutes later, he returned with the coffee and looked at Maisie saying, 'Weren't you in here the other night with old Shakespeare?'

He knew she had not been, and he didn't know Carrie Brown at all, but he now reckoned from the sight of notebook and pencil that the man with them was a reporter and by adding to the women's credibility, he had just earned himself a tip. It was how things worked in Manhattan.

'Ladies,' began the reporter, who was impressed by what the waiter had said. He was experienced enough to hide the excitement he was feeling at interviewing at least one person who knew the victim. 'Might either of you know the clerk at the East River Hotel, one Eddie Harrington?'

They looked at each other nervously. The darker of the two, Bella, shot back at him,

'You saying that Eddie did it?' Was she asking him for information, or was she expressing incredulity at his stupidity, he wondered.

He smiled, beginning to doubt that these two knew anything and were not worth the cost of breakfast. 'No, he was the clerk on duty when Mrs. Brown checked in with a man who might have been the killer. I wondered if you knew him and could say whether he would be the sort of man to remember things, names, faces, details of dress, and so on.'

The women had started eating from plates of bacon.

'I never heard of anyone taking names or signing the register. You just pay your money and get a key,' said Bella off-handedly.

'Are you saying he would not have seen Mrs. Brown?' asked the reporter.

'Well, from what we hear,' continued Maise, not wanting to be excluded from the conversation with this obviously stupid man who had money to spend, 'Eddie was busy serving the drinks in the bar and he told Mary to do the checking in, which in truth, is no more than handing over the key and taking orders for drinks. Folks tend to get a pitcher or bucket of beer to take up to the rooms if they are staying a while.' Maise delivered this, the longest speech she had made on the subject to anyone other than Bella, all without taking her eyes from her plate of food. She slurped her coffee.

Bella, agitating to be an important part of the conversation, added to her companion's statement, 'You see, no one is going to sign in with a real name in a dump like the East River. Anyway, they know all of us who work the area and use the place from time to time. It's not a doss house, but it isn't really a hotel either, not like respectable people think a hotel should be. It's just lots of rooms, a bed, an old chair and somewhere to hang a coat, oh and a table to put your drinks on. Some of the rooms have pull-down blinds and some have drapes. It is not what you might call a particularly clean place.'

Maisie, struggling to manage the bacon as she was missing most of her teeth, warmed to the subject. 'If you want Eddie, he is in jug. The police took him off with them for questioning and to stop him blabbing to you lot. He was in a bad state, shaking and sweating, crying like a baby and saying he had seen things he would never be able to forget. You were slow off the mark there, mister. Some of the local reporters arrived at the same time the police did from what we heard and got the name of the killer and saw the body and everything.'

'I know about that,' he agreed sharply. 'Tell me, you ever come across a fellow named something like Mr. C. Knick?'

They conferred silently and with puzzled looks.

'Is that the name in the register? You going to believe it's a real name? You going to believe that it was even written in the book when they say it was?' Bella was contemptuous of this man's credulity. 'I'd be asking Mary about that if I were you.'

Part Two: Panic in New York

'So, you don't know him, this Mr. Knick, or you don't believe there is such a person?' asked the man who was finally getting somewhere even if it was not where he wanted to go with the story.

'Right on both counts,' snapped Bella.

He tried again. 'Ok, let's forget about the name in the register for now, but this Mary Miniter, she says she got a look at this one fellow who went up to the room with Mrs. Brown. What do you say to that?'

'Well, you will have to ask her about it. If old Byrnes has got her, she will probably say anything he wants her to say by now.' Bella had resumed her position as principal witness.

He knew who they meant. With resignation, he accepted the story wasn't going anywhere. There was a witness called Mary Miniter who probably wasn't a witness, an unreliable one anyway: there is a name in the register which might not be the name of the killer and might not even have been written by him from what these two implied, but could he believe anything these two said? This was a tough case to write about other than give the lurid details of what had happened. Still, Byrnes was the man to crack it by all accounts, so best to stick close to him; that was where the story would be.

'Thank you, ladies. Oh, incidentally, do you know where Mrs. Brown was living before she died so tragically?'

'Flop house on the Bowery. Nowhere fixed. We were with her when she spoke the Shakespeare, you know, after a drink or two.' Bella added the last piece of information in the hope he might extend the interview and buy them whisky.

He nodded; a vision of the three crones in Macbeth came to him. A moment later, he nodded to the waiter and offered him some money. He dropped more coins onto the table as he stood to leave.

'Have a drink to wash it down, ladies,' and with that, he left.

Maisie didn't look at him but at Bella. 'Seems like a nice fellow,' she said. Her companion shrugged. She dismissed him from her life as readily as she did those who paid for a different service.

The Abandoned: *Victims of Jack the Ripper*

CHAPTER THIRTY-ONE

THE GREAT DETECTIVE

Byrnes was a painstaking detective.

He reviewed the reports from his detectives with as much thoroughness as he dissected the statements of witnesses and suspects.

What seemed of immediate importance was the testimony of Mary Miniter, an employee at the East River Hotel. Her statement could be the key to unmasking the killer. He placed the transcript on his desk in front of him.

According to her, the killer had a name or an alias of *C. Knick*. What language was that? Where in the world did such a name come from? It didn't matter so much if it was a made-up name because when he caught him, he could compare the handwriting in the register and catch him that way if indeed he had written in the register. But somehow, Byrnes doubted he had.

What else?

According to Mary Miniter, she did not get a good look at him, and yet could say he was about five feet eight inches tall and wore a Derby hat with a dented crown. He was of slim build, wore a dark brown cut-away coat, and black trousers. The man had a long, sharp nose and a moustache, which was possibly blond. For some reason, she thought him German. Putting an age on him, she would say he was 32. Byrnes sighed and shook his head. For someone who had not had a good look at the man, she seemed to have noticed an unusual amount.

It didn't add up.

Byrnes pushed back his chair and opened the door of his office. Two of his detectives sat on either side of the diminutive witness. Byrnes stood over her. He had suggested to his men that they be kind to her and protective, bring down her defences, and that it would be his part to drag the truth out of her. Not only small, she was young, thin with straggly dark blond hair, nervous and close to tears. He didn't know much about her, but she was afraid and that was a good start.

He worked on her in two sessions, first questioning her memory, then the details of her statement, getting her to contradict herself. He brought in the hotel register and set it in front of her. He pointed at the signature.

'Did he sign the register with that name?' He was very stern.

She looked at one of the other detectives as if for comfort.

Byrnes spotted it. He barked at his men, 'Leave us. I'll handle this alone.'

They left without comment. Mary Minter did not realise that this was all part of the process of isolating her, breaking her down. As the door closed, Byrnes carried on.

'I don't care whether the hotel kept its register up to date; none of the places have. But I do care if you are going to carry on lying to me. I'm going to make it hot for you, and all I need to do is drop a hint to the Press outside that maybe I think you were in on it, or maybe you are covering up for someone. You are covering up, aren't you?' It was not a question but a threat. His voice was full of certainty.

The woman folded. Her head went down; the weeping started. He was unmoved.

'Who wrote the name in the register?' more of a demand than a question.

In a feeble wail of a voice, she replied without looking up

'I did. Please don't tell anyone. I was scared after the body was discovered cos I hadn't done the names; I was busy getting the beer, so I wrote it later. I made up the name. I couldn't spell a foreign name, so I just put that.' Terror was taking hold of her.

'The description, is that a fabrication too?' he barked.

Part Two: Panic in New York

'I know he spoke with an accent, like a German, but I didn't really see him. He paid for the beer. I heard him talking to Carrie, but it was mostly she doing the talking.' All her words were sobs now. 'Carrie asked for Room 31. It was her preferred room. I don't know why.' Her words came out between sobs. 'I'm sorry' was all Mary could think to say.

He eased the tone of his voice as he pressed on.

'Could the man she was with have left and another taken his place? Could Carrie Brown herself also have left and returned with another? Or maybe another could have joined her in Room 31 after her friend had left?' He handed her a glass of water, a gesture showing he could be kind if she would be helpful. He saw her thinking over his questions.

'Yes, there could have been comings and goings, although it is not allowed because it isn't a brothel, you know. Anyway, I don't know. I didn't see anything else. I don't know when the man I saw left. Ask Eddie, he might know.' Her sobs had subsided.

'Your friend, Eddie, is not up to much at the moment,' said Byrnes in his matter-of-fact tone of voice. He let the observation hang, implying he had reduced Eddie to some sort of hopeless state. It rebuilt the fear in Mary. She shook, recommenced sobbing and pleaded to go home.

Byrnes wrote out a statement. 'Sign this,' he said, handing her a document.

With a trembling hand, she signed her name without reading what he had put. Byrnes checked it and grunted. Then, instead of placing it in the folder on his desk alongside the other statements, he put it in the top left-hand drawer of his desk, locked the drawer, and slipped the key into his vest pocket. It was his custom to use only the evidence which suited his purpose, and he did not know yet whether this was of value to him.

'You can go. Don't speak to the Press, or I'll have you arrested. My advice to you is to find another profession.' She knew she was nothing to him.

She got up to leave when Byrnes spoke again.

'Wait,' he said. This was one of his favourite techniques, cat and mouse, letting his subjects think they could scurry off only to feel his claws pulling them back into danger.

'There is something else. Carrie Brown had other men she serviced. Was one of them staying in the hotel that night?'

'I don't know.'

'Do you know a man called Frenchy, and wasn't he staying at the hotel?' His detectives had already ascertained this was the case.

'Eddie will know. But yes, I know him, a rough customer.'

'According to the register, if we can believe it, he was in the room across the hall from Mrs. Brown. Does that seem right to you?'

'That is Room 33. Eddie will know. I didn't sign him in, but if he arrived early that day, then anyone could have signed him in.'

'I take it Frenchy is not a German?' Byrnes was not being ironic.

'No, he has a strong accent, but different to the man I heard.' Her fears were welling up again.

'You can go, but not from the police house, for your own protection for now.' He called in the detective who had been kind to her to take her away.

After she was led away, Byrnes turned to the police reports from the morning. The night porter, this Eddie Harrington, was in no way a suspect and was so shaken by his experience that he would be unlikely to be given to fabrication.

At the end of his shift, at about 9 in the morning, he routinely checked that the room keys were back on the hooks. The key to Room 31 was missing. He went up to the room and knocked. There was no reply, so he used his pass key, but he wished he hadn't. He opened the door to a scene of utter horror. On the bed lay the disfigured corpse. Harrington closed the door and ran for the police. They turned up bringing with them the Coroner and made a detailed list of what they saw, and what they saw accorded to what Byrnes knew of the work of *Jack the Ripper*.

This association had already driven the Press to a frenzy. What made the story difficult to contain was that members of the Press had also arrived alongside the police at the crime scene. This was a familiar problem with just about every cop in the city on a retainer to the local newspapers to tip them off about big stories. He could only imagine the chaos of police and reporters falling over each other until his detectives took control. He dreaded to think what evidence had been obscured or destroyed by press intrusion.

And on the subject of evidence, what evidence did he have? A *Ripper*-like killing; a long-bladed knife left in the room, different to the London crimes as the London *Ripper* did not drop his weapon, as far as he knew. There was also a hatchet in the room and might have been used in support of the knife. Not so different to the last

Part Two: Panic in New York

of the London murders, where a hatchet was found. The locked room was in a place where the killer would not be disturbed, again, like the last of the London killings. An older prostitute murdered, slit open and then the corpse violated. No reliable witnesses. It felt like *Jack the Ripper,* but leaving that knife behind didn't seem right. He needed to get down to the site and see what he could find. Although too senior now to normally involve himself in day-to-day murder inquiries, he took personal control of this one.

He set out a sheet of paper and drew a timeline of Carrie Brown's last few days from everything his detectives had found out so far. On the 23rd of April, Brown had been with another well-known prostitute named Alice Sullivan. They spent the afternoon together. Brown had not been working and had not eaten for three days, she said. More likely, she had spent her meagre earnings on drink. Sullivan says she bought Brown a cheese sandwich from a saloon, but by the evening, they were both at a Christian Mission Station having salt beef and cabbage. They left the mission mid-evening, possibly about 8 p.m., to pick up customers. She last saw Carrie Brown with a man she called 'Frenchy', a man she had seen around quite often.

Confusingly, Sullivan reckons others saw Brown later still with another man called Isaac Perringer.

Frustratingly, Perringer was also known as 'Frenchy'.

His detectives were also holding a prostitute called Mary Healy in 'protective custody' because after Brown had left the Sullivan woman, she had been drinking with Healy on the evening she died. Healy also saw her with a man she knew as Frenchy. Her description of Frenchy did not match that of the man Mary Miniter had first described, but Miniter was not a reliable witness.

Looking further into the case notes, he could see his detectives had done a fair job of piecing together the movements in the hotel. They thought the name written in the register as *C. Knick* might have been Nicolo. Byrnes knew differently and the name on the register was fictional.

Nevertheless, from what followed, they estimated he left Room 31 at about 2 a.m. and judging by spots of dried blood on the floor that they followed, they reckoned he had made for the stairs and the exit. Partway down the stairs, it seemed he changed his mind, probably because there was someone about and he couldn't slip away unnoticed. The blood trail indicated he went back up the stairs as far as he could and got out onto the roof. What comes next is speculation based on police instinct.

At some time in the early hours of the morning, a man appeared in the lobby of the adjoining Glenmore Hotel and asked the Night Clerk, a Mr. Kelly, for a room. Kelly apparently didn't like the look of him, or maybe the man had no money (Kelly said both things) and stated that his hands and clothes appeared to be smeared with blood. He refused him a room. Had the killer simply climbed over the roof and come down the stairs of the Glenmore? His detectives thought as much.

Next, he picked up the statement from Kelly. It was short and to the point, but one thing stood out. Kelly's description of the man in blood-smeared clothes exactly matched that Mary Miniter had given, the description he had bullied her into retracting. Kelly was adamant the man had a German accent. Byrne's logic told him he was looking for a German or Germanic accented man, sharp featured and probably blond. Could this be the London killer, too?

Meanwhile, he needed to put out a story in the newspapers. He needed to protect his own reputation and he didn't want any of his associates in Tammany Hall getting the jitters. There was an anti-corruption campaign growing in the background of political life being stirred up by a damned Protestant, a Dutchman, not even a native New Yorker, so not someone he could lean on or influence readily. His sources in Tammany Hall told him that this man, Riis, was encouraging a lot of discontent over the way things were being run in the city and he had the ear of a Republican Party bigwig called Roosevelt. They couldn't do him much harm yet as Roosevelt was busy with Party in-fighting. Some seemed to think he had sympathy with the Reds, socialists causing trouble in Europe, but this *Ripper* story could be just the thing to let him get at the police and dish his opposition. It made a fine distraction from political squabbling. He regretted ever having spoken to the Press about the *Ripper* case some months earlier and how he would have solved it; it was coming back to haunt him.

He opened the top left-hand drawer of his desk again and withdrew a folder. He put the statement from Mary Miniter on one side and took out some press cuttings. He had been interviewed about the killings in London and had let his self-belief run a little too freely. As Acting Superintendent of Police for New York as well as overseeing the Detective Bureau, he had been too full of himself.

Part Two: Panic in New York

Now, he had to get control of this case before it affected his credibility. He read the quotes in which he told about having had copies of the infamous *Jack the Ripper* letters titled *From Hell* and *Dear Boss* sent over from London. He boasted that no one would get away with such crime in New York City because he would 'have him in 36 hours.' His views were repeated and slightly varied in several newspapers across America, but much of it was taken from a single interview in the New York Times in October of the previous year.

Underneath the cuttings were photographs of the infamous, taunting 'Letter from Hell,' apparently written by *Jack the Ripper* as it contained detailed knowledge of the crimes. The London police tended to the mind that it was a hoax, but he wondered if they were correct in this assumption.

Genuine or fake, he didn't want any such letters appearing in the American newspapers. He also had a transcript of the previous *Ripper* letter, the so-called *Dear Boss* letter. It was chilling, and it introduced the world to the name *Jack the Ripper*.

It had arrived at a London news agency at the end of an inquest into the death of the murder of a prostitute called Chapman. At all costs, he wanted to avoid this sort of thing happening here and happening to him. He could imagine the pressure publication of these letters had put on the London police, the panic they caused in the general population, and he knew he must avoid it for New York.

Now, all he could do was hope for the best until he caught the man, which must be soon.

He collected the documents and locked them back in the drawer. He realised grimly that even though a letter-writing campaign had not yet started in New York, this old letter from the *Ripper* was cause enough to worry.

Once letters like this got out, there would be widespread panic, questions asked of him, and demands to justify his reputation as the great detective. It was time to visit the East River Hotel with some of his trusted detectives; he needed to get this case moving to a conclusion.

The Abandoned: *Victims of Jack the Ripper*

CHAPTER THIRTY-TWO

POLITICS, CORRUPTION, GANGS, AND JACOB RIIS

Smoking, lounging around, excitedly gossiping, the Press hacks were waiting outside the station house. Indeed, they were not only outside the station house, but many were inside too, having coffee with some of the cops. It was hard to keep anything a secret for long.

A clerk handed Byrnes a message in an envelope and from the sealing wax on the back, he could tell it was from Tammany Hall. He thought for a moment, and then took the envelope with him back into his office.

Everyone in the outer office who had stood up at his appearance went back to doing whatever had occupied them before his door had opened. Byrnes felt that problems were mounting, and he had to keep a clear head.

Still, he smiled, he was good at keeping a clear head. He sat at his desk and opened the envelope. The message was from one of the ward secretaries. It was more trouble from this guy named Riis.

Riis, supported by two or three assistants with cameras, had been in the alleyways and in some of the tenements in Manhattan, taking pictures. He was publicising the poverty of the area and pointing the finger of blame for the state of the immigrants, crime, and moral latitude toward the landlords and tavern owners.

Unfortunately, the properties Riis targeted were legitimate businesses owned by local politicians, amongst others.

One of the up-and-coming local Tammany Hall leaders, Big Tim Sullivan, was getting spooked by this interference and was concerned that with the big-news murder taking all his time, Byrnes wouldn't have the inclination to shake off young Riis.

Instead, Sullivan was thinking of employing a young local boxer, Paul Kelly, to frighten him off.

Young Kelly already had quite a following amongst the local teenage thugs and was keen to be part of the Tammany Hall group.

'No, no, no,' said Byrnes out loud. He pushed back his chair and walked over to the window. It was bright outside. He didn't think there was much he could do about Riis, who was a nuisance but nothing more, at least for now.

As for Paul Kelly, well, he might be useful at some point, but right now, his emerging gang was a cause for alarm amongst the established gangsters as well as the police. This was a complication Byrnes did not need.

'Does Big Tim know nothing?' he thought. Kelly isn't even Irish. His name is really Paolo Antonio Vaccarelli, an Italian immigrant, a good Prize Fighter though. He had chosen the name Kelly so he could get onto the fight cards which the local Irish bosses controlled.

Ever since then, he stuck to the name as it made him more acceptable to both the Irish, who thought he was one of theirs, and the Italians, who knew otherwise. He went back to his desk and quickly wrote a note to Sullivan.

'Stay away from Riis. You will bring a heap of trouble on us all. Kelly is trustworthy to a point, but he has a lot of uncontrollable friends in his gang that you do not want to be associated with. For now, at least, stay clear of young Johnny Torrio, Al Capone, Bugsy Siegel, Frankie Yale and especially young Salvatore Lucania, whom you might hear called Luciano, a mad Sicilian kid. From memory, these are the least reliable. I don't want another murder on our hands while I am sorting out the big one. Tell all members it's not Jack the Ripper, though. I will have the culprit soon.'

There was too much gang violence going on and Byrnes was going to run them all out of town. The trouble was, he had to solve this murder first before he could get a handle on anything else. New York City was a violent place. He sealed the letter with wax.

Part Two: Panic in New York

Much as he did not understand what Riis was about, and although Byrnes deplored the reporter's soft-hearted feeling for the scum of the earth, he would not encourage crime, including physical harm directed at Riis. Byrnes liked police work, not politics, though Tammany Hall politicians paid him well for his services.

Thus, refusing to be distracted by pressure from Tammany Hall, Byrnes gathered his elite group of three detectives and some uniformed cops and headed out to the Lower East Side. A gaggle of reporters followed on.

At the hotel, he noted that although he had posted a guard on the door of the hotel and another outside Room 31, the guard at the entrance to the hotel had wandered down the street a little to talk to a couple of men and was probably enjoying a cigarette with them.

When he saw his colleagues arrive, he seemed to be not much bothered, but when he saw it was Byrnes, he hurried back. Byrnes glared at him and then proceeded into the seedy interior with its smell of lamp fuel and burnt candles. He looked in the lobby where the possible killer had stood in the shadows. He positioned himself behind the counter and looked out at the view Mary Miniter would have had. It depended on the lighting, of course, but it was possible that Mary Miniter could have had a look at the German just as she said. He went slowly up the stairs and stopped at the point where his men said the bloodstains stopped. The evidential blood had been cleaned away—probably the first time in years these stairs had been washed.

From the landing, he walked the short distance to Room 31. At least his police guard was still there, sitting on a stool outside the locked door. The man jumped smartly to his feet as Byrnes approached.

'Unlock the door,' said Byrnes. The constable produced a key from his pocket, unlocked the door and stepped to one side. Byrnes took only a couple of steps inside and carefully looked around.

In the far corner, to the left of a grimy window, was an iron bed with a thin, heavily stained mattress on top. The room had been cleared of body and gore, but the bare floorboards were stained with the result of the barbarity, and a heavy stench hung about the room. He thought he heard the buzzing of flies.

There was a chalk mark showing where the knife had been found, another where the hatchet had been abandoned. He took in the whole scene.

In many ways, it was no different to the countless murders he had investigated over the years. It was only the savage attack on the body that was different. He was not happy. Too many features made this similar to the *Jack the Ripper* murders, and he did not want this to be one. It could be a savage coincidence as, after all, other bodies had been hacked about in murders in cities all around the world. He stepped back from the room and made a mental note to chase up the coroner's report. He looked up and down the corridor and saw reporters being held back by cops at the stairs. Opposite him was Room 33.

'Open that one,' he said.

Room 33 was a mirror image of Room 31 but faced onto the street. His detectives had searched the room on his instructions, all the rooms, in fact, but this one was of particular interest to him, it was where the mysterious Frenchy had stayed. His team had found nothing and no trace of Frenchy.

From the corridor, he trod the stairs to the roof and here some of the blood stains remained. When he asked if anyone had searched the flophouse next door for blood stains, he had an equivocal answer that stains had been seen there but were now washed away.

So now he had two main suspects—this person, Frenchy, who had been seen around with Carrie Brown and who had used the room opposite her during the murder, a man now disappeared, and the blond German who no one seemed to know anything about. He knew that Frenchy had been around New York for a long time, several years, so he could not be the notorious *Ripper*. He would be found. The other man, well, how reliable were the witnesses? How many fair-haired foreigners might there be in an immigrant area? He would take the easiest path in his elimination of suspects. As he went out onto the street, he spoke to his detectives and to the waiting Press.

'I am looking for a man of dark complexion, known as Frenchy. It is my belief that he was a resident in this establishment, in the room opposite the victim. He waited for her guest to leave her, and then, probably in a drunken state, he gained admittance to her room. Carrie Brown knew this man and had probably taken payment from him in recent times. I strongly suspect that his intention was to rob her of the fee she had just earned, but in a drunken struggle, he strangled her and in frustration at finding little or no money, he cut her up. He then left her room and returned to his own before going into hiding. We know who this man is and will hunt him down. Good day to you all.'

He took two detectives with him and walked down to the Brooklyn Bridge. With them, he walked onto the bridge so he could look back at the scene. He knew how he wanted this to play out. He was not at all convinced in his own mind he had the right man, but as they were all thieves and cutthroats, then, at the very least, it would be another worthless irritation removed from the city. The Great Detective would have his man, even if it was possibly, even likely, not the right man.

Back in his office, Byrnes found the Carrie Brown autopsy report waiting on his desk. As was now the custom, there were photographs of the corpse attached. He was not moved by the pictures, but he spent a good amount of time reading the report from Dr Jenkins. It was not the most thorough report ever produced, as it seemed the doctor didn't know where to begin or end with his examination. The body was not completely naked; some clothing was still around the neck and throat of the victim, but the doctor had noted that the clothing had become so entangled about the throat that the killer had probably struggled to remove it and it had impeded his attempt to slash her throat. She probably died from strangulation, but it might have been from a severed artery in the throat or neck.

The killer had then taken a great deal of time in hacking and cutting the body to remove the sex organs and disembowel the corpse. Marks and crosses were carved onto the body. The victim had eaten earlier that day.

In the opinion of the doctor, she had been about 60 years of age at the time of her death.

All this worried Byrnes. He had read about the London murders and some features of this murder were horribly similar. He would have to be careful which parts of the evidence he stressed.

As this would be a public document and would be presented to the court, he did not put it in his private file but in the official file.

Obviously, there had been a lot of blood. He took the original descriptions of the murder scene and noted where the tracks of blood had gone. It would be very useful indeed if his detectives now remembered that they led into Room 33, Frenchy's room.

The Abandoned: *Victims of Jack the Ripper*

CHAPTER THIRTY-THREE

FRENCHY

By the 26th of April, all newspapers were declaring that police were searching for a man in his 30s, a desperado called 'Frenchy'. Byrnes had put out the word to every police district to arrest and hold anyone of this name. He would then use witnesses, even Mary Miniter, indeed anyone who knew Frenchy from the East River Hotel to identify him. Within the week he had two men, both named Frenchy. He termed them Frenchy1 and Frenchy2 and It turned out that they were cousins. It didn't take long to establish that it was Frenchy1 who had stayed in Room 33 on the night of the murder. Byrnes hedged his bets though, and put out Mary Miniter's description of the blond German. Since visiting the hotel lobby he had become less dismissive of Mary Miniter's description of a man Carrie Brown had been with that fateful night. He would be happy to pull in either or both suspects.

Byrnes set up an interrogation, but it wasn't easy to communicate with Frenchy. He had a police record but under different names. One of the arresting officers recognised him as one 'George Fronk', but it might have been George Frank. He didn't seem to speak much English, was swarthy, down-at-heel and shifty. Everything about him told Byrnes that this was an out and out scoundrel. He had to get a translator so naturally found one who spoke French, only to be told that the language was not French or if it was, was of so strong a dialect it made it difficult to understand. One thing for certain was that he was not French from the continent of Europe, nor was he Canadian or Cajun. In the opinion of the translator, he was an Arab, probably from Algeria. Eventually, painstakingly, the name emerged. He admitted to being Ameer Ben Ali, an Algerian from the French colony who had arrived in New York several years earlier and since then had led a precarious hand-to-mouth existence. All he did in interrogation was to hysterically plead innocence and claim not to understand anything. Still, Byrnes let the word leak out to the Press that he had his man.

The case had to be built without confession, but Byrnes was ready for that. He would rely on forensic evidence from three doctors. He arranged for them to analyse scrapings from under Ben Ali's fingernails which they did. He presented them with socks said to belong to Ben Ali which seemed to have blood stains on the sole. He also announced that police had indeed found blood splatter leading from Room 31 to Room 33. This latter announcement caused alarm in the Press. Quite a number of reporters had been at the hotel when the police first inspected the scene and they saw no such trail. They pointed out that the police who tried to follow the blood-spot trail similarly made no reference to blood leading to Room 33. Byrnes ignored them; he placed the trail to Room 33 as being central to his evidence. Within a very short time the medical evidence came back to support his view. Surprisingly, after several days had passed, blood and faecal matter similar to that found in the room was found under Frenchy's fingernails. The stains on the socks turned out to be blood which could have come from the murder scene. Again, the Press asked how the scrapings had survived so long and asked why there were not clear footprint smears of blood in Room 33; in fact, they again disputed any trail of blood there.

News came to Byrnes from the Sherriff of Queens County to the north of the city. He had recognised the name Fronk and was able to show he had the man in custody during March that year for vagrancy. He had been released twelve days before the murder. Moreover, two convicts still in prison claimed that Fronk had smuggled a knife into prison, and they had seen it. Immediately on receipt of this news, Byrnes sent two detectives to the prison with the knife found in Room 31. The detectives met with the two convicts, but neither could positively identify the knife. One of the detectives was convinced that they were lying about ever having seen a knife. Neither prisoner wished to give evidence. It would have helped, but it only went to show in the mind of Byrnes that the criminal class were all liars and could not be trusted or believed whatever they said.

Byrnes was about to charge Frenchy with the murder of Carrie Brown when a curious diversion arose. One of his detectives picked up information that a man named George Chapman might well have been in the area at the time of the murder. Chapman, real name Kaminski, was a person of interest to the police, not least because he had once been arrested by the police in London on suspicion of being *Jack the Ripper*. The case against Chapman in London collapsed and he was known to boast that the police had to pay him compensation which enabled him to settle for a while in America. He was then living in New Jersey. The local police were diligent in finding him and detaining him, but he gave an alibi. Police in New Jersey visited his alibi, a dubious source, and said it stood up. Byrnes did something apparently uncharacteristic of him, he did not have his detectives question the alibi, but took the word of the local Captain that it put Chapman in the clear. Sometime later Chapman left the country and returned to England.

On the 30th of April, only about five days after the most gruesome murder anyone in New York City could recall, Frenchy was formally charged with the murder of Carrie Brown. Byrnes was confident that the forensic, scientific evidence he could muster would be sufficient to send his man to the Electric Chair. Still, though, there was disquiet on the street and in the Press. Nevertheless, it would now be a matter for the courts. On his way from his office, the Press pack surrounded him and between calls of congratulations at solving the matter so quickly, there were also questions about why Frenchy had done it.

'How sure are you Mr. Byrnes, that you have the right man?'

'Certain,' he replied with all the confidence a great detective might command.

'Well, what about the blond-moustachioed German guy, did he never exist and if he did exist could he have been the killer?' they asked.

'It doesn't matter whether he exists or not. We searched hard for him and questioned many suspects who loosely matched that description. But as for evidence and a description, it must be remembered that the people we depended upon to give it were a drunken lot, without enough intelligence to remember how the man looked. If the fair moustache did exist, he left before the murder. We have the evidence taken from Ben Ali's hands, a blood trail to his room, blood on the outside of the door handle to his room and on the inside, blood splatter on his clothing. It was him. His motivation was probably robbery, but he got angry, he couldn't find much to steal, and he did her in. He was almost certainly drunk and in a frenzy.'

'Some might say you didn't search so hard for the German guy once you pulled in this Frenchy character within a couple of days. Isn't it true that a conductor on a train out of the city on the morning after the killing saw a fair-moustachioed man with blood-stained shirt? Isn't it the case that Detective Kilcauley from Jersey City Police contacted the New York City Police with the news that a train conductor had positively identified the blooded man on a train to Easton? Why was that not followed up?'

Byrnes ignored the questions.

'Is it true that Frenchy was unarmed when your police took him?' asked another.

This time Byrnes responded.

'Irrelevant. He had left the instruments of murder behind him anyway. He did, of course, have a reputation for carrying a knife and there have been claims he even smuggled one into prison with him. Make no mistake, this is a violent and unstable man.'

He pushed his way through the crowd whilst continuing to speak.

'We have considered all the evidence and all the stories. Some accounts are far less reliable than are others and when dealing with the populace of the streets I think it fair to say that in my experience you learn to take a lot with a pinch of salt. What is more, I would take the evidence of medical men, scientists, over the drunken rabble any day. There will be opportunity in court to gainsay the evidence. Justice will be done. That is all.' He tried to be dismissive.

Then came the real question, the one he had been expecting.

'Is this man the notorious *Jack the Ripper*?'

Byrnes stopped and paused, weighing his words. He looked directly at the mob about him and with great authority said,

'No. I do not believe such a person has been in New York. We cannot yet say for certain of course, but I very much doubt it. You have all made much of what has been one of hundreds of murders. What I do say is this, criminals in my jurisdiction had better beware'.

With that he determinedly left them to write their columns and await the trial.

His denial that it was the demon killer did not sit well with the newspaper men. Byrnes was deflating the biggest crime story of their careers.

The Abandoned: *Victims of Jack the Ripper*

CHAPTER THIRTY-FOUR

CASE CLOSED?

Interest in the case remained high.

Speculation that Byrnes had caught *Jack the Ripper* continued to circulate and newspapers did very well indeed in keeping the story going, just as it had in the London newspapers.

The allegations of the prisoners who had claimed Frenchy had a knife in prison leaked out. The Star-Journal ran the story announcing that *Jack the Ripper* had been a resident of Queens County Jail for a while.

It printed that the man now arrested and awaiting trial had been arrested for vagrancy in Newton just a month or so before the murder and had used the name George Fronk or Frank. The vagrancy conviction had resulted in his incarceration. The paper gave full credence to the allegations of the two prisoners who had claimed they saw Fronk with a knife. It kept the sensationalist nature of the story alive by stating that Queens County Jail had enjoyed the honour of housing *Jack the Ripper* and then named him Fronk.

As far as selling newspapers was concerned, it was worth establishing that the murder of poor Carrie Brown was indeed a continuation of the career of the *Ripper*, no matter what Byrnes said. The victim herself, as was the case with the cruelly murdered women in Whitechapel, was all but forgotten.

Frenchy's interrogation was a waste of time. He did not communicate much other than by hysterical outbursts and fits of wailing. His means of expressing himself did him no favours in court either. The trial opened on 24th of June, the prosecution in the hands of Assistant District Attorney Wellman and Assistant District Attorney Simms. They also represented Byrnes and four of his detectives.

In a two-pronged attack, first, they did everything they could to discredit the defendant by calling an array of witnesses from the slums, all of whom had nothing good to say about Ben Ali and all of whom had been brought along by Byrnes' men. The second prong was the *scientific* evidence. As Ben Ali was without means, the State provided him with a lawyer.

Facing the experience of the State prosecutors was a man handling his first murder case, a Jewish lawyer, and a man unknown to Byrnes. Abe Levy was a man who went on to defend over 300 murder cases in a legendary career.

Indeed, he mounted as robust a defence as he could given that he had no funds, no independent experts and had to rely on the defendant who simply could not contain himself from saying anything, true or obviously false, which might get him out of this predicament. The newspapers loved it. The Press benches were packed, and the lurid stories rolled out.

Levy took the character witnesses apart. Their role had been to establish the wickedness of his client but also to seed a story that Frenchy was known to wander around the East River Hotel rooms at night when everyone else had gone to sleep. It was also suggested that on the night of the murder, the candle in his room was seen to be still burning in the early hours.

The implication was that he was waiting for something, perhaps for Carrie Brown's client to leave.

After the witnesses had been paraded, the words of Byrnes that none of them *was capable of telling the truth* must have echoed in the court room.

If nothing else, Levy was able to imply the use of such witnesses was nothing more than a crude attempt by the prosecution to show *mens rea,* the criminal intention to commit an offence; he was waiting up to rob Carrie Brown. Levy was dismissive. Not one of the police witnesses from the slums was believable; their testimony did not show intention for murder and butchery, or anything else for that matter. Levy had a more challenging time with the medical evidence.

Then, for whatever reason, from 1st of July, the prosecution of the case was assumed by the District Attorney himself, Anthony Nicoll. The prosecution was becoming jittery.

On the face of it, the medical evidence was compelling. The police reported finding blood on the door handles, on Frenchy's person and on his socks. The medical experts stated that a chemical analysis of fingernail scrapings matched the analysis of the blood found on the mattress where the corpse had lain. The stains showed 'the intestinal contents of food elements, all exactly identical. The logical conclusion was that the blood came from Carrie Brown.

The question was, how had the blood got under his fingernails (how had the scrapings been taken, and the specimens secured for analysis) and how had the blood got onto socks and onto the door handles and floor of Frenchy's room?

The defence asserted that no blood stains were seen on the door handles when the police, coroner and reporters first visited, and no independent person secured the socks either. There was no link between Frenchy and the murder weapon and where was the key to Room 31? The killer had locked the room when leaving and the key had not been found. The police assumed Frenchy had disposed of it but could not prove he had ever had it.

The prosecution was resolute, however, dismissing doubts raised by the defence whilst never properly saying anything Levy said. That left only Frenchy to give evidence on his own behalf and all agreed, both defence and prosecution, that he was a disastrous witness. He tried to explain away any scrapings from his fingernails by clearly making up stories. He shook and pleaded in his own language and avoided answering questions.

Most damning of all, when under severe pressure from Nicoll, he did not wait for his interpreter to translate but shouted out denials in English. The jury and all in the court took the view that his claim to speak little English was untrue and so everything he said was probably a lie.

It was a hot summer. The Jury was sent out on 3rd of July to consider its verdict. The court hearing was at risk of running into the 4th of July celebrations.

In the jury room, only one man expressed serious doubts about Frenchy's guilt. He agreed that Frenchy was a criminal and possibly beyond redemption but was not convinced he was the murderer. He did not like the appearance of the blood evidence when earlier, there had been none. He was not convinced by motive. The Press had been full of stories that this was *Jack the Ripper*, after all, the crime was like the *Jack the Ripper* atrocities in London, but there was nothing else connecting this man with London.

Was this why the police were now ignoring the grisly details of the crime, denying it was a *Ripper* crime because that would afford this man a defence, as Frenchy seemed to be in New York City at the time of those murders?

Moreover, this defendant knew the victim, and though not friends, they were on friendly terms, acquainted through circumstance and whilst the juror accepted that this would not preclude an argument and even murder, why the butchery?

Another prostitute, Mary Ann Lopez, even claimed that Frenchy had availed himself of Carrie Brown's services the previous week in Room 31. Evidence for his innocence stacked up if one took into account that, according to witnesses, Frenchy was seen leaving the hotel at about 5 a.m., or 'slinking out' as they put it.

Why wait so long if the butchery had taken place probably at about 2 a.m.?

There was no sense in it. The whole case was too neatly contrived, the evidence focusing only on what the police wanted to find. Nothing belonging to the victim was found amongst Frenchy's meagre belongings. Not one of the general witnesses who had spoken against him was credible.

Despite voicing his reservations to the other members of the jury, he stood alone, just as Frenchy did.

Every other member of the jury was convinced by the testimony of the police, backed up by the scientific reports; this must be the man.

Consequently, the dissenting lone voice of doubt became increasingly convinced that this jury had been 'packed'. He felt that hardly any of them had considered the evidence at all but were there to ensure a conviction.

Jury rules demanded that there be a unanimous verdict, but they were stuck, and the other jurors thought that this one juror, and not the holes in the case, was the problem. They did not want to go back into court and seek clarification, and neither would they shift their opinion that Frenchy was guilty. They wanted no further delay.

The next day would be 4th of July, a time to be spent with friends and families, not in a courthouse. A deal was struck. It was agreed that Frenchy would be found guilty of second-degree murder, which in English Law would be manslaughter, but not guilty of first-degree murder, which would certainly have resulted in the electric chair. They knew the verdict made no sense, was illogical, but it was a compromise. They returned in short order to the court, where they delivered their surprise verdict. Spared the death penalty, Frenchy, Ameer Ben Ali was sent to Sing Sing Prison for the rest of his life: case closed.

The conviction was not met with the universal acclaim for which Byrnes had been hoping. Disgruntled newspapers had not had their *Ripper* story, the police had not had the definitive verdict of first-degree murder they had wanted; the populace of lower Manhattan thought a miscarriage of justice had occurred. The story in the taverns followed one of two paths. The popular one was that *Jack the Ripper* had come to New York City to taunt Byrnes and had got away with it. Frenchy had been set up by Byrnes to save his own reputation with his friends in Tammany Hall and because of his own sense of self-importance. They believed it didn't matter to Byrnes, who had done it as long as he seemed to solve the case and could take the credit for it. The second story, and the two overlapped at times, was that the real killer was a guy with a fair moustache, not a local, either a merchant seaman or some other out-of-towner. The word from the docks was that he had slipped away a few days after the murder, working on a steamer to Shanghai. No one believed Frenchy was guilty.

Thomas Byrnes sat in his office, his private file on the Carrie Brown murder on his desk. He was not at peace. He didn't know who the fair-moustached man was, the man rumoured to be the actual killer of Carrie Brown, but now it did not matter. He heard the man had left the country, and if that was so, it was all well and good.

Byrnes's self-belief was unshakable and as far as he was concerned, he had caught the right man. True, and not for the first time, there had been a problem with the evidence, but he had overcome that. Frenchy was the only one who could have done it. Frenchy knew Carrie Brown had a client with her, and maybe he was jealous. Who could tell with people like that? Either the door to Room 31 had been unlocked, or she simply let him in because she knew him and might make a little extra by entertaining him; who could tell?

Byrnes had no idea why Frenchy had mutilated the body and Frenchy gave nothing away by simply denying everything. Byrnes had confronted him with the photographs of the mutilations that had threatened him, but it was all so difficult because the man played his part of being unable to understand so well. He got him, though. With a little manipulation of the evidence, he got him, and it was a good thing, too.

The sentence though, well, that was a mystery. What on earth were they playing at? He closed his file and locked it away, this time in the lower, deeper, left-hand drawer, alongside a few others he kept there to remind himself of what had been fact and what had been improved upon. All this stuff about *Jack the Ripper*? Yes, he had found himself dragged down that line of speculation, but where was the evidence for it being the *Ripper*? The murders were similar, but that was mere chance. Maybe Frenchy had copied the crime, or maybe he was mad. Word from Sing Sing was that Frenchy was to be moved to a prison hospital for the criminally insane. Who was to say that if he was mad or bad? Byrnes had no opinion on it. He thought again about his secret file. His experience and instinct told him to be ready to destroy it. A group of liberals, including the irritating Riis, had started to review the Ben Ali trial and conviction. He was irritated rather than threatened by this, and watched the situation from a distance, without public comment, dismissively. He had every confidence that given time, the fuss would abate, and the conviction would stand as another success for 'The Great Detective'.

Still, he wished he could do something about Riis. The man stirred up trouble everywhere with his bleeding-heart sense of liberal justice. Byrnes got up from his chair, put on his hat and went home to his wife and five daughters.

***

Out in the countryside, on the outskirts of New Jersey, was a farm in the little town of Cranford. The farmer was annoyed that a farmhand he employed had gone missing.

Indeed, he had left the farm on the night of the East River Hotel murder, coming back a day later but only to suddenly leave again for good, without warning, without a goodbye. The farmer had waited to see if he would return but, after a few days, decided he would not, so he cleared his room.

Part Two: Panic in New York

In there, he found a bloodstained shirt and a hotel key. The key had a label with a room number on it:

31.

The farmer never saw the worker again but later described him as Danish or possibly German, a man with a heavy, fair coloured moustache.

There were no more *Jack the Ripper* types of killing in New York City.

The Abandoned: *Victims of Jack the Ripper*

Part Two: Panic in New York

PART THREE

A *RIPPER* LEGACY

The Abandoned: *Victims of Jack the Ripper*

Part Three: A *Ripper* Legacy

CHAPTER THIRTY-FIVE

CHICAGO AND NEW YORK CITY

In Chicago, it is always very cold in February. It is said that when the north wind blows across the great lakes, tears freeze to the eyeballs.

In 1897, a young lawyer named William Sanford Lawton walked off the pathway in Lincoln Park. It was seven o'clock in the evening. He reached a lonely spot, took a pistol from his pocket, pressed the muzzle to his right temple and blew out his brains. The shot attracted attention, and he was soon found, but he was declared dead three hours later in the Alexian Brothers Hospital. In writing the death certificate a doctor remarked to a colleague that it was yet another suicide committed on St Valentine's Day. Although, he was a day early.

While the story made the morning newspapers, no one in Chicago thought much of it. The lawyer had been only about 28 years of age and, although raised in Chicago, had moved to New York City many years before and studied law there.

He had been staying at the City Hotel on State Street back in his hometown of Chicago for a week before his death, apparently on his way to see his mother in California. The Chicago police made enquiries about him, perturbed at finding no suicide note.

According to the hotel staff, he had seemed happy enough until the day of his death. On that day, he had sent a telegram to his office in New York, the law firm of Foote and Lawton in the Home Life Building and had anxiously awaited a reply. When no reply came, he seemed to staff to be ever more anxious and gloomy, yet no one had cause to suspect he would shoot himself.

According to his partner in the firm, Mr. Foote, Lawton had left New York with a large sum of money to be used in a property transaction; no trace of which was found.

What the Chicago police did discover from their colleagues in New York was a curiosity. Lawton had been the junior defence lawyer representing one Carl Feigenbaum in a murder case in 1894, a man who, having lost his appeal against conviction, was sent to the electric chair two years later.

Following the execution, Lawton had caused a sensation when he had announced in the New York press that his client had confessed to him to be the notorious *Jack the Ripper*. The final victim, said Lawton, had been one Mrs. Hoffman, a middle-aged widow Feigenbaum had been rightfully convicted of murdering. One year on from breaking the story, Lawton too was dead.

When his claim to know the identity of *Jack the Ripper* had come out, although it made headlines, enthusiasm for such revelations had waned. The murder which sparked the Lawton proposition had barely been reported outside New York City. Once the young lawyer put out to the Press his inside information, interest did pick up and for a while was widely commented on, though without the energy the story once had.

Lawton became well known for a brief time as the man to whom the *Ripper* had confessed his evil ways, but soon his moment of fame was over, and his name did not appear again outside New York City court reports until he shot himself on that cold winter night in Chicago. His claim that he had definitive proof of the identity of the *Ripper* was not believed by police who wanted no more of the matter and somehow it never captured the public imagination which once had burned so brightly with the death of Carrie Brown.

***

Juliana Hoffman at the age of 56 was a widow. She was an immigrant from Budapest who like so many others from central

Part Three: A *Ripper* Legacy

Europe had found her way to the Lower East Side of Manhattan, to East Sixth Street, not far from the notorious Bowery area, just south of Tompkin Square Park. She was on the edge of the growing Hungarian area, in what was widely known as Klein Deutschland, an area more populated with German speaking people than anywhere outside Berlin or Vienna.

She was desperately poor, renting two rooms above a small store. Her only income was the pittance earned by her 16-year-old son Michael who lived with her. One room overlooked the street, the other was at the back and overlooked a yard. Knowing that there was ever a shortage of places to live, they decided that Michael and she would live in just the one room, the room to the front of the building, and they would rent out the second room to bring in a little more money for food. Mrs. Hoffman never resorted to the life endured by Carrie Brown, nor did she drink. She and her son had only each other. They put up a sign in their front window advertising a room to let.

On Wednesday, 29th of August, a man called and asked for the room. He was apparently as poor as they were but he spoke in German, so he did not seem so much a stranger. He told them he had just arrived in the city and had a job starting that week at a florist's shop. He could not pay the one dollar a week for the room in advance but would pay on Saturday as soon as he received his wages. He also opted for breakfast each morning for an additional eight cents a day.

For some reason, Mrs. Hoffman trusted him to do as he promised and let him have the room. He gave his name as Herr Carl Feigenbaum. He did not say, but she might have supposed it, that he had been sleeping in the open in Tompkin Square Park.

The living arrangements for the three occupants were cramped. The front room which served as the Hoffman's bedroom, was also the parlour, kitchen and dining room. The lodger sat with them on the first night until bedtime and again on Friday night.

It was the first day of September, and it was still hot, even at night. Mrs. Hoffman had to buy some basic provisions for supper for herself and her son and Feigenbaum saw her take a few coins from a small purse in a closet. At about ten o'clock that night, he went to bed in his own room and the Hoffmans did the same in their shared room, Mrs. Hoffman having used a daybed and her son the couch at the foot of her bed. They slept with a window open in the hope of a cooling breeze.

What followed was sadly predictable.

Around midnight, the lodger crept back into the Hoffman's room and tried to silently open the closet containing the purse with its few coins, Mrs. Hoffman's total wealth. He did not succeed past opening the closet and locating the purse because she awoke to see him there and screamed, waking her son. Michael sat up and saw the lodger with a carving knife in his hand. He sprang up to protect his mother, jumping on Feigenbaum from behind.

In the struggle which followed, the boy realised he was no match for the robber with a knife and escaped through the open front window onto the cornice over the shop beneath them, shouting for help. Feigenbaum silenced the screaming woman by stabbing her in the neck, dragging the knife forward to cut her throat. The awful scene was witnessed by Michael.

In what seemed like panic, Feigenbaum then ran from the room to his own room, climbed out of the back window, dropped onto a shed roof, and then into the yard. He quickly washed blood from his hands at the pump in the yard, then ran into the connecting alleyway at the back of the shop, discarding the murder weapon.

Michael's screams of murder and pleas for help were heard by neighbours who came out onto the street to investigate. He was also heard by the local beat police officer just in time for the policeman to see a barefoot, coatless Feigenbaum run from the alley. Feigenbaum was then trapped and easily caught.

Mrs. Hoffman was already dead, murdered for a few pennies.

Feigenbaum was caught near the scene obviously in a panic, the knife was found in the alleyway he had just vacated, and the police had an eyewitness to the very act of murder. He had no credible defence; and everybody knew he was done for. That is, except for the lawyers, Hugh Pentecost and William Lawton, who were appointed to defend him.

Remarkably, the case was heard by Recorder Frederick Smyth, the same man who had presided over the trial of Ameer ben Ali, a.k.a. Frenchy.

The two lawyers had differing ideas about their client. Pentecost thought him a rogue and not a particularly intelligent one. He never believed anything that Feigenbaum said, but gaining any information was difficult as the prisoner would communicate only through an interpreter. He did understand some English but struggled to speak in anything other than German, which was a surprise to Pentecost as the man claimed to have been in America for about six years, mostly working as a gardener. The lawyer's view of the man as being an inveterate liar was supported by the police records. It did not take them long to discover previous names for Feigenbaum, suggesting his real name was Anton Zahn, a 54-year-old German of swarthy appearance.

Why he was living rough and roaming around was not known because he did have a bank account and some property upstate.

Nevertheless, he persisted in being known as Carl Feigenbaum just as he stuck to a preposterous story that he was innocent and the murder had been carried out by a friend of his. Pentecost found him exasperating and wondered if he might be insane.

Lawton was fascinated by Feigenbaum. He was attracted by the convoluted stories of his origins, his whereabouts over the years, his true name, and his outrageous defence to the charge of murder by claiming a friend was the murderer. Feigenbaum dismissed from his mind the facts of the case, even that young Michael Hoffman had witnessed the killing. When he could not answer a direct question, he simply clammed-up.

When told he had been caught literally red-handed because he had not managed to wash away the blood from himself, he merely shrugged, saying nothing until he had time to think of another implausible excuse. Lawton could see that this man had long made a habit of hiding his past and wondered what else he might have been up to and until now, had gotten away with. He probed away but did not elicit any information he felt worthy of sharing with Pentecost or the jury.

Feigenbaum was held in The Tombs prison, a stinking place of incarceration near the courthouse, built on an extension of the Five Points area. Called The Tombs because its design was based on ancient Egyptian pharaoh tombs, it was a disaster of engineering.

Constructed with enormously heavy masonry, it did not sit on granite foundations as did much of Manhattan but was sited over the same poorly drained swampy area that added to the Five Points reputation for being the unpleasantly smelling place it was. The foundations were piles of giant hemlock trees, but the structure was always too heavy for them to support the stone above and soon after completion, it began to sink into the boggy ground. The whole building stank of decay.

The drama that followed, such as it was, involved Carl Feigenbaum and his lawyer, but it did not emanate from the trial itself. The trial was an almost pointless affair because the defendant had no defence.

Once he was convicted, an attempt to have a retrial was quickly ruled on as having no merit. The only hope the lawyers had was to move for a finding of insanity. This certainly delayed matters and Feigenbaum was examined to see if he could be adjudged insane.

This move also failed when he was pronounced sane, knowing right from wrong and deliberate in his actions.

That was it.

In Sing Sing prison on the 27th of April 1896, Feigenbaum suffered death by electrocution. And that should have been the end of things, but it was not.

Lawton, the young lawyer who had fought hard to save his client, came out with the astonishing statement that Feigenbaum had admitted to being *Jack the Ripper*.

Part Three: A *Ripper* Legacy

CHAPTER THIRTY-SIX

SEEKING FAME

The plan had been forming in Lawton's mind for quite a while. After the trial, he knew the only hope of avoiding the death penalty for Feigenbaum was the acceptance of a plea of insanity, but that remote prospect soon enough disappeared. He could not save him.

From then on, not able to advance his career through the legal procedures representing a man such as Feigenbaum, he tried another tack. He would put himself in the headlines for something else: he would be the only man in the world to be trusted by *Jack the Ripper* with the answer to one of the world's greatest mysteries, his true identity.

Carl Feigenbaum would admit to the horrors of his past only to Lawton. Lawton would create the impression that it was his dedication to his client's lost cause that impressed Feigenbaum and even so guarded a villain as he would trust him.

Thus, from then on, he was sure that clients would flock to him for his services, a dedicated, tireless representative. It was a great effort of self-publicity resting on the deeds of a serial killer, uncaring of the victims caught up in the story.

Lawton planned the revelation carefully. He developed just enough information to make the statement that Feigenbaum was the *Ripper* credible.

He was not an expert in the history of the killer, but he had read articles in the newspapers over the years, who hadn't? He began to believe his own hypothesis that this man might have been, no indeed was, the *Ripper*.

Subconsciously, he started to make the facts fit the story. He also planned how to market his story. His theory alone was not enough, he had to make it sound convincing. He was unsure that most newspapers would take him seriously, so he cultivated reporters from the New York Advertiser, making them feel important enough to receive his revelation. The time to strike was whilst Feigenbaum was still newsworthy at his execution.

As the body lay in the mortuary, Lawton took the New York Advertiser reporters aside. They were attending Sing Sing only to report on the death of the killer of the now forgotten Mrs. Hoffman, to comment to prurient readers on the use of the electric chair. What he gave them was a far more sensational story. The Advertiser was so impressed with his sales pitch that he sent out a press release to news agencies, building the story.

He told them he would stake his professional reputation and that if the police had carefully traced Feigenbaum's movements for the past few years, their investigations would have led them to London and Whitechapel.

He explained that Feigenbaum seemed at first acquaintance to be simple-minded, yet the man was crafty and cunning. He had means of his own, as was proven by a will he made before his death, yet he always professed extreme poverty. It was hard to say why this was so.

Then, according to Lawton, he told him, 'I have for years suffered from a singular disease which induces an all-absorbing passion. This passion manifests itself in a desire to kill and mutilate every woman who falls in my way. At such times, I am unable to control myself.' The introduction to the notion that this was the *Ripper* was set.

Lawton told the press that he subsequently looked up the details of the Whitechapel murders so that when he saw Fiegenbaum again, he asked, 'Carl, were you in London from this date to that one?' while naming some dates.

Part Three: A *Ripper* Legacy

'Yes', said Feigenbaum. Lawton then asked directly about the Whitechapel murders. Feigenbaum's reply, according to Lawton, was that the Lord was responsible for his acts and that to Him only could he confess. Mr. Lawton was convinced that the prisoner was no other than *Jack the Ripper*, the man who, for more than a year, had terrorised London. He was also responsible for some of the mutilations in Wisconsin where other murders were reported to have occurred; that he was the killer of 'Old Shakespeare'.

Despite the excitement of The Advertiser, despite all his hopes, neither newspapers generally nor the police took much notice of the claims.

At first, it seemed he had support for his claim from Assistant District Attorney Vernon M. Davis, who had prosecuted Feigenbaum.

When approached, he supported Lawton's theory and was quoted in the news report. 'If it were proved that Feigenbaum was indeed *Jack the Ripper,* it would not greatly surprise me because I always considered him a cunning fellow, surrounded by a great deal of mystery, and his life history was never found out.'

Apart from that, Lawton's assertion fell apart. Especially damning was the opinion of his defence colleague, Hugh Pentecost. He simply pointed out that the conversations probably never took place.

'I do not like to spoil a good story, but I take no stock in my colleague's story myself, while, as to facts, Mr. Lawton, of course, is able to tell more than I, as I only knew our client to talk through an interpreter.'

In other words, Lawton was a liar. He went on saying, 'In Feigenbaum, I found nothing in his homicidal method to remind me of *the Ripper.*'

Yes, one fact, perhaps the absence of blood on him after the killing. Of course, as was brought out in the trial, he had an opportunity to wash himself at a sink, and a policeman said, 'At the First Avenue Station House, Feigenbaum had what appeared to be blood on one of his hands. That Feigenbaum killed Mrs. Hoffman, I haven't a particle of doubt.'

It was devastating for Lawton; no one of note took him seriously, and some even doubted his integrity.

On the 29th of April 1896, by which time he had expected his value to be lauded, the New York Times dismissed his theory. It gave a balanced explanation of the facts and, whilst not being so bold as to suggest the discussions between Feigenbaum and Lawton were fiction, left little doubt that there was nothing in his claims.

The days went by and although sometimes, rumours of *Ripper*-like murders emerged from around the world, they were without foundation.

Lawton had himself become yet another secondary victim of the *Ripper*.

APPENDIX

LOOSE ENDS

The Abandoned: *Victims of Jack the Ripper*

THE POLICE

Sir Charles Warren
On leaving the Metropolitan Police, replaced by his enemy and rival, James Monro, Sir Charles served the government in Singapore before being recalled to virtual retirement in England. With the outbreak of the Boer War in 1899, he was surprisingly appointed commander of the 5th Division of the South African Field Force. In 1900, he was accused of bungling an attempt to relieve the besieged town of Ladysmith. He had operational command of forces at the battle of Spion Kop, which proved to be a disaster for British forces. He was reviled amongst other senior officers as being incompetent as a field commander. Recalled again to Britain, he was appointed to his specialism in charge of The Royal Engineers and was never again permitted to be a field commander. In 1908, in retirement, he worked with Baden-Powell in founding the Boy Scout movement.

James Monro
Following a long feud with Warren, Monro succeeded him as Commissioner. Monro was responsible for the development of the Secret Service and believed in making the detective service of the police a credible and professional organisation. He was much admired by his staff but had little to do with the investigations into the *Ripper* killings, as his appointment occurred only as the killings ceased. Fiercely independent, Monro would not tolerate any interference in his management of the Metropolitan Police, an attitude which led to his resignation only eighteen months later.

Inspector Frederick Abberline
Having risen to the rank of Chief Inspector, Abberline retired from the police in February 1892. He received 84 commendations and awards during his service as a police officer. Despite serving all his police career in London, on leaving the Metropolitan Police, he

worked as a private enquiry agent for three seasons in Monte Carlo before being appointed the head of the European branch of the Pinkerton National Detective Agency of America.

Inspector Edmund Reid
Forced by poor health to retire from the Metropolitan Police in 1896, aged only 49, Reid became the landlord of 'The Lower Red Lion' pub in Kent but soon gave it up to become a private detective. In 1903, Reid moved to Hampton-on-Sea and was known as an eccentric. From a wooden kiosk in his garden, which he called the *Hampton-on-Sea Hotel,* he sold soft drinks and postcards of himself. Because of erosion of the cliffs caused by the incursion of the sea, he had to move from his home to Herne Bay in 1916. His wife had died in 1900, but he married again in 1917, only to die himself in December of that year.

Superintendent Donald Swanson
Swanson was involved in many high-profile police actions in his career, including preventing Fenian (forerunners of the IRA) terrorist attacks in London during the 1870s and 1880s. In particular, he worked on the cases of the so-called Rent Boys, who attempted to blackmail homosexuals or were themselves blackmailed for being male prostitutes. Blackmail flourished as a direct consequence of the perverse criminalisation of homosexual activity. He retired in 1903 and died in London (New Malden) in 1924. He had oversight of all investigations and was satisfied he could name the killer but not prove it.

Sergeant William Thick
Once retired from the police in April 1893, he went to work as a Railway Police Inspector. In 1902, he was a guide and advisor to author Jack London, who was researching his book, *The People of the Abyss.* He died in December 1930.

Thomas Byrnes
In 1895, as part of his drive to rid the police of corruption, the new president of the New York City Police Commission and the future President of the United States, Theodore Roosevelt, forced Thomas Byrnes to resign. Byrnes, a reasonably wealthy man by then, became an insurance investigator on Wall Street.

THE OTHERS

Rose Mylett
Long sought by Inspector Reid as a witness in the Emma Smith murder, Rose was found dead in Clarke's Yard just off Poplar High Street on the evening/morning of 19th-20th December 1888, just a few weeks after the Mary Kelly murder. The cause of her death was disputed, the police insisting that she died of natural causes (probably associated with alcoholism), but the coroner refused to accept that opinion. The Inquest recorded that she was murdered. Of course, everyone assumed it had been a *Ripper* murder, although there was nothing to tie the case to the notorious killer.

Frenchy
After eleven years of incarceration, he was suddenly pardoned, paid compensation and allowed to leave the country.

Jacob Riis
Continued to work as a social reformer and journalist. He was a major cause of the demolition of the slums around the Five Points district in NYC. He died in 1914.

'Jacob Riis, whom I am tempted to call the best American I ever knew, although he was already a young man when he came hither from Denmark.'
— *Theodore Roosevelt.*

Sir Charles Matthews, Home Secretary
Matthews continued as Home Secretary until 1892 when the Conservative Party lost the General Election. When the Conservatives returned to power in 1895, Queen Victoria was again keen for him to be Home Secretary, but opposition within the Conservative Party

itself prevented it. Instead, he was ennobled as Viscount Llandaff of Hereford. He never married and died in 1913.

Annie Besant
One of the most remarkable people of a remarkable century. Annie campaigned for equality and justice throughout her life, always facing great opposition from the Church and governments in a conservative, misogynistic society. She eventually went to live in India, where she campaigned against the British for Home Rule and died there in 1933.

Eleanor Marx
Known as Tussy, Jenny Julia Eleanor Marx was the multi-lingual, intellectual, social activist daughter of the philosopher Karl Marx. She played important roles in the formation of the modern Trades Union movement, especially in the East End of London, and was a powerful advocate of women's rights and social justice all her life. She died at the age of 43, apparently by her own hand.

John McCarthy
The notorious landlord and local 'boss' stayed in Dorset Street until it was redeveloped in 1927. He moved to Clapham in South London to live with one of his sons. He died in 1934. Ironically, he is buried in St Patrick's Cemetery in Leytonstone, near the grave of Mary Kelly (if indeed it is Mary Kelly). McCarthy may have been distantly related by marriage to the author of this book.

Appendix: Loose Ends

THE LETTERS

There were dozens of hoax letters claiming to be from the killer, most of them hopelessly amateurish but published by a press addicted then, as now, to sensationalism. The most notorious letters, including *Dear Boss* and the *Postcard From Hell,* were forged by a journalist, almost certainly Tom Bulling, a well-known crime reporter of that time, perhaps as a means of undermining Sir Charles Warren, pressuring him to step aside as Commissioner of the Metropolitan Police in favour of Bulling's friend, James Monro. This eventually happened. It was Bulling, then, who invented the name *Jack the Ripper*.

Monro must have known he owed much to Bulling's support, and subsequently, it is likely that he rewarded him with a great deal of inside information about crime in the city. Such exclusive information might explain why Bulling was much sought after as a crime reporter and why the Metropolitan police were never criticised by him in any article he wrote, at least during Monro's short tenure.

Bulling did not admit at the time to writing those letters (he may have done so later in life) either to help get his friend appointed Commissioner of the Metropolitan Police, build his own reputation as a great crime reporter, or simply to sell newspapers.

To admit to that would imply the subjects of the stories, the victims, the unfortunate women, the desperate men of the East End who suffered the reign of terror, who continued to suffer the degradation of life there, were cruelly used in pursuit of power, reputation, and money. He was not an immoral man, though, and neither were his friends; they were men of their era.

JACK THE RIPPER

In London, the *Ripper* murders stopped, and no one knew why. Reid continued in his belief that no Jew could be responsible, and in doing so, he and others missed the possibility that the incarceration in an asylum for the insane by his family of the violent Aaron Kosminski ended the terror. In later years, Swanson named him as the killer. Once Kosminski was locked away, the killings stopped. He had lived in the killing fields so he could escape home quickly. He fitted descriptions of the suspect given by prostitutes in the area and was a man deranged by a childhood that suffered the brutality of the pogroms in Poland. He was protected by his disbelieving, frightened immigrant refugee family, most of whom spoke little English until he attempted to murder his own sister with a knife.

Thus, the year of terror passed. He died in the asylum.

Charles Cross

Charles Allen Cross, more properly Charles Allen Lechmere, was the man seen leaning over the body of Mary Ann Nichols, a *Ripper* victim he claimed to have stumbled upon. He gave evidence at the inquest into her murder. It seems no one at the time questioned why he used the name Cross (his stepfather's name) or why he lied to police about the request for police assistance from a non-existent officer. In recent years, Lechmere has become a prime suspect in the case. He was a delivery driver (carman) in the area, often transporting butchered meat and possibly wearing a leather apron at times. He could be placed in the vicinity of each murder albeit I know of no strong evidence that does so at the times in question, although it is possible to make a case that he could have been around at those times. However, Lechmere did not die until 1920, so the question is, if he was *Jack the Ripper*, why did he stop?

Appendix: Loose Ends

SPITALFIELDS

It is still there. My daughter has an apartment there. The market is now gentrified, full of restaurants and shops. White's Row is easily found, as are Hanbury Street, Commercial Street, Wentworth Street and Brick Lane. Dorset Street is still there, if you know where to look as it is much changed and has no name to proclaim its sad past. The Church still stands aloof, in silent witness to the past, whilst on the corner is The Ten Bells public house where I sat and thought of those who populate this book.

The Frying Pan pub, too, is still to be found. Although it is a restaurant now, it can be recognised by the stone sign of frying pans high on the cornice.

The sites of the murders can still be found, especially poignant being Mitre Square, surrounded by modern buildings, a small place where workers eat their lunchtime sandwiches, unaware of its tragic past.

If you want to come to London, maybe we can walk together around these places where life never stands still.

TABLE OF VICTIMS

These are the women police were confident had been murdered by *Jack the Ripper**

Martha Tabram**
Born on the 10th of May in 1849 in Southwark, London.
Last resided on 19 George Street, Spitalfields.
Died on the 7th of August in 1888 at the age of 39 at George's Yard.

Mary Ann Nichols (Polly)
Born on the 26th of August in 1845 in Shoe Lane, London.
Last resided on Thrawl Street, Spitalfields.
Died on the 31st of August in 1888 at the age of 43 at Buck's Row.

Annie Chapman
Born on September 1841 in Paddington.
Last resided on Dorset Street, Spitalfields.
Died on the 8th of September in 1888 at the age of 47 at Hanbury Street.

Elizabeth Stride
Born on the 27th of November in 1843 near Gothenburg, Sweden.
Last resided on Flower and Dean Street, Spitalfields.
Died on the 30th of September in 1888 at the age of 44 at Berner Street.

Catherine Eddowes
Born on the 14th of April in 1842 in Wolverhampton.
Last resided on Fashion Street, Spitalfields.
Died on the 30th of September in 1888 at the age of 46 at Mitre Square.

Appendix: Loose Ends

Mary Kelly
Born in 1863 in Ireland.
Last resided on Dorset Street, Spitalfields.
Died on the 9th of November in 1888 at the age of 25 at Dorset Street.

*Several other victims were possibly also the prey of the Ripper, but the police at the time doubted he was the killer.

**not originally attributed to the serial killer but now widely accepted as being the first victim.

FACT AND FICTION IN *THE ABANDONED*

All the main characters in this book are real. The victims, their backgrounds, locations and circumstances are all based on research and are accurate as far as I can tell. Similarly, all the police officers, landlords, husbands, lovers, partners, vigilantes, politicians and newspaper reporters in this story did exist and were involved in the events described..

The dialogue, however, is fictitious. It is used to carry the story and sketch the personalities of the protagonists, carefully avoiding distorting the known facts about them. It was always my intention to show women struggling in desperate circumstances, who lived lives typical of so many at that time, were daughters, mothers, partners, each worthy of sympathy and consideration, not noteworthy merely for being victims of the *Ripper*.

In the entire work, only three characters are fictitious, Bella and Maisie, the women who make meagre wages from selling their stories about the East River Hotel murder victim, and the reporter they speak with. Their use is a simple device to centre the story and colour the background.

The events are true in both London and New York (and later in the book, Chicago), with the exception given below. Although the book is centred on the agreed upon five victims of *Jack the Ripper*, it could have extended to several other vicious murders, some of which are also possibly attributable to the serial killer. I include Martha Tabram in the story as it seems to me, and to many *Ripper* students, that she was likely to have been his first victim.

Appendix: Loose Ends

In America, Old Shakespeare did exist and was the victim described, though not a victim of *Jack the Ripper*. The circumstances around the killing in New York, as with London, are accurate. If anything, the violence and miserable living conditions in Manhattan at that time, is underplayed. The politics and corruption behind the misery of the city is only touched upon, though I could not resist mentioning certain gang members who originated there and developed criminal careers elsewhere. The story of the lost key from the hotel is also documented, leaving yet another mystery unresolved.

In London, the story concerning Mary Kelly is fiction, wishful thinking on my part. It is a fact that witnesses claimed to see her after the murder was committed, and I use that evidence (disregarded by the coroner) to invent a different ending for her. It would be nice if it were true.

Overall, *The Abandoned* treads a careful path between documentary and fictional drama.

As a screenplay, it might be referred to as a *docudrama*.

BIBLIOGRAPHY & RESEARCH

E. P. THOMSON
The Making of the English Working Class
Penguin

PETER ACKROYD
London the Biography
Chatto and Windus 2000

EVANS, S.P. & SKINNER
The Ultimate Jack the Ripper Sourcebook
Hodder & Stoughton 2013

JACK LONDON
The People of the Abyss (1903)
Tangerine Press

JACOB RIIS
How the Other Half Lives (1890)
Simon & Schuster

FIONA RULE
The Worst Street in London
Ian Allen Publishing 2008

REG BEER
Bryant & May Strike, 1888
National Museum of Labour History, 1983

Appendix: Loose Ends

JOSEPH ROGERS
Sickness and Cruelty in the Workhouse
Amazon Books

BENJEMIN LEESON*
In the Old East End: Memoirs
Amazon Books

I highly recommend Casebook: Jack the Ripper, an online guide to all matters associated with the murders. Provides source material, dissertations, and opinions.

https://www.casebook.org.

There are dozens, if not hundreds of YouTube explorations of the killings. Most are concerned with identifying the Ripper, but amongst them are details of the victims and the main characters of this story.

* Leeson was one of the police officers to attend the Mary Kelly murder in Dorset Street.

ACKNOWLEDGEMENTS

My interest in the victims stems from Fiona Rule's book about the area, The Worst Street in London, given to me by my partner, Nicky. That thoughtful gift started my journey into the subject. She accompanied me on many research trips to the area.

I am grateful to my friends, Peter, Jill, Elizabeth and Halcyon, who, over the years, allowed me to walk them around the sites mentioned in this book as I established my knowledge of events and locations. Thanks too, is owed to Grant who read the original, tumbling, complicated manuscript and encouraged me to complete the work as we sat in the Ten Bells one summer day.

Similarly, I am deeply appreciative of the faith shown in me by my children, Ruth and Jack.

Faye, the editor of this book, has been enormously helpful in encouraging me to streamline and improve the work.

Thanks too to Sofie from Woodbridge Publishers who has managed the process from submission of the original manuscript to publication.

ABOUT THE AUTHOR

David Stephens was raised in the English Midlands. He attended the University of Warwick, and then Birmingham University. He has undertaken many occupations, eventually working as a Senior Manager assisting Family Courts across London to safeguard the welfare of vulnerable children. He is the father of the musician, Jack Stephens (leafcuts), and the New York/London based photographer, Ruthie Stephens.

He currently lives with his partner in the southwest of England.

David Stephens is also the author of the novel What Friends We Were, available on Amazon.

Printed in Great Britain
by Amazon